THE COMPLETE IDIOT'S GUIDE® TO

Saltwater Aquariums

b   *ot*

I would like to dedicate this book to my wife Emmanuelle and to Greg Meyer for being my partner in fish crime (the legal kind, of course).—M.M.

I would like to dedicate this book to my wife Karen, without whom there would be no illustrations in this book and little joy in my life. I would also like to dedicate this book to Jonathan Meigs, Alan Tousignant, Mark Cartland, Bruce Rinker, and my formative years spent at the Trevor Zoo at Millbrook School where I first learned animal husbandry. —RdePTIII

ALPHA BOOKS

Published by the Penguin Group

Penguin Group (USA) Inc., 375 Hudson Street, New York, New York 10014, USA

Penguin Group (Canada), 90 Eglinton Avenue East, Suite 700, Toronto, Ontario M4P 2Y3, Canada (a division of Pearson Penguin Canada Inc.)

Penguin Books Ltd., 80 Strand, London WC2R 0RL, England

Penguin Ireland, 25 St. Stephen's Green, Dublin 2, Ireland (a division of Penguin Books Ltd.)

Penguin Group (Australia), 250 Camberwell Road, Camberwell, Victoria 3124, Australia (a division of Pearson Australia Group Pty. Ltd.)

Penguin Books India Pvt. Ltd., 11 Community Centre, Panchsheel Park, New Delhi—110 017, India

Penguin Group (NZ), 67 Apollo Drive, Rosedale, North Shore, Auckland 1311, New Zealand (a division of Pearson New Zealand Ltd.)

Penguin Books (South Africa) (Pty.) Ltd., 24 Sturdee Avenue, Rosebank, Johannesburg 2196, South Africa

Penguin Books Ltd., Registered Offices: 80 Strand, London WC2R 0RL, England

International Standard Book Number: 978-1-59257-826-9
Library of Congress Catalog Card Number: 2008929020

11 10 09   8 7 6 5 4 3 2 1

Interpretation of the printing code: The rightmost number of the first series of numbers is the year of the book's printing; the rightmost number of the second series of numbers is the number of the book's printing. For example, a printing code of 09-1 shows that the first printing occurred in 2009.

Printed in the United States of America

Note: This publication contains the opinions and ideas of its authors. It is intended to provide helpful and informative material on the subject matter covered. It is sold with the understanding that the authors and publisher are not engaged in rendering professional services in the book. If the reader requires personal assistance or advice, a competent professional should be consulted.

The authors and publisher specifically disclaim any responsibility for any liability, loss, or risk, personal or otherwise, which is incurred as a consequence, directly or indirectly, of the use and application of any of the contents of this book.

Most Alpha books are available at special quantity discounts for bulk purchases for sales promotions, premiums, fund-raising, or educational use. Special books, or book excerpts, can also be created to fit specific needs.

For details, write: Special Markets, Alpha Books, 375 Hudson Street, New York, NY 10014.

Contents at a Glance

Contents

Appendixes

Introduction

The Complete Idiot's Guide to Saltwater Aquariums is unlike other beginner books about the saltwater aquarium hobby. Many of the reasonably priced books for beginners, we have found, remain useful for about 10 minutes after the tank is up and running. That may be fine if all you want to do is set up a simple marine aquarium, but most aquarists we know want to grow with their tank, and that's where *The Complete Idiot's Guide to Saltwater Aquariums* comes in.

While this is a book for beginners, it is also a book with which you can grow. For one, we've included a CD-ROM, which provides the most comprehensive catalog of marine species for the aquarium in any currently available beginner book. More importantly, we have taken an approach that gives you all the information you need to make the right decisions about setup for the type of species you plan to keep. In other words, we believe a tank is not a tank is not a tank, and instead of telling you what to do, we give you the information and guide you through the process of making choices appropriate for you.

That's not to say that we don't offer plenty of advice along the way—we most certainly do. Many saltwater aquarium books go out of their way to not mention or endorse specific products. That has not been our approach. We frequently mention products by name in the text, but we only recommend those products with which we have firsthand experience. We are not claiming these are the best products, but it is our belief that these products work well because we have seen them work well. In most cases, we have spent many hours on the phone or in person interviewing the designers of these products so that we can fully understand how they work and pass that information on to you.

We, Mark and Ret, approach this hobby from two very different angles. Mark is the founder of one of the leading online retailers of marine livestock, and his resumé demonstrates his involvement with nearly every aspect of the marine aquarium industry from collection to importation to policy work. Ret, on the other hand, is a hobbyist with a passion for researching and writing about the marine aquarium hobby. Together, we approach every aspect of setting up, stocking, and maintaining a marine aquarium from both sides of the hobby. The result is that you get cutting-edge insight into best practices from an industry insider and no-nonsense, applicable advice from a hobbyist. Because Mark and Ret are strong advocates of a sustainable hobby and conservation of ocean environments, all of this is presented in a manner that values the natural ecosystems upon which the hobby depends and by which it is inspired.

While this is a different type of saltwater aquarium book, it does cover all of the basics of planning a system (Part 1), equipping and building that system (Part 2), aquascaping and filling the aquarium with water (Part 3), stocking the aquarium with fishes, corals, and other invertebrates (Part 4), and caring for the system (Part 5). In short, it is an A-to-Z guide that will remain a useful tool for years to come.

This book was written for people who are seriously considering adding a saltwater aquarium to their home, dorm room, or office. It is also written for people who have started down the road of planning or even setting up an aquarium but who are frustrated or confused with the apparent complexity. In addition to these two groups, it is intended to be a valuable resource for any aquarist's bookshelf, given that some of the information and ideas that appear in the book are appearing in print for the first time. As always, the marine aquarium hobby is a work in progress—new ideas and techniques are constantly emerging, and it has been our hope to contribute to that dialogue.

What this book does not do is provide the sheer volume of husbandry practices, advanced techniques, and cutting-edge science that other books cover. That is why we have included a reading list in Appendix B. While many of these books are expensive and written for an intermediate to experienced (sometimes even scientific) audience, they will be books you will eventually want to purchase as you progress further into the hobby. Finally, we have created a website called TheSaltwaterAquarium.com where we will continue the dialog begun in this book. We hope you will join us there, as we all strive to increase our own knowledge about the hobby and the ecosystems we attempt to replicate in our aquaria.

Extras

Throughout this book, we will discuss some concepts that may seem intimidating or confusing at first, but really are not. We think it's important for you to get the complete story instead of some dumbed-down version of the facts, but we also firmly believe that you shouldn't need to be a scientist or expert aquarist to set up a successful marine aquarium. That is why we have included four types of sidebars throughout the book to clarify the text and, in places, expand on ideas.

def•i•ni•tion_____

These explanations provide additional assistance for understanding the text.

Eco Tips _____

These ideas and facts point out intersections of the hobby and the environment.

Warning _____

Pay attention to these sidebars! They warn you about dangers to the aquarist, livestock, and/or the system in general.

Pearls of Wisdom

These notes contain further information to enrich your knowledge of selected topics in the text.

Acknowledgments

The authors would like to thank Mark's business partners, Thad Jones, Leighton Chalmers, and Dave Palmer, for giving him the time to pursue this project. The authors would also like to thank Chris Irwin and Todd Haney for their tireless support in all things scientific and marine (and for the darts).

Ret would also like to thank his aquarist grandfather, P. L. Spruance, who, under the auspices of Villie Vacuum, Grand Wizer, and Chaley Cardinal, Grand Wizer's Scribe, helped induct Ret as an Honorary Member of the International Piscatorial People Fry and Swimming Society at the tender age of five (the plaque hangs beside Ret's 135-gallon reef tank).

Finally, the authors would like to acknowledge the hard work of the editorial staff, especially Jan Lynn, Julie Bess, and Tom Stevens. Without their help, these musings would be little more than scratching on a page.

Special Thanks to the Technical Reviewer

The Complete Idiot's Guide to Saltwater Aquariums was reviewed by an expert who double-checked the accuracy of what you'll learn here, to help us ensure that this book gives you everything you need to know about saltwater aquariums. Special thanks are extended to the godfather of the marine aquarium industry, Mr. Robert Fenner.

Trademarks

All terms mentioned in this book that are known to be or are suspected of being trademarks or service marks have been appropriately capitalized. Alpha Books and Penguin Group (USA) Inc. cannot attest to the accuracy of this information. Use of a term in this book should not be regarded as affecting the validity of any trademark or service mark.

Part 1

A Glass Box—A Primer to Building Your Mini Sea

In Part 1, our goal is to introduce you to the hobby and give you the information you need to make an informed decision about what type of marine aquarium setup is right for you. We'll avoid complicated terms and technical details in this part of the text, but we will introduce the major concepts and recommend several approaches to planning your system. By the time you finish Part 1, you should know if this hobby is for you, how much it will cost in terms of money and time, and how best to go about planning a successful marine aquarium that will become a centerpiece of your home for years to come.

A Primer to Building Your Mini Sea

In This Chapter

- Introducing the marine aquarium hobby
- Mark's glass box—a simple approach
- The natural reef ecosystem
- The costs and benefits of the hobby

If you're just starting out in this hobby, know that you are in excellent company. It is not everyone who endeavors to bring the sea into his or her home. It takes a special person—someone keenly aware of beauty and with more than a trifling curiosity. Certainly it takes someone willing to commit the time and money to adequately care for the living things they acquire. More important, however, this hobby requires someone who has an explorer's passion, an inventor's ingenuity, and a scientist's inquisitiveness. That's not to say you have to be an explorer, inventor, or scientist to be successful, but to get the most out of marine aquarium keeping, you will need to be able to envision your new aquarium as something more than furniture or art.

The Woman Who Brought the Sea to the City

The first saltwater aquarium *hobbyist* was perhaps not the person you might expect. Her name was Anne Constantia Beresford, a mother of eight and the wife of the subdean of Westminster Abbey in London. It was 1846, and the Thynne family—that was her married name—was vacationing on the coast in Torquay, England. Of all the entertainments this fashionable Victorian seaside resort had to offer—Torquay was commonly called the English Riviera—it was the tide pools at the base of the cliffs that drew the curious minds and attention of Anna and her children.

Pearls of Wisdom

If you decide to pursue this hobby, people will refer to you as a hobbyist or an aquarist. Sometimes you'll even be called an aquarium hobbyist! As with any hobby, there are lots of people dedicated to the marine aquarium hobby, and they are a great resource for you as you move forward. You can connect with other hobbyists online or through your local fish store.

Scampering amongst the exposed rocks at low tide, they marveled at the curious world of the marine life living there. Each pool a miniature sea—a world unto itself of beauty and wonder. Perhaps it is not so surprising that Anna became the first successful saltwater hobbyist.

At first it was Anna and the children on the floor of their vacation villa staring into shallow, saltwater-filled pie trays teeming with tide-pool life. When it was time to return to London, Anna and the children would usually release their "pets" back into the sea. But then one fall, Anna, inspired by her own interest in the popular Victorian pastime of coral fossil collecting, decided to attempt to bring some live corals with her back to the city. Safely sewn onto a large sponge and packaged in a stone jar filled with seawater, the corals safely made the journey to London. Upon reaching their new home, the corals were transferred to two glass bowls and kept in the family's parlor. Extra seawater, which had been brought from Torquay, was used for every-other-day water changes.

Mark's Glass Box Theory

As you embark on this hobby, keep Anna's glass bowls in mind. Mark often talks to beginning hobbyists about his "glass box theory." In essence, it is Anna's story. The theory is simply this—an aquarium is a glass (or, as is often the case today, acrylic) box filled with saltwater. Add life to this box—a fish or a snail or a coral—and you're going to see some changes in the quality of the water. If you don't address these changes, your animals will soon die.

When an animal dies, ask yourself why it died, and then strive to fix that problem. The animal will no doubt live longer next time, but it, too, will eventually die. Again, ask yourself why it died, and address that problem.

Of course, we're not suggesting that you actually do this—that would be nothing short of torture for the poor animals you use as guinea pigs—but we are suggesting that this is a good way to think about a successful marine aquarium because it keeps it simple. It's so easy to get overwhelmed by pages upon pages in aquarium catalogs of high-tech equipment like calcium reactors, metal halide lights, UV sterilizers, and protein skimmers. Don't worry, we'll cover what you need to know about this equipment, but we'll also constantly encourage you to return to the basics. After all, an aquarium is really just a glass box.

Pearls of Wisdom

In the early chapters of this book, we will mention various pieces of equipment by way of example. It is not important that you know what these pieces of equipment are, at present, but if you want to know, you can always look them up in the glossary. Don't fret; we will explain each piece of equipment we mention in the appropriate chapter.

The Wonder of Tropical Reefs

That which drew Anna to become the first successful marine aquarium hobbyist in the 1840s is what still draws people to the hobby today. It is the absolute amazement one feels when afforded a glance beneath the surface of the sea. Whether you are fortunate enough to have snorkeled or been diving on some of the world's coral reefs, or simply have marveled through the glass at a public aquarium, you know what we mean. The array of colors, the almost extraterrestrial forms taken by strange plantlike animals undulating in the sweep of the current—this is another world, and once you've seen it, you really can't get enough.

Perhaps that's why you are now considering starting a marine aquarium in your house, and guess what? We're glad you are! We are looking forward to giving you the information you need to be successful in this hobby. Before we start talking about the aquarium, however, we think it's well worth taking some time to look at the natural ecosystems we will be replicating in the aquarium. Our approach, as we've said before (and we'll say again and again), is to keep it simple, but to do this, it helps to understand the basic principles of how it all works in the wild.

What's a Reef?

Most marine aquarists, even if they are not intent on creating a reef aquarium, will keep reef-associated fishes. Generally speaking, these are the animals that are more frequently collected and are more interesting from the aquarists' perspective. Likewise, most aquarists, especially beginning aquarists, will be dealing only with tropical reef species. In most cases, when we talk about reefs in this book, we are therefore going to be talking about tropical reefs.

def•i•ni•tion

> **Reef-building corals,** known as hermatypic stony corals, build their own skeletons by making calcium carbonate. When the coral dies, this calcareous skeleton becomes porous rock colonized by a variety of organisms including other corals. Over time, a reef is formed in this manner.

Coral reefs have been around for a long time. Scientists believe the first coral showed up somewhere around 650 million years ago. It's very important to understand that a reef is not just a pile of rocks—it is, in fact, a living thing. Corals are alive, and, yes, they are animals. Some corals are known as *reef-building corals,* and it is these corals that, as their name implies, build reefs over time.

Where Are Reefs?

A very long time ago, a continuous belt of coral reefs circled Earth. Then, somewhere between 200 to 500 million years ago, the shifting of continents and the formation of Eurasia and Africa interrupted that one continuous reef. As the continents continued to shift, a second barrier was formed by North and South America, resulting in two distinct bodies of water. We refer generally to these today as the Atlantic and Pacific oceans. Even these oceans, however, are separated into smaller reef systems. The western Atlantic reefs are cut off from the eastern Pacific reefs by Central and South America, and the western Pacific is separated from West Africa by deep ocean. Likewise, the eastern Pacific is distinct from the Indo-Pacific. The result is that the marine aquarist has four major areas from which to choose when replicating a natural reef ecosystem:

- ◆ The Indo-Pacific
- ◆ The Caribbean (western Atlantic)
- ◆ West Africa (eastern Atlantic)
- ◆ The eastern Pacific

While each of these areas shares the same environmental conditions that allow reef-building corals to grow, each is also quite unique as a result of its separation from other coral reefs. It is very rare that a species from one of these distinct areas makes its way into one of the other areas. The continents and deep oceans that separate these areas have generally proven to be insurmountable barriers to the animals indigenous to each. When you purchase fish, coral, or other invertebrates for your aquarium, most retailers will identify for you from which of these four regions the animals originated.

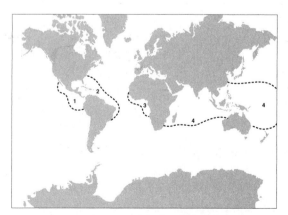

A map of the world showing the world's tropical reefs and the four main collection areas.

(Courtesy Karen Talbot.)

Pearls of Wisdom

Despite the barriers of continents and deep oceans, some species have moved from one area to another as a result of human impact. The creation of the Suez Canal, for example, has caused the migration of more than 100 species of marine life from the Indo-Pacific to the Mediterranean Sea. Unfortunately, the marine aquarium hobby has been responsible for the introduction of some non-indigenous, invasive species like the introduction of the lionfish to the western Atlantic.

Reefs in Trouble

As you can see, reefs have a long history on Earth, and over time those reefs have faced many challenges. Ice ages, for example, have dramatically shifted the level of the sea. Sea level change affects coral reefs because most reef-building corals need both to be submerged and to have access to sufficient light. This means that many reefs are quite shallow, and, as such, even small changes in sea level can be disastrous. In one scenario, the sea level drops and the reef is fully exposed to the air and the sun, killing the corals. In the another scenario, the sea level rises, the sun can no longer reach the reef with sufficient strength, and the corals die. This is why, of the 7,000 or so known species of coral, more than half are extinct.

This fact, in and of itself, shouldn't necessarily make us all that worried. Yesterday, Ret took a walk over the ridge behind his house in Laguna Beach, California, and visited a fossilized reef from the Miocene era. Fossils of extinct coral species can be found there, despite the fact that this fossil reef is located about $4\frac{1}{2}$ miles inland from the Pacific.

The demise of this reef, and the corals which inhabited it, was certainly not the result of carbon emissions as it happened long before the first European crossed this land in 1769. Rather, this reef's death resulted from the natural ebb and flow of geologic time. The problem today is that human influences are increasingly taking a greater toll on the world's reef systems than geologic forces. Global climate change, for example, is already having a documented detrimental impact on coral reefs by way of coral bleaching and ocean acidification. In addition, coral reefs are also struggling because of overfishing, destructive fishing methods (e.g., fishing with dynamite and cyanide), unsustainable tourism, coastal development, and pollution.

It's a sad fact that the marine aquarium trade has been responsible for the degradation of certain reef systems in the past. Unsustainable collection methods have turned some reefs from true "rainforests of the sea" to barren underwater deserts. In the twenty-first century, the marine aquarium industry has the potential to either contribute positively to the understanding and conservation of coral reef ecosystems worldwide,

Eco Tips

Because ocean acidification is directly related to carbon emissions, driving less can help save the world's coral reefs. Ocean acidification refers to a decrease in pH in the ocean with the more acidic seawater causing stress for calcifying organisms like coral.

or to contribute to the continued destruction of one of Earth's most incredible ecosystems. We believe the marine aquarium hobby should and can do the former, and throughout this book, we will be pointing out ways you can contribute to the knowledge and understanding of coral reefs and their conservation worldwide, while, at the same time, pursuing the marine aquarium hobby in an ethical and responsible manner.

Eco Tips

Coral bleaching is the result of the failed symbiotic relationship between corals and algae called zooxanthellae that live within the cells of the coral. The outcome is that the coral, which often gains its color from the zooxanthellae, whitens or "bleaches." Coral bleaching is caused by rising sea surface temperatures. Major coral bleaching events occurred in 1982, 1987, and 1992. In 1998, the most significant coral bleaching event on record severely stressed or killed nearly half of the corals in the western Indian Ocean.

The Costs of Bringing Nemo Home

We were at the Aquarium of the Pacific in Long Beach, California, the other day looking at the tropical reef exhibit when we heard the following exchange:

Daughter: What kind of fish is that, Mommy?

Mother: That's a blue Nemo fish, Sweetie.

A blue Nemo fish? That was a new one for us. Of course, what the mother meant was that the blue tang *(Paracanthurus hepatus)*, which had attracted her daughter's attention, was indeed the fish named Dory that Ellen DeGeneres played in the 2003 animated movie *Finding Nemo*.

The marine aquarium trade has grown dramatically in recent years thanks to popular cultural icons like Nemo, advances in technology and *husbandry*, and the explosion of online retailers selling marine livestock. Today the aquarium industry in the United States is worth over $1 billion. While freshwater aquarium keeping is still more popular—14.7 million homes and offices in the United States have a freshwater fish tank—more than 600,000 homes and offices now have a marine aquarium.

def•i•ni•tion

The term **husbandry** refers to the care and breeding of livestock. For the aquarist, it generally refers to caring for your animals, be they fishes, corals, or other invertebrates. In books about the hobby, the husbandry section will tell you how to care for the animals you are considering purchasing.

Whether you decide to get into this hobby because of a movie, a diving vacation, or simply because you're curious, it is our belief that you should enter the hobby with full knowledge of all the costs associated with keeping a marine aquarium. While it is not our intent to discourage you from bringing a slice of the ocean into your home, we have seen far too many people get excited about keeping a clownfish after seeing *Finding Nemo*, only to find out that they are unable or unwilling to commit the space, money, and time to maintain the saltwater aquarium long term. Bringing Nemo home isn't cheap, but if you're up for the costs, it sure is rewarding, and we can (and will) show you how to do it right.

A "Blue Nemo Fish," better known in the hobby as a blue tang (Paracanthurus hepatus), *a.k.a. Dory from* Finding Nemo.

(Courtesy Karen Talbot.)

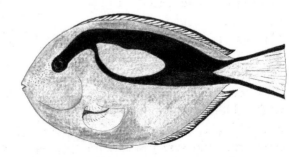

How Much Space Will I Need to Bring Nemo Home?

While so-called *nano reefing*—keeping tanks less than 30 gallons—has become very popular as of late, the beginning aquarist should be warned that the less water in the system, the harder it is to maintain. Twelve-, ten- and five-gallon tanks (and smaller!) are readily available, and, while they may seem like the ideal starter tank (they are less expensive and require less space), these smaller systems are generally harder to keep stable. Because they are less forgiving than a larger system, we believe that, where the novice is concerned, bigger is truly better. This is not to say that you can't have success with a nano tank if you are just starting out in the hobby, but know you will need to commit more time in terms of maintenance and monitoring for your nano tank than you will with a tank 55 gallons or larger.

If you decide to go with a nano system, you can set it up in a space roughly the size of the tank's footprint, as many manufactured nano setups are all-inclusive (all the filtration equipment is actually inside the tank itself). As you will learn more about in Chapter 6, however, we recommend that nearly all systems employ the use of an external reservoir of water called a sump. If you plan to use a sump with your nano setup, you will need to make sure you have room (usually under the tank) for the sump. It is not uncommon for a sump to be housed in the aquarium stand.

If you decide to go with a larger tank, and we recommend you do, you will need to do a little more planning. A larger tank obviously has a larger footprint, but with a larger tank, you will also probably need to have more space for filtration and other equipment. This is because, with a larger system, the filtration equipment is rarely internal or even hung on the back of the aquarium, as we often see with freshwater systems. Be sure to read Chapter 6 on filtration before deciding where your tank will go so that you make sure you have the space you need. At the very least,

def•i•ni•tion

Nano reefing refers to keeping fishes, corals, and other invertebrates in a small aquarium called a nano tank. You will find a variety of opinions about how small an aquarium needs to be to be considered a nano tank, but for the purposes of this book, we consider everything under 30 gallons to be a nano tank.

you will want to have all of the space within the aquarium cabinet dedicated to tank equipment.

If space is an issue, or if for some reason you can't fit the necessary equipment under the tank itself, you can run the tank from a remote location such as an adjacent bathroom, a garage, a cellar, or a dedicated fish room. Plumbing your tank in this manner requires more knowledge and is more expensive, but if you're careful with your planning, it is not outside the realm of possibility for someone who has read this book cover to cover.

How Much Will It Cost to Bring Nemo Home?

This is a nearly impossible question to answer definitively because there are so many choices based on what type of saltwater tank you are setting up (Chapter 3), what equipment you plan to use (Chapters 6 and 7) and how you anticipate stocking it (Chapter 3). Having said that, Mark, whose company started as a custom marine installation business, suggests that if somebody is starting with absolutely nothing, then a regular old saltwater tank is going to cost something like $10 per gallon. Using the same formula, it's safe to assume that a basic reef tank is going to cost you in the neighborhood of $15 to $30 per gallon, depending on options. Having said that, a smaller tank may cost more per gallon even though the bottom line is less. Mark's experience dealing with thousands of customers is that 100 gallons is the average size for a marine aquarium.

Regardless of how big your system is, or how much you plan to spend, here are some basic tips.

 ◆ **Don't buy cheap equipment.** In general, what you pay for a piece of equipment is directly proportional to how well that piece of equipment will function over time. This doesn't mean to go out and buy the most expensive equipment you can find, but certainly don't base your decisions on price as the sole determining factor.

 ◆ **Don't buy every bell and whistle.** There is a lot of marine aquarium equipment available, but when you are starting out, keep it to the basics. It's much better to buy excellent filtration equipment than to buy mediocre filtration equipment so you can also afford a bunch of equipment you don't really need.

◆ **Don't rush.** Rather than buying everything all at once, plan your system carefully and build it one step at a time. This way you will save money by only buying what you know you need as opposed to buying everything you think you need and then only using some of it.

How Much Will It Cost to Stock an Aquarium?

Stocking your aquarium refers to adding livestock—fish, coral, and other invertebrates. It is possible to have a beautiful and interesting aquarium with nearly no intentional stocking at all, provided you add *live rock*, appropriate lighting, and a heater. Live rock, discussed in detail in Chapter 12, is not actually alive—but it is (or should be) teeming with life when you get it. If you are patient and take note of the details, you will see literally thousands of small macroorganisms, those you can see with the naked eye, emerge from the rock over the course of days, weeks, and months. Admittedly, it will take years for the live rock to really mature into even a small reef, and, as such, this approach is definitely not for everyone.

Stocking your aquarium will usually be an ongoing process, but, in our opinion, it's worth coming up with a comprehensive stocking plan from the outset. You know, for instance, that you are going to need to add live rock followed by snails and other beneficial invertebrates early on. The price of this so-called clean-up crew depends on the size of your tank and the species you purchase. To do it right, however, you will probably

def•i•ni•tion

Live rock refers to rock that is loaded with life. Often this rock is collected directly from reef rubble zones and shipped wet to preserve much of the life. We recommend that live rock be used in almost every marine aquarium because it serves as such a valuable biological filter. It's great looking, too!

spend anywhere from $60 to over $400 on a comprehensive clean-up crew for tanks ranging in size from 30 gallons to 200 gallons respectively.

You may also choose to add a fish or two (depending on the size of your tank) as part of your initial clean-up crew. A yellow tang (*Zebrasoma flavescens)*, for example, is an excellent grazer and will help control hair algae in the maturing aquarium (75 gallons or larger). A small- to medium-size yellow tang will cost around $30. Adding a small *shoal* (three to seven) of hardy fish such as green chromis *(Chromis viridis)* may also be appropriate early on if you just can't wait for fish. These guys should cost you between $3 and $12 each, depending upon their origin and the number you purchase.

def•i•ni•tion

Is it a **shoal** of fish or a school of fish? Starting in the sixteenth century, the word "shoal" came into being in English. It was a derivative of the Old English adjective *scolu*, meaning "band, troop, school of fish." The word "school" is a late fourteenth- or early fifteenth-century word derived from the Dutch word *schole*, meaning "group of fish or other animals.'" The terms sometimes refer to the behavior of the group rather than the group itself.

From this point on, you really do need to take it slow. Adding many fish at once is a sure recipe for disaster. There is a definite science to adding livestock, and we explain this in detail in Chapters 15, 16 and 17. For the purposes of this section, however, here are a few favorite fish and the amount you should plan to spend on them.

Top 10 Marine Aquarium Fishes

Common Name	Scientific Name	Cost
Ocellaris clown pair	*Amphiprion ocellaris*	$60
Blue tang	*Paracanthurus hepatus*	$25–$115
Yellow tang	*Zebrasoma flavescens*	$25–$80
Green chromis	*Chromis viridis*	$3–$12
Flame angel	*Centropyge loricula*	$45–$75
Percula clown	*Amphiprion percula*	$12–$28
Lawnmower blenny	*Salarias fasciatus*	$14–$25
Neon goby	*Elecatinus oceanops*	$25
Sixline wrasse	*Pseudocheilinus hexataenia*	$15
Copperband butterfly	*Chelmon rostratus*	$25–$90

If you are planning a reef tank, most popular corals are around $25. Three of the most popular are mushrooms, zoanthids, and brain corals.

How Much Will It Cost to Keep Nemo and His Buddies Happy?

Too many people don't calculate the cost of maintaining an aquarium before setting it up. There are electrical bills and water bills, synthetic salt mix, and various supplements. There is fish food and there are filter pads. The list goes on and on. Be sure to consider how much it will cost to keep your tank up and running. Later in the book, we'll tell you how to figure out exactly how much your electric or water bill will be, but a ballpark figure based on the percentage of your initial setup cost is sufficient at this point.

How Much of My Time Will It Take to Clean Up After Nemo?

We're glad you asked! Regular maintenance is essential when it comes to saltwater-aquarium keeping. It's not like the sink, where you can allow dishes to pile up and then clean them all at once. If you do not follow through religiously on a regular maintenance regimen, you will lose animals. We discuss aquarium maintenance in detail in Part 5, but for the purposes of understanding how much time your new tank will require, plan on at least 15 to 30 minutes of daily maintenance. In addition, plan on at least one hour additional time per week for larger tasks. If you plan on keeping a reef tank, you should probably double the maintenance times. If you cannot commit to this, then you may want to look into hiring an aquarium maintenance service.

We tend to think of aquarium maintenance as "hobby time" rather than work, and we hope you will, too. There is nothing like immersing yourself in your underwater world to make a long, difficult day fade into the past. While you are maintaining your tank, observe your animals. Note any changes in behavior, shape, size, or color. You will quickly learn to spot something that is out of the ordinary, and this is your best line of defense against developing problems with water quality, sickness, or disease.

Granted, maintaining your aquarium is not quite like taking a vacation to some reef-fringed tropical island every day, but it's close (especially if you make yourself umbrella drinks).

The Return on Your Investment

As you can already see, this is not an inexpensive hobby in terms of money or time, but it is, in our opinion (and in the opinions of the more than half a million Americans who now keep a marine aquarium), a hobby that repays you many times over in enjoyment, knowledge, and for the erstwhile aquaculturists, possibly even money.

The Enjoyment

Few things in a home are as relaxing and intriguing as a marine aquarium. A marine aquarium is always changing and growing, and you will marvel at the way the inhabitants establish their routines and resume some of the extraordinary symbiotic relationships they pursue in the wild. One of our friends calls her aquarium a "living work of art," and we wholeheartedly agree.

When you consider the amount most people spend on recreational activities like going to the movies, playing a round of golf, or spending a day at the amusement park or on the ski slopes, it's pretty easy to justify the expenses associated with a marine aquarium. The best part is that your aquarium only gets better over time.

The Knowledge

Aquarium hobbyists quickly become experts on many aspects of marine life. Because we know how to sustain marine life in the captive environment, we can provide invaluable services to scientists looking to set up controlled experiments in the lab. We can also share our observations with marine scientists who are studying the same animals and ecosystems in the wild. And who knows, the next Jacques Cousteau may be a girl from Iowa who grew up with a marine aquarium at home.

Cottage Industry

While you probably won't get rich doing it, many an aquarist has successfully traded or sold fish bred in his or her aquarium to other aquarists. You can often even trade them in for credit at the local fish store. If you have a reef tank, the time will come when you will need to "prune" your corals by "fragging" them, and these so-called "frags" can also be sold or traded. We're not suggesting you put out a shingle, but selling or trading animals raised in your tank can be a fun way to reinvest in the hobby.

The Least You Need to Know

♦ The marine aquarium hobby has been around for a long time and can be approached in a fashion much simpler than it often is.

♦ Knowledge of natural reef ecosystems improves the hobbyist's success and the integrity of the world's reefs.

♦ While not an inexpensive hobby in terms of money or time, the marine aquarium hobby is one that is well worth the investment.

2

If They Could Do It, Then So Can I

In This Chapter

- ◆ The short history of keeping marine fish
- ◆ How to keep a fish alive
- ◆ The basic components of a marine aquarium

Remember Anna from Chapter 1? We said that Anna was the first successful marine hobbyist way back in 1846. That's a true statement in many ways, but she was not the first person to keep marine fishes. The earliest known aquarists were the Sumerians. They kept fishes in artificial ponds at least 4,500 years ago. Records of fish keeping also date from ancient Egypt and Assyria. It probably started something like this: monsoon floods pushed fish up into interior lagoons, and these lagoons were then blocked off from the sea by industrious fisherfolk. Ever heard of shooting fish in a barrel?

The earliest records of purposeful fish farming (sometimes called *aquaculture* or *mariculture*) come from China in 2,000 B.C.E., but these dealt primarily with freshwater species. Ancient Egyptians kept and bred fishes for their aesthetic value, and Egyptian tombs dating back to roughly the same period feature frescoes of ornamental fishes. Ornamental saltwater ponds were not uncommon for both wealthy Egyptians and Romans. According to Pliny the Elder, a Roman by the name of L. Licinus Murena raised marine eels in saltwater ponds early in the first century B.C.E. Antonia (the daughter of Marc Antony and mother of the emperor Claudius) is said to have fastened earrings to the pectoral fins of her favorite pet eel.

def•i•ni•tion

Aquaculture is the intentional cultivation of fish and other aquatic organisms in a controlled environment. **Mariculture,** as a subset of aquaculture, is the intentional cultivation of marine aquatic life in a controlled environment. Worldwide, aquaculture (freshwater and marine) makes up more than 30 percent of the total production of fisheries, but it has yet to have a significant impact on the marine aquarium industry.

The Chinese started what we would come to call goldfish about 1,700 years ago, and it was this fish, although not a marine species, that would spur the aquarium hobby in Europe in the eighteenth century. As you can see, keeping marine fishes is really nothing new, which, perhaps, begs the question of how all these ancient people successfully kept marine species without all of the high-tech aquarium equipment you will read about in this book.

How Did They Do It?

Before we figure out how they did, consider this question: Is it a coincidence that the best public aquaria in the United States are in coastal states? Absolutely not! Most public aquaria the world over are located near the ocean where there is plenty of natural seawater. There are inland public *aquaria*, such as the Shedd Aquarium in Chicago, but many of these rely on seawater being shipped to them (it comes by rail to the Shedd). The Georgia Aquarium, which opened in 2005, was one of the first big aquaria (at more than eight million gallons, it's currently the world's largest aquarium) to take a different approach. They use city water that is then mixed with commercially available salt—basically the same thing most aquarists do.

Let's take a quick look at the Aquarium of the Pacific in Long Beach near where we live in Southern California. This aquarium is right on the harbor. The aquarium's Tropical Reef exhibit, which in many ways is the most interesting to the marine aquarist, holds 350,000 gallons of water (overall the aquarium uses more than 1 million gallons of seawater). Remember in Chapter 1, when we said that the smaller the system, the harder it is to keep it stable? Well, apply that same concept here. Whether it's a 350,000-gallon tropical tank at the Long Beach aquarium or only a 100,000-gallon coral reef exhibit at the Georgia Aquarium, these are *huge* aquaria by anyone's standards, and their size, combined with their access to limitless saltwater, is perhaps their greatest asset in terms of their success.

Now think back to the early fish keepers we mentioned at the beginning of this chapter—the Sumerians, Egyptians, Assyrians, and Romans. What do these civilizations all have in common? (Think about the aforementioned question: Is it a coincidence that the best public aquaria in the United States are in coastal states?) That's right! All of these civilizations have coastal access, and all of the successful marine fish keeping in these civilizations occurred on or very near the coast in enclosures that were generally quite large (e.g., ponds and even small bays like the fish ponds of Tusculum built by the Roman general Lucullus near the Bay of Naples around 65 B.C.E.).

> **def•i•ni•tion**
>
> Throughout this book, you will see us refer to the plural for aquarium as **aquaria** instead of aquariums. While you may see the word "aquariums" quite frequently, the aquarist knows that the proper term is aquaria—spread the news!

> **Warning**
>
> In this text we generally prefer the metric system, but we do use gallons as well, as this is what you are most likely to see when purchasing a tank in the United States.

So we now have an answer for the question we asked at the outset of this chapter. How did they do it without all the fancy, high-tech equipment many marine aquarists think of as "essential equipment" today? Like most of the best public aquaria, they had access to limitless

supplies of fresh seawater, and they kept their fishes in very large enclosures. This situation is a far cry from today's heartland hobbyist trying
to keep a tropical marine species alive in a 135-gallon tank in her living
room in the winter (much the less a 10-gallon nano tank in her Wichita
office). Whew! We were beginning to worry that there was no longer a
need for this book!

A Fish in a Glass Box

Successfully keeping a marine fish alive in an aquarium is all about
understanding the fundamentals of what that fish needs to survive.
Remember Mark's glass box theory? In Chapter 1, we hypothesized
that if you put a marine fish in a sterile glass box filled with saltwater, it
would initially do quite well, but over time (8–24 hours or so, depending on the size of the glass box), the fish's condition would deteriorate,
and, eventually, it would die.

Why? Over time, the chemistry of the seawater would change as a
result of the fish's normal biological functions, and, if left unchecked,
that water would no longer support the fish's needs. Mark shares his
glass box theory with beginning aquarists because it is a simplistic
approach that demystifies the apparent (and often seemingly overwhelming) complexities of the marine aquarium hobby. In many ways,
it's as simple as asking you what would happen if you were placed at the
bottom of the ocean without any breathing apparatus. You'd die, right?
Duh.

You would die because, although oxygen is present in water (H_2O), the
oxygen in water is attached to two hydrogen atoms, making it unusable
for human lungs (of course, you'd also die because it is 2°C, and the
immense pressure alone would kill you). Fishes, on the other hand, can
"breathe" underwater because the fishes are using dissolved oxygen by
way of their gills. So why did the fish in the glass box die?

Oxygenation

It's possible that the percent of dissolved oxygen (DO) in the glass box's seawater dropped too low to support the fish's respiration. Dissolved oxygen is a gas, one of two principle gasses found in seawater (nitrogen is the other principle gas). Oxygen is captured by seawater at the surface of the ocean through wave action and produced by photosynthetic organisms. Oxygen-rich surface water gets mixed by waves and currents, and sinks as the surface water cools and the seawater becomes more dense than underlying layers (cold water is more dense than warm water). As it sinks, fishes and other organisms consume this oxygen, decreasing the concentration of DO in the water.

In our glass box, a certain amount of dissolved oxygen already existed in the seawater when we added it. Let's say the DO starts at somewhere around 7 ppm (that's the saturation point). The concentration of dissolved oxygen was increased by the process of pouring the seawater into the glass box (similar to wave action trapping oxygen through air-seawater interaction in the ocean).

> ### Pearls of Wisdom
>
> Fishes require oxygen to survive, but they don't "breathe" the same oxygen we breathe. Instead, a fish uses oxygen gas or dissolved oxygen, which is diffused into its blood as the water passes by its gills. In the event that the concentration of dissolved oxygen in the water is too low, the transfer of oxygen cannot happen, and the fish will die.

Over time, the percent of DO in the glass box decreased as a result of the fish's respirations. It's also possible that the glass box, which perhaps we put in a sunny window so it looked nice, got warmer. As the temperature of the seawater went up, the percent of DO decreased even further as cold water "holds" more oxygen. Finally, because we were careful not to disturb our new friend, we kept the kids and pets away from the glass box so that the surface of the water was absolutely still. However, with minimal air-seawater interaction, surface oxygen concentrations decreased dramatically. Since the rest of the water column's percent of DO depends on surface oxygen concentration, the oxygen available to the fish in the glass box decreased even further. At a point (only hypothetically speaking, of course), the fish in the glass box would essentially suffocate as a result of the concentration of oxygen falling well below four or five parts per million.

Now that's not that complicated, is it? It sure is a lot simpler than talking about trickle filters, dosing ozone, ReDox potential, ORP (ORP is RedOx Potential), and UV sterilization (although we do cover some of these things in Chapter 6). While modern aquarium technology can make aquarium keeping easier than ever before, its misuse can be deleterious, especially in the hands of someone who doesn't understand the fundamental principles first. Bear with us, and let's stick with the basics a little longer.

Aeration—Renourishing Seawater

Remember Anna with her live corals safely sewn onto a large sponge and packaged in stone jars filled with fresh seawater? As it turns out, a good 15 years before Dmitry Mendeleyev figured out the periodic table of elements, Anna figured out that one key to successfully keeping marine life alive in a glass bowl was something, like Mendeleyev's elements, essentially unseen. The Sumerians, Egyptians, Assyrians, and Romans knew this, too, even if they didn't articulate it as such. They knew that keeping marine fishes in large outdoor enclosures with lots of surface area for air-seawater interaction resulted in successful fish keeping, but there is no evidence that they applied this knowledge to keeping marine fishes in smaller vessels indoors. As early as 1790, Sir John Graham Dalyell had successfully kept a marine aquarium in his flat in Edinburgh, Scotland, but the success of his efforts was largely the result of a servant filling an earthenware pitcher from the sea and bringing it back to his flat several times per week.

> **Pearls of Wisdom**
>
> Sir John Graham Dalyell was one of the first known people to attempt to keep marine species in his laboratory, but he relied on a servant to constantly collect fresh seawater. It is estimated that the seawater-fetching servant tread an estimated 39,650 miles in the service of Dalyell's aquaria. Without this, his aquarium never would have succeeded.

Anna, a member of London's fashionable Victorian society, also relied on a servant, but her ideas about how to "renourish" her aquarium were still quite revolutionary. The ocean was not a quick jaunt down the street from their London home, and while she sent for seawater from the coast for a time, eventually she came up with a new plan.

"I thought of having [the seawater] aerated by pouring it backwards and forwards before an open window, for half or three quarters of an hour between each time of using it," said Anna. "This was doubtless a fatiguing operation; but I had a little handmaid, who, besides being rather anxious to oblige me, thought it rather an amusement."

This simple process of pouring seawater back and forth in front of an open window mimicked wave action and increased the percent of DO in the water column through air-seawater interaction. In Anna's terms, it "renourished" the seawater. In modern terms, it aerated the water and increased DO.

Circulation

As we have demonstrated (actually, Anna did the demonstrating), oxygenation of the aquarium water is essential. We can achieve oxygenation in the marine aquarium today through circulation, especially at the surface where the seawater absorbs the oxygen (and releases the carbon dioxide, but that's a different story). Good circulation also doesn't allow dead spots, places where water remains stagnant, to develop in the tank and ensures that all of the oxygen-depleted water that has settled through the water column is constantly forced back to the surface where it is "renourished." We discuss how to create effective circulation in Chapters 8 and 10, but for the time being, know that oxygenation through circulation is one critical component to keeping marine life alive in an aquarium.

Waste Management

Now that we've figured out the importance of circulation and its effect on the percent of DO in the aquarium, let's return to our glass box with a fish in it. By adding circulation to the system, the percent of DO in the water has risen, the fish is no longer "gasping for air." We took the glass box out of the window so that the little guy wouldn't boil, and we're keeping the water temperature at about 26°C (79°F).

Things are progressing swimmingly, at least for a time. But then we notice some solid matter on the bottom of the glass box. Next we see a long piece of string-like material coming from the aft portion of the fish's underside. Yep—we all do it. It begins with "s" and ends with "t"; it comes out of you and it comes out of me; Hey! Don't be rude and call it that, be scientific and call it "scat."

Fishes, like people and all other organisms, produce waste. Some of this waste takes the form of carbon dioxide produced through the fish's respiration, and some of this waste takes the form of liquid and fecal matter and, even more importantly, *ammonia*. Even if the fish is not fed and does not produce feces, it can still die as a result of ammonia poisoning because every time a fish flaps its gills, it releases small amounts of urine, which contains high concentrations of ammonia. Over time, this waste builds up in the glass box until it reaches a critical level and becomes toxic to the fish. If you do not intervene, the toxicity will reach a level where the fish dies. Even with plenty of circulation in the glass box, producing lots of oxygen exchange, you're going to still need to get rid of the ammonia.

def•i•ni•tion

Ammonia (NH_{3+} and NH_4OH) is toxic to fish and other aquatic organisms. It is produced by fish waste and decaying organic matter (e.g., uneaten food, dead animals, etc.). In high concentrations, it can easily kill nearly all aquatic life. The successful aquarist must deal with this ammonia before it becomes toxic enough to kill.

Frequent Water Changes

We discuss the process of ammonia breaking down in the aquarium in Chapter 13—this is called the nitrogen cycle, and it is an absolutely essential process for the aquarist to understand. For the present discussion, however, suffice it to say that you remove waste in two main ways. The first way is the way Anna and all the first marine aquarists did it—frequent large water changes. Today's aquarist still relies heavily on regular water changes (we discuss this in Chapter 18). Water changes are one of the easiest ways to partially remove waste from the system, although over the past decade, a number of products have been advertised as eliminating the need for water changes. In our experience, none of these products are as effective as regular water changes, but it may be worth researching some of the new "Zero Water Exchange" products.

Filtration

The second way to remove waste from the marine aquarium is through filtration—both biological and mechanical (there is also chemical filtration, which we discuss in Chapter 6). While biological is more important than mechanical, we'll talk a little about mechanical filtration first, because it's an easier concept to grasp.

Think of a sieve or a coffee filter (we drink a lot of coffee). A coffee filter keeps the ground coffee beans inside the filter, and allows the coffee to flow through the filter. This is how we avoid grounds in our coffee, and it is essentially how solid waste is removed from the aquarium. The water is pumped or drains into a mechanical filtration device and is then pumped or drained back into the aquarium. If all the water in the tank is pumped through this filtration device, and if the filtration device is fitted with a *filter medium* with pores small enough to catch the solid waste but large enough to allow water to pass through, then, theoretically, all of the solid waste will be captured in the filter media. This is called mechanical filtration. The aquarist can then come along and clean or replace the filter medium, which effectively removes the waste from the system.

def•i•ni•tion

The media in **filter media** is plural for medium. In the marine aquarium world, a filter medium is an intervening substance through which your aquarium water passes. The medium separates out substances and gasses from the water that would otherwise harm the aquarium inhabitants.

There are other kinds of waste that need to be dealt with through other filtration methods besides mechanical filtration (e.g., biological and chemical filtration), and we discuss these in detail in Chapter 6. Remember we discussed previously how a fish excretes ammonia every time it flaps its gills? Well, the ammonia produced in this fashion could easily kill the fish long before its feces break down into toxic ammonia. This is why biological filtration is so essential, and it's why we need to allow our tanks to begin this process—called cycling the tank—before we add any fish. Don't worry, we cover all that in gratuitous detail in Chapter 13.

Temperature and Light

Our glass box is now full of saltwater that is being circulated and mechanically filtered, and the fish seems quite content. Two other critical factors will impact the fish's prolonged health and well-being.

These factors are temperature and light, which often are intrinsically connected in the marine aquarium. Of these two factors, temperature is the more decisive for the fish's immediate health, but light becomes equally important when we start dealing with many invertebrates. A fish will be fine for a period of time either fully in the dark or always in the light (although interrupting the normal photoperiod for a prolonged period of time will cause undue stress that can lead to disease and ultimately death), but without the right temperature, the fish will deteriorate quickly.

Most fishes can tolerate a fairly wide range of temperatures, but losing the ability to control the temperature of a saltwater aquarium for a period of time can lead to the death of the animals. Stability of temperature is even more important to a fish than matching exactly the temperature of the ocean in the fish's wild habitat. This is because, while ocean temperatures may vary over the range of a particular species, a given point in the ocean maintains a very stable temperature throughout a 24-hour period. Once again, we see the advantage of a large system in terms of stability, and we are again confronted with the challenges of maintaining stability in a much smaller enclosure that is far more affected by environmental conditions.

In the case of marine aquaria, especially invertebrate and reef tanks, lighting becomes another absolutely essential element. Many invertebrates such as anemones and various corals need light in order to survive. Not only do they need light, but not any light will do. These lights must be capable of providing the same intensity and wavelengths of light as one might experience on a shallow reef in the Tropics. We discuss lighting in Chapter 9, but it's worth mentioning here that these lights, in addition to being quite expensive, generally add a fair amount of heat to the aquarium. In most cases, by the time you add up the heat coming from the lights, pumps, and other equipment in your system, you find that you again have a temperature problem. There are a number of ways to combat rising temperatures in your aquarium, but the most effective is a chiller, which we discuss later in Chapter 7.

The Basic Components of a Marine Aquarium

Okay, let's take one more look at that glass box to see how the fish is doing now. We find the glass box on a table away from a window in a room with a stable temperature. Because we only have a fish in this tank, we do not have any special lighting—just your standard aquarium hood fluorescent light that contributes very little heat to the system. We have set up a pump that is circulating the tank water and running it through a filter, taking care of both oxygenation and filtration. Finally, we have a submersible aquarium heater with a simple thermostat that keeps the tank at 26°C (79°F).

With this basic setup, the fish will live for quite some time (although he sure would like some decorations—maybe a few pieces of rock). We feed the fish twice a day and only as much as he will completely consume in two to three minutes. The fish produces solid waste, which is captured in the mechanical filter media inside the filter housing. We—correction, you ... we have our own fish to attend to—change the filter media regularly, and you siphon off and replace about 10 percent of the water every week. Success!

The system works because it has the basic components necessary for sustaining marine life in captivity:

♦ Oxygenation

♦ Mechanism for removing waste

♦ Mechanism for converting toxic ammonia

♦ Temperature control

♦ Light

Notice that we are not talking about all the fancy pieces of equipment you will read about in Chapters 6 and 7. There are no protein skimmers, fluidized bed filters, or calcium reactors, and guess what? The fish is alive. So is this all you need to know to jump into the saltwater hobby?

Absolutely not. While this so-called glass box aquarium will function for quite some time, eventually, even with the equipment and regular maintenance discussed previously, the water quality will begin to change and, most likely, deteriorate. This is especially true if you want to keep more than a single fish, and we know you probably are imagining a full-blown reef tank or a fish-only system with beautifully colored angelfishes drifting about. As your bioload goes up, your system may become less stable (at least initially), and it definitely requires more intervention from you. In a nutshell, that's what the rest of this book is about.

As we get into the complexities of water chemistry, aquarium equipment and species-specific requirements, keep Mark's glass box in mind. Even though the problems will become more complex as your system grows and matures, this basic way of thinking about problems and solutions will serve you well. In addition, it will save you a little money if you don't immediately run to the local fish store or hop online to figure out what new piece of equipment you need to solve your problem. Most problems can be solved with common sense, patience (you're going to hear a lot about patience being a virtue in this hobby), and research. No doubt you will eventually add some high-tech equipment, but by the time you do, you will be knowledgeable enough about your system to resolve the new issues created by the new piece of equipment you bought to solve the old issue you used to have.

Finally, if it ever gets to be too overwhelming, don't get too discouraged without first thinking back to how Anna brought the sea to the city in 1846. If she could do it, so can you.

The Least You Need to Know

- People have been keeping marine fish for almost 5,000 years, and they didn't have modern aquarium equipment.

- Fish need oxygen just like us, but they need it in the form of dissolved oxygen, or DO.

- Oxygenation, filtration, temperature control, and light are all critical components of successfully keeping marine fish.

Chapter 3

Categorizing the Hobby— Before You Buy

In This Chapter

◆ General categories of aquaria

◆ General categories of livestock

◆ How to create a stocking list

Now that you've made it to this point in the book, you know you're in this hobby for the long haul. You are already armed with some solid information, and it might be tempting to run right out and buy that aquarium. We'd recommend, however, that you don't do that just yet.

We know you're excited, but you're going to have to be patient in this hobby. We won't sugarcoat it for you—there is a lot of hurry up and wait for the marine aquarist, and it's best to get used to it early on. In our opinion, waiting is not a downside to the hobby. Being patient affords us the opportunity to do what we love best—research, scheme, and dream really big.

Obviously we've done a lot of the research for you, but there is still plenty for you to do. In fact, this would be a good time for you to start a notebook, a blog, or just a Word document on your PC. Call it "(your name here)'s Reef," and use it to try to capture all your ideas regarding your soon-to-be very own slice of the ocean. Even if something seems completely out of the question, write it down. Collect pictures from aquarium magazines and the Internet. Leaf through books (we've included our favorites in Appendix B). Sketch your dream tank. Ask your kids to sketch their dream tank. Talk to people already knowledgeable about the hobby. This stage can be really fun—enjoy it!

As you begin the planning in earnest, we are going to try to make some broad generalizations to help you plan effectively. In this chapter, we will attempt the impossible—breaking the hobby down into categories. Please understand that any attempt to do this will fail in some way, and therefore use our categories only for what they are—a tool to help you plan what sort of system you are going to build and what will inhabit it.

Stocking Stuffers–How to Create a Stocking List

While there is nothing wrong with going out and buying an aquarium and then figuring out what to put in it, we prefer to frontload the process by planning the entire system before buying anything. Mark always asks new customers what they want their tank to look like in a year. Do they want a reef tank densely populated with small color-ful fish? Do they want a tank with big impressive fish that can be seen from across the room? How you answer these questions has everything to do with the system you design and the equipment you purchase.

From Chapter 1, you have a good sense of generally what you need and how much it might cost, but we would now like to take it a step further and think through what you intend to keep in the aquarium. That way, you can be sure you are buying the right equipment. In this chapter, we discuss three approaches to socking a marine aquarium: the "must-have" species approach, the *biotope* approach, and the *habitat* approach.

A "Must-Have" Species Approach

So you're a diver, eh? Or maybe you just returned from a Caribbean cruise where you had the chance to snorkel over a tropical reef. Or per-haps you just got the new issue of *CORAL*, the leading reef aquarium magazine. Or, okay ... we'll go there ... you just saw *Finding Nemo*, and now you really, really, really want a clownfish. Regardless of where the inspiration struck, you now can't get that one species out of your head.

This is one approach to stocking an aquarium. On the positive side, you will be able to design a setup that really shows off that one species. On the negative side, you will be limiting yourself to what you can keep in the aquarium based on that one fish's profile. For example, you may really want to have that Red Sea Picasso triggerfish *(Rhinecanthus assasi)* you saw at the public aquarium—it's just such a cool-looking fish! When you consult the species profile on the enclosed CD-ROM, however, you learn that a lot of fish and invertebrates can't live in the same aquarium with this species of triggerfish.

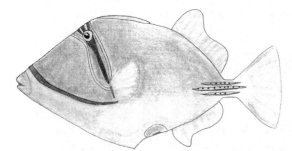

The Red Sea Picasso trigger-fish (Rhinecanthus assasi) *is a beautiful fish but will severely limit what else you can keep in your aquarium.*

(Courtesy Karen Talbot.)

When consulting the CD-ROM, you also notice that the Red Sea Picasso triggerfish is not reef compatible. This means you can't keep it in the same aquarium with certain invertebrates commonly found on a reef because your Picasso triggerfish will eat just about everything. You also learn from the fish's profile on the CD-ROM that this fish will need a tank of at least 75 gallons (although we think a tank over 100 gallons would be much better), and you find out the tank will need to be aquascaped so as to provide lots of hiding places and lots of swimming space. Finally, you discover that the Picasso triggerfish is a really messy eater that likes to eat frequently. This means you will need superior filtration, and you will need to clean the filter frequently (as in daily).

As you can see, choosing a "must-have" species ensures you will have a species you really want, but, in most cases, it also seriously limits what else you can keep in that system or even what kind of system you can have. Are you prepared to spend the money on not only purchasing this beautiful fish but also maintaining the aquarium in which it lives?

A Biotope Approach

The word *biotope* comes from the Greek and translates as "life place." In the biotope approach to stocking, you choose a species that is either *sessile* or which lives its entire life in a very limited space. This may not be your favorite species (although it might be), but it's the species that defines the portion of the ocean you are going to replicate in your aquarium.

Most fish species (like the above-mentioned Red Sea Picasso trigger-fish) do not make a good biotope species, because they range over a large habitat (a tropical reef habitat, for example). A biotope is a much more precise definition of place than a habitat. A species such as the Red Sea Picasso triggerfish may swim through your chosen biotope, and, as such, it may be an appropriate addition to your aquarium, but the Red Sea Picasso triggerfish won't define your biotope.

Say, for instance, you think you would like to keep anchor coral *(Euphyllia ancora)* in your aquarium. Anchor coral, like all coral from the genus *Euphyllia*, is a sessile invertebrate, and, as such, it is a good animal to consider when taking the biotope approach to setting up your aquarium. Does the biotope approach also limit your options in the same way that the "must-have" species approach does? In some ways it does. For example, you know from referencing the CD-ROM that anchor coral is mostly *photosynthetic* and requires strong lighting and moderate water movement. You also know from the CD-ROM that anchor coral possesses an offensive weapon in the form of tentacles that will sting and damage other corals with which they come into contact. You will need to provide the anchor coral with reef-ready lighting (expensive) and moderate flow. You will need to give it sufficient space so as not to damage other corals, and this may limit what other corals you can keep in the tank.

def•i•ni•tion

A **sessile** animal is usually attached to a solid object or makes its own solid object to which it remains attached. While some sessile animals are able to move about at some stage in their development, most are fixed in place as adults.

A **photosynthetic** coral relies on light for the survival of algae (called zooxanthellae) that lives within the coral's cells. These algae provides, in some cases, up to 90 percent of the coral's diet.

The biotope-minded aquarist is interested in what species live in close relationships with one another in the wild, and they take their cue from these interactions. Many of those same relationships which work in the wild will also work in the aquarium. For example, adding a few sexy shrimp *(Thor amboinensis)* would be a natural choice in the anchor coral biotope, as these shrimp are often found living in anchor coral in their natural habitat. Taking your lead on stocking from the natural eco-system is very rewarding for most aquarists. Not only do you tend to learn a lot about the natural marine ecosystem, but given the challenges those ecosystems face today, the more you know, the better equipped you will be to make a difference.

*Anchor coral (*Euphyllia ancora) *is generally con-sidered a common beginner, albeit aggressive, large-polyped stony coral.*

> ![Warning] **Warning**
>
> Not all species will act in captivity as they do in the wild. There are many species of fishes, for example, that shoal together in the wild but which would fight to the death if confronted with another adult of the same species in an aquarium. The popular yellow tang *(Zebrasoma flavescens)* swims in large shoals on tropical reefs, but two adults in the same home aquarium probably spells trouble.

To create the rest of your stocking list using the biotope approach, you might continue to look for other relationships building on the original biotope species. Look at pictures online and in books of reefscapes with anchor coral and see what other organisms are in the same frame. A Google image search for "anchor coral" may yield some interesting ideas.

Eventually, you may also choose to add some larger species that move through many biotopes on a given day in the wild. A Watanabe's lyre-tail angelfish *(Genicanthus watanabei)*, for example, will not spend its entire life swimming around a single anchor coral colony, but part of its territory may include the anchor coral biotope. As such, you could add a fish such as the Watanabe's lyretail angelfish to this biotope (if your tank is sufficiently large, of course).

This brings us to the last point we will make about the advantages of a biotope approach. With the biotope approach, the order of your stocking list will probably be close to the order in which you should introduce each species. With the "must-have" species approach, you most likely won't want to introduce the "must-have" species first, especially if it is something like a triggerfish. Most of these fishes are boisterous and aggressive enough as is without inflating their egos by making them think the whole aquarium belongs to them. A fish such as a triggerfish (or even a Watanabe's lyretail angelfish) should be amongst the last species you add to the tank so that everyone else has a chance to settle in and establish their territories before the bruiser enters the scene. With the biotope approach to stocking your aquarium, you are usually building up through the ecosystem, and, as a result, predators will often be the last species you choose and the last species you add.

Overall, we like the biotope approach to stocking your marine aquarium because it increases your chances of having few (if any) compatibility problems. It also increases your knowledge of the natural ecosystem, and it establishes an appropriate stocking order. We're not saying this is the only way to do it, or even the best way—it's just the way we like to do it.

A Habitat Approach

The last of the three stocking methods we will discuss is what we term the habitat approach. This is probably the most common approach taken by marine aquarists, and, in many important ways, it is quite similar to the biotope approach.

Using the habitat approach, you first choose a habitat to replicate. Instead of something as specific as an anchor coral's biotope, you might consider something as broad as a tropical reef habitat, a sea grass habitat, or a mangrove root habitat. The first step in this approach is to re-create the physical characteristics of your chosen habitat.

Suppose you want to recreate a coral reef habitat, for example. It doesn't have to be as specific as a reef slope, reef pinnacle, or reef flat. Rather, your aquarium simply has to have the physical characteristics of a typical tropical reef. In general terms, we're talking about moderate to strong water flow, intense lighting, live rock, and warm water. This habitat approach to stocking is not as specific (some might say limiting) as the biotope approach. This approach gives you the flexibility to decide what might live on your ideal coral reef rather than replicating the exact relationships found on an Indo-Pacific reef slope or a western Atlantic reef flat. For instance, you may keep two species that would never meet in the wild together in your ideal coral reef aquarium.

Taking this habitat approach is really about creating a specific set of physical environmental conditions and then adding species that will thrive in those conditions. There certainly is the potential for compatibility issues, given that you may be putting species together that never would encounter one another in the wild, but consulting the compatibility chart on the CD-ROM should help you avoid any major problems. In some cases, in fact, mixing species from the same families but from different regions may be the only way to keep multiple members of the same family together (e.g., angelfishes).

The last thing we'll say here about the habitat approach is that we encourage you to be creative. While most people enter this hobby with the image of a coral reef tank in their mind, there are many marine habitats worth recreating. Biologically speaking, sea grass habitats, mangrove habitats, tide pool habitats, and lagoon habitats are all incredibly diverse and interesting.

Categorizing the Fish

Now that we have discussed three different approaches to stocking your aquarium—the "must-have" species approach, the biotope approach, and the habitat approach—let's talk about the really fun stuff: the fishes themselves. Later we'll discuss categories of corals and other invertebrates.

Fishes can generally be broken down into two categories: peaceful fishes and aggressive fishes.

You will see on the CD-ROM that we also refer to some species as semi-aggressive, but for now, we'll just deal with the extremes.

Peaceful Fishes

Peaceful fishes are … well, peaceful (generally speaking). Peaceful fishes make excellent inhabitants of a peaceful community tank. It may be a fish-only tank, or it may be a reef tank, but it will be dominated by nonaggressive fishes. Examples of peaceful fish for a peaceful community reef tank might include clownfishes, blennies, gobies, small angelfishes, some chromis, many tangs, cardinalfishes, fairy wrasses, some dottybacks, basslets, and mandarinfishes.

The clownfish (Amphiprion ocellaris) *is the single most recognized fish in the hobby.*

(Courtesy Karen Talbot.)

Now, remember how we said these are just general categories and there are exceptions to every rule? It actually gets a lot more complicated. Although the above list represents some commonly available peaceful marine aquarium fishes, it is not a stocking list for a peaceful community aquarium. While each of these fishes may be listed as peaceful (or, in some cases, semi-aggressive) on the CD-ROM, if you put them all together, you would probably have trouble. In fact, some of them may well become the terror of the tank, constantly harassing and even killing the other fishes. For example, a wrasse such as the black fin flame fairy wrasse *(Cirrhilabrus condei)* may have compatibility issues with dottybacks, and dottybacks may tangle with small reef-safe angelfishes.

To make matters more confusing, there are sometimes issues with keeping certain members of the same species together. For example, two adult yellow tangs should not be in the same aquarium unless that aquarium is very large, but the yellow tangs' Atlantic cousin, the

Atlantic blue tang (*Acanthurus coeruleus*), prefers to be in pairs or a small group. And guess what? An adult yellow tang often does just fine with other tang species. Oh, boy!

Try to keep focused on the guiding principles here rather than getting into the "can-this-fish-go-with-this-fish" game. For example, the aggression between two so-called peaceful fishes may have to do with the fishes' appearances. Fishes that are similar in shape and size (and in some cases color) are, generally speaking, more likely to fight with one another, and if those two fish are from the same genus, watch out! Likewise, two fishes from the same genus that are dissimilar in color may do fine together.

To really determine what fishes are appropriate in a peaceful community reef tank, you have to go beyond checking a fish's disposition on the CD-ROM. While knowing if the fish's disposition is peaceful, semi-aggressive, or aggressive is a good starting point, you will need additional information. Read the species descriptions carefully and consult your local fish store or online dealer of marine livestock.

Aggressive and Predatory Fishes

It's important to point out that the vast majority of marine fishes are aggressive when they need to be. The ocean is a pretty hostile environment, and most saltwater fishes have developed certain aggressive characteristics to deal with this hostility. That's not to say that some fishes are not more aggressive then others—they certainly are. These more aggressive fishes often occupy the predator niche on the reef, and while they may adapt their behaviors to the captive environment and act quite peaceably (hand-feeding a moray eel or a triggerfish comes to mind), all of the fishes we term aggressive are fully capable of aggressive predatory behavior (which is why you should not hand-feed your moray eel or triggerfish).

When we talk about predatory aquarium fishes—those fishes that, by nature, prey on other animals in the aquarium—we generally think of two subcategories: fishes that nip their prey to death, and fishes that eat their prey whole.

In the first category, we have fishes such as triggerfishes. These fishes will go after something much larger than they are if they feel like they can get away with it. They will also often nip and pick at your corals and other invertebrates. In short, they are perpetually hungry and curious fishes, and, as a result, most may try just about anything at least once. Most aggressive fishes in this category therefore should be kept in a fish-only system with other fishes that are larger and more aggressive.

The second category of fishes, those that eat their prey whole, will not view something larger than their mouth as prey (be aware that some of these fishes can open their mouth pretty wide to accommodate a meal). Lionfishes are a good example of this second category of fishes. Most aggressive fishes in this category can be kept with peaceful fish, so long as those peaceful fishes are significantly bigger than the aggressive fish's mouth.

Some relatively common fishes that are generally considered to be aggressive include triggerfishes, lionfishes, groupers, large angelfishes, eels, pufferfishes, some large tangs, and large wrasses.

But wait a second, you say. I just saw a bunch of those so-called peaceful fishes together with some of those so-called aggressive fishes in the Tropical Reef Habitat at the Aquarium of the Pacific in Long Beach. Remember, the Tropical Reef Habitat at the Long Beach Aquarium is 1.3 million liters (350,000 gallons); the tank you are going to put in your home is probably quite a bit smaller. In most cases, the smaller the tank, the higher the chances of aggression. While tropical reefs are wildly diverse ecosystems, the density of fishes per section of reef is actually less than many people think (and certainly less than what some people try to cram into their marine aquarium). Even when the density on the natural reef is high, there is (quite literally) a whole ocean in which to escape.

As we said at the start of this chapter, there are exceptions to every rule. Anyone who has been around this hobby for long enough will tell you that individual fishes are, like people, individuals. We could have the nature versus nurture argument until the cows (or cowfish) come home, but for what it's worth, some individual fish will act nothing like you were told they would act. We wish we had a dollar for every aquarist who told us about their triggerfish's "puppylike" behavior—how that triggerfish lived for years in a community reef tank and never touched a coral or went after another fish. How can this be? Mark has children and Ret doesn't, so we're not going to take this conversation any further—suffice it to say that every fish (and child) is special and unique.

Pearls of Wisdom

While lionfishes and eels are listed as aggressive fishes, they are, in reality, essentially peaceful. While some species of eels are decidedly aggressive, most behave themselves so long as the other fishes in the system are significantly larger than their mouth. The same is true for lionfishes—in fact, lionfishes are often the target of harassment from triggerfishes, larger angels, and puffers.

Categories of Coral

Up until this point, we have not talked a lot about coral. Sure, we've mentioned it in passing and alluded to it every time we talk about a coral reef, but we have not really jumped in, so please indulge us a minute while we get some of the basics down. Then we'll move on to species of coral that are peaceful and species of coral that are aggressive. We'll also divide corals into the other categories by which hobbyists commonly refer to them.

As we discuss in Chapter 1, coral reefs have been around for about 650 million years. Keep in mind that the oldest known human remains have been dated at only 195,000 years old. Coral reefs are the most diverse of the marine ecosystems and second only on earth to the diversity of tropical rain forests.

Coral reefs are not just piles of rock with life growing on them—natural coral reefs are built over millions of years by hermatypic stony corals (reef-building corals) that make their own skeletons. When a coral dies, its calcareous skeleton becomes part of the reef and is colonized by a phenomenal abundance of life. It has been estimated that there may be over three million species of reef organisms, the vast majority of which have yet to be discovered.

Contrary to what many novice aquarists think, every saltwater aquarium is not a reef tank. Not only are there saltwater tanks that are designed to replicate other habitats (such as those discussed earlier in this chapter), but there are saltwater tanks full of reef species with no intentional coral living in them. These aquaria that do not intentionally contain coral (we say intentionally, because coral can make its way unintentionally into the system as a so-called hitchhiker on live rock) are not "reef tanks" insofar as the nomenclature of the hobby goes.

Pearls of Wisdom

The coral we recommend you include in your reef tank is alive. There is also dead coral or, more correctly, dead coral skeletons that are sold as part of the so-called curio trade. It used to be quite common to use coral skeleton in the marine tank. We recommend you use live rock and, in a reef or invertebrate tank, live coral.

A reef tank is a tank in which you intentionally introduce and grow coral that will share the aquarium with carefully selected fishes and other invertebrates. Some aquarists choose to have only coral and other invertebrates like snails and shrimp in their aquarium and no fishes. Such a setup is also—technically speaking—not a reef tank. A tank with coral and invertebrates, but no fish, is called an invertebrate tank.

Aggressive Corals

Like fishes, corals can be broken down into peaceful and aggressive categories. Given their bucolic appearance, it's sometimes hard to believe that some corals are aggressive, but remember that coral reefs are expensive real estate, and competition for space is at a premium. As such, most corals can (and will) fight for superiority both on the reef and in your aquarium. How do they do that? Some corals use stinging sweeper tentacles while other release toxic soluble compounds into the water column. Some corals simply grow over weaker, more submissive corals. Scientists have estimated that on a naturally existing reef, close to 40 percent of the corals present may be "at war" at a given point in time.

Understanding what these corals are up against in the wild makes their aggressive behavior in the aquarium seem a little less sinister. Of the aggressive corals commonly available, galaxy coral (*Galaxea fascicularis*), torch coral, frogspawn coral, anchor coral (all from the genus *Euphyllia*), and Bubble Coral (*Plerogyra* spp.) all bear mention.

This is not to say that you should not keep these species. In fact, species from the genus *Euphyllia* are amongst the most popular corals in the hobby owing to their showy appearance, relative hardiness, availability, and low price. If you do keep more aggressive corals, however, be sure to give them the space they need so as not to feel threatened. Most corals (even some very aggressive ones) would rather save their energy for growth and reproduction.

The CD-ROM covers most of the commonly available coral species and, like the fish descriptions, includes details about each coral's disposition. Make sure to consult this resource when planning your stocking list for an invertebrate or reef aquarium.

Warning

Some corals can cause injury to humans. It is therefore best to handle corals carefully. Reactions can range from a mild skin irritation to a serious, even life-threatening, response depending on the individual's sensitivity. Always read up on a coral before purchasing or handling it.

Peaceful Corals

As already stated, most corals are adept at both defending themselves and going on the offensive. There are some corals, however, that are quite peaceful, and the only real risk they pose is their vulnerability to being killed by more aggressive corals. Some species of coral, such as those from the genus *Porites*, actually use their passivity as a survival technique. These specially developed corals can sustain a fair amount of damage and continue to thrive, unlike most passive corals that quickly succumb and die when confronted with an aggressive neighbor.

Is Coral Hard or Soft?

In addition to categorizing coral species by their disposition, it is common for aquarists to talk about coral as belonging to one of the three following categories: soft or leather coral, large-polyp stony (LPS) coral, and small-polyp stony (SPS) coral.

These are imprecise terms at best (go ask a marine biologist for the real scoop), but they are the current nomenclature in the hobby. Soft corals are generally the easiest to keep and usually quite peaceful. These are, for the most part, good beginner corals, although keeping many soft corals may preclude your ability to later keep some of the stony corals. The species guide on the CD-ROM provides information on most of the commonly available soft corals.

Soft corals are differentiated from stony (hard) corals, and stony corals are commonly divided into LPS and SPS corals. The name implies that the differentiator is the coral's polyp size, but unfortunately that's not necessarily the case. LPS corals are generally considered easier to keep, and many also make good beginner corals, but it would be incorrect to categorically say that corals with large polyps are always easier to keep than corals with small polyps. You will hear a lot of people in the hobby say that LPS corals require less intense lighting and less current velocity than SPS corals, and this is often true with the commonly available species. Nonetheless, you should consult the CD-ROM or other resources for specifics.

While perhaps easier to care for, LPS corals do tend to be more aggressive as a result of their long sweeper tentacles. For this reason, it is not uncommon to give LPS corals a 15-centimeter buffer zone in all directions. The species guide on the CD-ROM provides information on most of the commonly available LPS corals.

SPS corals are generally considered more difficult to keep than soft corals and LPS corals, but they generally also require less space because they do not possess the same stinging tentacles. SPS corals need a much smaller buffer zone in most cases. The species guide on the CD-ROM provides information on most of the commonly available SPS corals.

Categories of Other Invertebrates

In addition to marine fishes and corals, you may choose to also include other marine invertebrates in your aquarium. In fact, it's common practice to add a number of invertebrates as the first inhabitants of a new aquarium. We discuss CUCs in detail in Chapter 14. In addition, you may want to add ornamental shrimp, urchins, sea cucumbers, sea slugs, and feather dusters, and, as you become more experienced, anemones, starfishes, lobsters, sponges, and bivalves such as clams and scallops. We discuss other invertebrates for your aquarium in Chapter 16.

Creating a Stocking List

Now that you have a general idea of the major options, feel free to start thinking about what you'd like to have in your aquarium. We'd suggest you choose one of the stocking methods described at the start of this chapter and then go to town. Don't worry about your list being too big initially. There will be plenty of time to pare it down as we progress into planning a budget for your new aquarium in the next chapter.

Warning

Avoid any simple formula for how many fish your aquarium can handle. The bioload changes dramatically based on the fishes' behavior, not just its adult size. Voracious eaters, for example, increase bioload beyond any of the common inch-per-gallon formulas, although the industry standard is 1 inch of fish for every $2\frac{1}{2}$ gallons of water. Your best bet is to add livestock slowly and test your water parameters frequently during the stocking phase.

The Least You Need to Know

◆ Develop a plan before you buy anything.

◆ Consider carefully what type of livestock you want in your system, and design it appropriately.

◆ Refer to the CD-ROM for specific information on the dispositions of various fishes, corals, and livestock.

◆ Create a comprehensive stocking list.

Chapter 4

The Dollars and Some Good Sense

In This Chapter

- ◆ Figuring the financial costs
- ◆ Figuring the maintenance cost
- ◆ Deciding where to buy

How much should you budget for this marine aquarium you are planning? Once you've decided on what animals you plan to keep, and therefore what equipment you need, where do you go to get all the stuff? Once the system is up and running, where will you buy your livestock?

These practical questions may not be as fun to ponder as whether or not you want a blue jaw triggerfish (*Xanthichthys auromarginatus*), but they are absolutely essential in our opinion. Establishing a realistic budget for your equipment, livestock and your system's maintenance is an important part of getting into this hobby in a responsible and sustainable fashion. There would be nothing worse than to design an amazing aquarium only to determine that you really can't afford to run it. So get out pencil and paper, or set up a spreadsheet, and let's get to work.

Financial Costs

There are three major categories of financial costs associated with having a marine aquarium: equipment, livestock, and maintenance

While it may be tempting to just start buying equipment, this hobby can get very expensive very quickly if you have not planned appropriately. In this chapter, we share some tips and tricks that will make setting up, stocking, and running your aquarium a little easier on the wallet and far more enjoyable in the long term.

Equipment Costs

While the aquarium itself is the most visible and often the largest single piece of equipment in the system, it is seldom the most expensive. Reef-ready lighting systems are notorious for draining your wallet at the outset, and then again with each electric bill. Appropriate filtration for fish-only systems loaded with waste-producing animals can easily cost more than a standard aquarium. Too often aquarists don't realize this up front, and it really sets them up for a world of hurt. It's a balancing act, for while bigger is better in terms of system stability, bigger is also generally more expensive in setup and operational costs. By planning out your equipment purchases ahead of time, you can strike the balance between the right system and the right price.

Mark indicated in Chapter 1 that, based on his experience doing custom aquarium installation, a fish-only saltwater tank will probably cost around $10 per gallon, while a reef tank costs between $15 and $30 a gallon depending upon how you set it up. Using that as a guide, consult the table below to get a general sense of how much the tank you are considering may cost.

Gallons	FOWLR	Reef
55	$550	$1,100
75	750	1,500
125	1,250	2,500
150	1,500	3,000

A very general list of the equipment will include an aquarium, lights, a stand and canopy, a return pump, additional pumps and/or powerheads, a protein skimmer, a sump, a hydrometer or refractometer, test kits, and two heaters. In addition, you should consider an ultraviolet sterilizer, a calcium reactor, and an aquarium controller.

Each system is going to vary in terms of the specifics, but most salt-water aquaria will employ the equipment listed above. In Appendix B, we have listed sample systems, and you may want to look at them now. While you may not know what a certain piece of equipment is or what it does at this point in the book, rest assured that we discuss each item in Part 2.

One final word on the cost of equipment: while it's tempting to let price be the deciding factor when comparing two pieces of equipment, know that all marine aquarium equipment is not the same. The money you save up front by buying protein skimmer A instead of protein skimmer B may be quickly lost when you figure out that protein skimmer A isn't really up to the task, and you end up purchasing protein skimmer B as well.

An inefficient, cheap piece of equipment will cost way more in the long run than a more efficient, albeit more expensive, piece of equipment. We discuss how to budget your system's energy requirements later in this chapter.

Livestock Costs

Aquarists refer to all of the living organisms in their aquarium as live-stock. While fishes are perhaps the most obvious organisms you might put in a fish tank, in the saltwater world, we also have many corals and other invertebrates from which to choose. In fact, some marine aquarists don't have any fish at all in their system, choosing instead to have an invertebrate tank loaded with colorful coral and interesting shrimps and other invertebrates.

Like equipment, it's difficult to generalize about the cost of livestock. Luckily, it's definitely worth going slow when adding livestock to your tank. Unlike equipment, where you need to buy the majority of it out-right, livestock will be purchased over the first four to six months of your tank's life (and then from time to time for as long as your tank is up and running). The reason for going slow with stocking has to do primarily with the amount of life a new system can handle. We call this bioload. It is essential to increase bioload slowly in a new aquarium so your system can catch up with each new addition. Adding all of your livestock to a new aquarium at once could cause your system to crash, killing all of your newly purchased animals in the process.

The second reason that your initial stocking should take up to six months is because some animals, like anemones and some fishes, need the stability of an older aquarium. While rock is certainly not alive and therefore not livestock, we mention it here because we strongly believe that almost every marine aquarium should contain a significant amount of so-called live rock. We discuss live rock in detail in Chapter 12, but for the purposes of budgeting, know that live rock is an early (and we believe essential) purchase.

Live rock costs in the neighborhood of $4–10 per pound depending on the quality, and you will want at least 1 pound of quality live rock per gallon of system water. This is not an area in which you want to skimp. Some aquarists choose to add 1.5 to 2 pounds of live rock per gallon.

Pearls of Wisdom

In Mark's experience, perhaps the most expensive aquarium fish is the peppermint angelfish (Paracentropyge boylei), which has fetched as much as $8,000. The most expensive fish per pound is perhaps the flaming prawn goby (Discordipinna griessingeri) which is 1 inch long and sells for around $150.

In Chapter 1, we suggested you budget between $60 (30-gallon tank) and $400 (200-gallon tank) for a comprehensive clean-up crew. This will be your first major livestock purchase (after live rock).

After you have live rock and a clean-up crew in your tank, you can pretty much go as slowly as you want. We listed the 10 most popular fish and their prices in Chapter 1 to give you a general sense of how much money you might spend on livestock. Those prices ranged from $3 (green chromis) to $115 (blue tang) per fish. You could certainly spend a lot more. It's really up to you. In general, the least expensive system in terms of livestock is usually going to be a fish-only system, and the most expensive system is usually going to be a reef system.

A trochus snail is a common member of an effective clean-up crew, or CUC for short.

(Courtesy Karen Talbot.)

Maintenance Costs

Maintaining a saltwater system can be quite expensive, so it's best to consider your monthly maintenance costs during the budgeting phase instead of when the first month's bills arrive. By taking the time to budget maintenance costs at the outset, you may well find that a more expensive piece of equipment will actually pay for itself in a short time because the costs to operate that piece of equipment are significantly less. A more expensive pump, for example, may require less electricity per month.

While electricity is a major cost of running your system, there are several other maintenance costs associated with running a saltwater aquarium. You will probably want to mix artificial saltwater from a commercially available salt mix, for example, and, you guessed it, salt is not cheap. Natural seawater is an option for some who live near the coast, but using natural seawater can bring its own host of problems, especially for the beginner. The best choice for most aquarists is to use a synthetic salt mix.

All synthetic salt mixes contain major elements, minor elements, and trace elements either essential or highly desirable for maintaining marine life in the captive environment. In terms of cost, you will have to mix up enough saltwater to initially fill your system, and then you will need to replace around 10 percent of your system water with freshly mixed synthetic saltwater each week. As of this writing, 160 gallons worth of synthetic salt mix costs between $30 and $40, so plan accordingly.

Pearls of Wisdom
If you use natural seawater, more frequent water changes are necessary, and you ought to quarantine the seawater in a dark place for a period of at least a week (or treat it) before using it. Many people use natural seawater, but you need to know what you are doing to avoid catastrophic problems with possible introduction of pests, parasites, and pollution. We recommend that the beginning aquarist use a synthetic salt

Water is free, right? Well, even if you have a private well, you're probably going to have to spend some money on prepping the water for your aquarium. In addition to filling the system and replacing 10 percent every week, you will need to top off the system daily with freshwater. This daily top-off is necessary because of evaporation, which can be significant (it's not uncommon to have 5 gallons of water evaporate each day from a large reef tank). All in all, even a 50-gallon aquarium can require between 12 and 15 gallons of water a week.

Unfortunately, you probably won't be able to simply top off your tank or mix your synthetic saltwater with water straight from your tap. Tap water (be it derived from a public or private source) often contains dissolved solids, liquids and gasses, sanitizers, nutrients, gasses, and other substances that can cause real problems in your marine aquarium. While there is debate about how significant the risk to your livestock might be, it's safe to say that the risk is lower in a fish-only system and higher in a reef system. It's also safe to say that the risk to your tank varies widely based on geography and how your water is treated before it comes out of your faucet.

We recommend that you use source water that has been processed with a reverse osmosis and deionization (RO/DI) unit for both mixing up synthetic saltwater and topping off your aquarium. You can either buy one of these units designed for home use, or you can purchase RO/DI water from your local fish store or another source. If you decide not to use RO/DI, and especially if your water is municipal water containing a sanitizer such as chlorine, at least consider using a dechlorinator. Dechlorinators are readily available at your local fish store.

Regardless of if you use RO/DI or dechlorinators, do consider the cost of water when budgeting for your tank. If you're not sure how to budget for water, you may want to jump ahead to Chapter 11 now. There we discuss water chemistry in detail, and that will help you decide if you want to invest in an RO/DI unit or not.

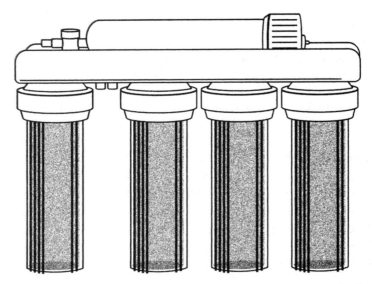

A reverse osmosis and deionization (RO/DI) unit prepares your tap water for the aquarium.

Some Common Sense About Where to Purchase

As you have seen in this chapter, you are going to make a significant investment in aquarium equipment and livestock. Another way to look at it is that some retailer is going to get your business.

The Local Fish Store—A 10-Point Inspection

Your local fish store may be in a strip mall, a basement of a private home, or on a rural route in the middle of nowhere. In other words, it is very hard to generalize about the local fish store. You may well be lucky enough to have a local fish store that is owned and staffed by knowledgeable hobbyists who run the business in an ethical and cost-effective manner. You may, however, find that you're graced with a local fish store full of algae-ridden tanks, diseased fish, and an ichthyophobic owner who has never kept a saltwater tank of his own. Chances are, your local fish store will probably be somewhere in the middle. Here are some tips you can use to assess the quality of the establishment just by walking in and looking around. We call it the Local Fish Store 10-Point Assessment.

1. Are there dead fishes?

2. Are the fishes' fins clamped to their body?

3. Are there blotches or blemishes on the fishes' skin?

4. Are there obvious wounds on the fishes' bodies?

5. Are the fishes' eyes clouded or dull?

6. Are the fishes' respirations fast?

7. Are the fishes swimming abnormally (e.g., on their sides, upside down)?

8. Is the water discolored? (Many medications will discolor the water.)

9. Do the fishes fail to respond to you moving in front of the tank?

10. Are the tanks overgrown with algae?

Warning

One reason it is so important to assess the health of livestock before purchasing is that sick or infested animals can spread disease and parasitic infestations in your tank. Don't buy a sick-looking fish unless you are prepared to attempt to nurse it back to health in a dedicated quarantine tank—not something the beginner should take on.

If you answer yes to any of these questions after careful observation, be cautious. Don't get us wrong, an occasional dead or sick fish is a reality, and there are always exceptions to the rule. For example, newly arrived fish need time to recover from the stress of shipment. If your dealer just received a shipment, you may see fishes exhibiting some of the signs mentioned above. Ask if those fishes just arrived. If so, come back in a day or two. If the fishes are healthy, they should have recovered by that time.

The biggest advantage of finding a good local fish store is that you will have a knowledgeable person willing and able to walk you through the process up setting up and maintaining a saltwater aquarium. Unfortunately, not all salespersons (or even owners, for that matter) know their stuff. While it's unfortunate, there are guys out there who are just trying to make a quick buck without really investing the time to know the hobby themselves. There is also an unlimited supply of unsophisticated, or less-knowledgable people looking for any job, and that job just may be at the local fish store.

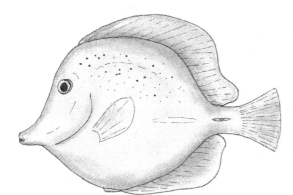

A yellow tang (Zebrasoma flavescens) *with clamped fins suffering from tang turbellarian disease or black spot, which is caused by the* Paravortex *flatworm.*

(Courtesy Karen Talbot.)

Rest assured that most local fish stores are staffed by fantastic people. People don't often get into the retail marine aquarium business if they don't also have a passion for marine aquaria and, more importantly, marine livestock. Likewise, most people simply looking for any old job won't want to clean disgusting-smelling protein skimmers unless they, too, have a passion for (and remarkable knowledge of) the hobby.

After doing your own 10-point inspection, it's time to do some talking. Think of your first visit to a new local fish store as a kind of interview. The store should want your business, and as such, they are probably willing to make an investment in time to get that business. Because you have done as we have suggested and planned a detailed stocking list and budget, you already know quite a bit about the equipment and livestock you intend to purchase. Now don't go thinking you're an expert already, but armed with the basic knowledge you already have, you should feel confident walking into the local fish store and engaging a salesperson in a dialogue about equipment and livestock. Don't act like a know-it-all (nobody likes that), but do question with confidence. It's fine to say you are a beginner—in fact, that will probably work to your advantage, as the salesperson is thinking that you may buy everything from him or her.

After a few minutes of conversation, you should be able to categorize the salesperson as 1) an expert from whom you are excited to learn a lot, 2) a person who knows the basics, but doesn't seem to really have a passion (or the time) for the finer points, or 3) a natural salesperson who has an answer for everything even when they have no idea what they are talking about. Seek out the first, give the second a second chance, and run from the third.

During that initial conversation, there are some questions to which you definitely would like to know the answer. Consider asking some of the following questions, as it will both make you appear an informed consumer and give you hard data to help you judge if this is the store for you:

Will the store test your aquarium water for free?

Does the store have a guarantee on the marine livestock they sell?

Does the store actively promote a community of aquarists through seminars, in-store educational events, and electronic (or hard-copy) newsletters?

Will someone at the store look at a piece of your equipment that is not functioning properly? If so, do they do repairs on-site (for a fee, of course)?

Are they willing to help you with custom jobs such as drilling your tank (we discuss why you would want to drill that expensive new aquarium in Chapter 8) or building/contracting a stand for your custom tank?

Do they hold hobbyists' hours instead of bankers' hours?

Do they provide aquarium maintenance services (where they come to your home and regularly maintain your system)?

Is the owner or a salesperson available for emergencies? By phone? By e-mail? Do they make house calls?

If you buy a complete setup from the store, will they install it for you (for a fee, of course)?

Do they only purchase livestock from reputable wholesalers that use collectors who practice sustainable collection techniques?

Do they carry captive-bred species in addition to wild-caught livestock?

Can you meet the owner?

Eco Tips

You should do your best to ensure that the retailer from whom you are buying livestock uses a reputable wholesaler who only buys fish from collectors trained in sustainable collection techniques. Ask your retailer about the so-called chain of custody from collector to retailer and steer clear of those retailers who boast so-called "secret suppliers."

It's not that you need to hear an affirmative answer to all of these questions, but the way the salesperson answers these questions tells you a lot about the kind of store it is. Local fish stores have to work hard to survive in this age of big-box pet stores and online retailers. Many local fish stores therefore differentiate themselves by offering outstanding customer service. Don't take advantage of this, but if you're prepared to make a sizeable purchase from the store, by all means take advantage of the services they offer to loyal customers.

The Big-Box, National-Chain Pet Store

The big-box, national-chain pet store has become a ubiquitous part of suburbia, and many of these megastores carry aquarium saltwater supplies. Some (although not many) even carry saltwater livestock. Often it is the case that the big-box pet store can offer a cheaper price for saltwater supplies and nonspecialized aquarium equipment. Less frequently is it the case that you will find a salesperson truly knowledgeable in the intricacies of the marine hobby, as most of the stores don't carry marine livestock. As such, rarely are these stores the place to go for marine livestock (although they often have great freshwater fishes!).

When it comes to stocking, few of the national chains deal in marine livestock. Those that do may have good prices but too often, in our experience, the quality is dubious at best. There are exceptions, however, and you may be lucky enough to have a local big-box pet store with an outstanding livestock manager well-versed in marine fishes and invertebrates. If the big-box pet store carries livestock, by all means use the same 10-point assessment listed above, and don't limit your 10-point assessment to the marine tanks. It's generally easier to care for freshwater aquarium fishes, so if you see any of the above warning signs in the store's freshwater tanks, you should probably be hypercautious about their ability to care for marine livestock.

When it comes to equipment, you may find better prices at some of the big-box pet stores. This is the result of the fact that they often handle more volume. For a product like synthetic salt mix, if you can save $5 and it's on your way home, go ahead and save the $5 and the extra trip. When it comes to more specialized saltwater equipment, however, be very careful about buying a product at the big-box pet store just because it says it is "for freshwater or saltwater." There are many products that say they are for saltwater that actually are not really designed for the marine environment. These products may work for a period of time, but you will end up replacing them much sooner than if you buy a product truly appropriate for saltwater. If you think you spotted a great deal, take the time to go home and get online to check out what other marine aquarists have to say about the product before purchasing. This will undoubtedly save you money down the road.

Overall, the big-box pet store has its place in the pet industry. When it comes to buying dog food and cat litter in bulk, there is really no better place. When it comes to marine livestock and specialty saltwater equipment, however, you may be better off looking to a more specialized store, especially as a novice in the hobby. These stores simply don't have the incentive to invest in the hobby the way a specialty local fish store does. With the exception of certain bulk goods, we recommend that, when possible, you take your business to the local fish store if there is a good one near you. The few extra bucks something might cost you at the local fish store is an investment in your relationship with a retailer who will probably end up saving you money in the long run.

Buying Online

Buying aquarium supplies online is really no different than shopping at Amazon or eBay. In fact, you can purchase aquarium supplies at both Amazon and eBay, but there are also a rapidly growing number of online aquarium supply stores. These stores can often offer a more competitive price on equipment than the brick-and-mortar local fish store for the exact same reasons that Amazon can often sell books cheaper than the brick-and-mortar local bookstore. Online shopping is not for everyone, however, and the beginner is often better served by developing a relationship with an excellent local fish store. In addition to the lack of face-to-face advice, shipping costs for aquarium equipment purchased online can get pretty expensive pretty fast.

Many people may, on the other hand, prefer the online shopping experience. For example, let's say you need to buy a protein skimmer. The local fish store may only carry one or two brands, and those are the brands they are probably going to recommend. When shopping online, you can literally look at every available skimmer, and read the manufacturers' marketing material, customer reviews, and online advice from seasoned aquarists. All this can get pretty overwhelming pretty fast, but if you go into it with a strategy, you can potentially make the most informed decision shopping for aquarium supplies online. Buying fish and other marine livestock online is controversial. The reality is that the number of online retailers of marine livestock has increased dramatically in the last decade, and, in our opinion, it will only continue to do so. There are some serious advantages to buying online *if* you buy from a reputable online retailer. Livestock are often less expensive (again, for the same reasons books are cheaper at Amazon), and an incredible assortment of species is available to anyone with access to the Internet. This is particularly nice for the biotope-minded aquarist who wants very specific species.

In addition, an often overlooked advantage of shopping online is that the beginning aquarist is going to get what he or she wants (not always the case at the local fish store). The beginning aquarist often has as much trouble with species identification as the beginning bird watcher. A flood of colors, behaviors, sounds, and common names makes even looking at the bird feeder overwhelming. The same can certainly happen in the local fish store (yes, some fish make audible noises), and unless you have a very knowledgeable salesperson committed to answering your questions, it's easy to feel your conviction about which species you intended to purchase when you walked in the door ebb like the tide. Unfortunately, it is also not an uncommon experience for the salesperson at the local fish store to sell you something that turns out to be something else when you get home.

When you buy online, you trust an expert to send you exactly the species you requested (notably different than pointing to that cool-looking fish in the display tank at the local fish store and saying, "I'll take that one"). You also trust their experience in selecting an individual that is healthy. You should have the same expectations at the local fish store, but we've both seen that salesperson get frustrated catching the individual you wanted and, instead, give you one that was easier to catch, assuring you it's just the same. A reputable online retailer bases its entire reputation on the fact that the animals that arrive in the box are the animals you ordered. Also, because most online retailers have guarantees on their livestock, it is in their best interest to select healthy individuals for you.

We recommend vetting online retailers of marine livestock in the same way you vet the local fish store. Take the time to give the retailer a call and talk to a representative about their business. Here are some questions Mark, the founder of one of the largest online retailers of marine livestock, suggests you ask:

> What shipping company and service do you use?
>
> What is the policy for items that arrive dead?
>
> What systems are in place to determine quantity of heat or cold packs used for shipments?
>
> Do you house your fish on-site?
>
> How long do you hold your fish between the time they arrive and the time they are shipped to end users?
>
> What systems are in place to control pathogen spread?
>
> How often are your fish fed and what exactly are they eating when they are shipped?
>
> How long have you been in the business of shipping livestock?
>
> Can I put a deposit on an animal and you hold it for me until it is healthy and eating?

In addition to being good sources of livestock, many online retailers are also great resources with species' pictures and descriptions.

The Least You Need to Know

◆ Budget everything before you buy anything.

◆ Don't forget to consider the ongoing monthly costs of operating the tank.

◆ Choose your retailer, brick-and-mortar or online, carefully.

◆ Be an informed consumer.

Part 2

Equipment

In this part of the text, we move beyond generalizations and get into the nitty-gritty details of equipment. We will cover every aspect of the hobby, from filtration and plumbing to lighting and water movement. While we assume you are a novice aquarist, we share with you many of the tips, tricks, and strategies that are often included in books written for the intermediate or advanced aquarist. While you will find the latest ideas about proper husbandry in this part, you will also learn about what simply works in no-nonsense, straightforward language.

Chapter 5

The Tank Itself

In This Chapter

- ◆ Aquarium kits versus do-it-yourself
- ◆ What size aquarium is right for you?
- ◆ Glass versus acrylic aquaria
- ◆ Placement of the aquarium
- ◆ Other considerations before you buy

So you thought this was what it was all about, eh? So how come it took us four chapters to get here? It's not called the marine *aquarium* hobby for nothing, and there is a reason you are now officially an *aquarist*. Yep, the aquarium itself is indeed the main attraction, but it's sort of like the polished newscaster who gets the airtime while all those people who put together the evening news actually remain in the shadows.

In reality, the tank is the most and least important part of the system. Without it you wouldn't have a system, but with it alone, no marine life could survive. When it comes right down to it, an aquarium is just a watertight box. It usually has clear sides, but we have seen some amazing tide-pool tanks where the only viewing was from the top.

Plug and Play, or Do It Yourself?

This is a very important decision. Let's say you've decided you want to set up a 90-gallon reef tank. Should you buy a complete kit that's plug and play, or should you build the system yourself, handpicking each component? We're going to recommend the latter, but first we'll show you what you might get with a plug-and-play kit.

Some Assembly Required

If you go online or to your local fish store in search of an all-inclusive, plug-and-play 90-gallon reef tank, you will probably find that a standard setup will go for around $2,250 dollars (not including shipping if you buy online). That's consistent with the estimate Mark provided in Chapter 1—around $25 per gallon. Let's take a look at what's included for that price.

This setup includes a 90-gallon glass aquarium, a stand and canopy, a 300-watt heater, a simple thermometer, a return pump, a wet-dry filter, plumbing accessories, and reef-ready lighting. Best of all, the system promises to "take the hassle out of creating a beautiful saltwater aquarium." Wow! That sounds great, doesn't it?

While "some assembly is required," a kit like this one generally comes with straightforward instructions and all the little pieces you need to get everything up and running in a day or so. It doesn't take an advanced aquarist (or really anyone with more than a sixth-grade reading level, for that matter) to get the system plumbed. Heck, some retailers even send a guy to set the thing up for you! Running it may be another matter altogether, but chances are, if this kit arrived Friday, you could plumb it on Saturday and fill it with saltwater on Sunday. The following weekend, presuming everything is running well and the temperature, pH, and salinity are all within acceptable parameters (we discuss this in Chapter 11), you could go ahead and add your live rock and begin the cycling process (discussed in Chapter 13). In four to six weeks (depending on the quality of the live rock), you would be able to begin stocking.

Wow! you exclaim. That was easy! So if the plug-and-play system is that easy and hassle-free, why do we recommend a DIY system?

Lots of Assembly Required

While the plug-and-play kit is pretty straightforward and hassle-free, the major drawback is you now have an aquarium designed to someone else's specifications. Is this really a problem? People buy cars and iPods and houses designed to other people's specifications all the time, don't they? And isn't it best to leave it up to the experts anyway? Why would someone try to build their own iPod when they could simply buy one designed by an engineer who knows what he or she is doing?

These are all good questions. For starters, there are not a lot of plug-and-play systems over 34 gallons on the market, so your choices are seriously limited if you go that route. Also, with most plug-and-play systems, you're going to want to upgrade almost immediately. For example, with the above system you would, at the very least, want to add a protein skimmer (a filtration device we recommend on nearly all saltwater systems). Likewise, we'd recommend a UV sterilizer as an immediate upgrade, and we'd probably also try to talk you into a calcium reactor, since you are planning a reef tank. It doesn't really matter that you don't know what these things do yet, just know that with most plug-and-play systems you will probably want to upgrade almost immediately.

Big deal, you say. At least I'll have my system up and running and then I can add to it. While this is true, have you considered that you might also have to take away from it? The above system, for example, comes with a filtration system (something called a wet-dry filter) that we would suggest you not use with a reef tank (we explain why in Chapter 6). Is this a huge deal? No, except that now you have this equipment that you're not going to use, and you don't have some equipment you want to use. Such is the experience of most people who buy a plug-and-play system. While it will work, and it will be up and running quickly, most aquarists will start upgrading almost immediately as they learn more

> **Pearls of Wisdom**
>
> A compromise between plug-and-play tanks and DIY tanks is to ask your local fish store to put a system together for you based on your specific needs and desires. Often they will be happy to do this for you, and they might even give you a break on the price since you are ordering all of the equipment through them.

about the hobby. We'd suggest you learn first, and then put your own system together based on your firsthand knowledge.

Is Bigger Really Better?

Bad jokes aside, bigger really is better when it comes to saltwater systems. The reason for this is that a bigger system is more stable and more forgiving. For starters, most large systems have more surface area for seawater-oxygen exchange (remember Anna's and Mark's glass box from Chapter 1?). In addition, a larger tank is not as limiting in terms of stocking the aquarium with fishes and invertebrates that need the space to swim. Most important, however, is that in a larger volume of water, it takes longer for anything catastrophic to occur.

Think about the world's oceans, for example. They are immense, right? The fact that they are so large is probably the only thing that has kept them going, considering everything we human have thrown at them, from trash to global warming to overfishing. Go back to the glass box we discussed at the start of this book, and answer this one question for us:

> Would the fish in the glass box with no filtration or circulation survive longer in a 10-gallon tank or a 55-gallon tank?

That's right—the fish will live longer in the bigger tank because, to oversimplify things, the fish will produce the same amount of waste in either tank, but the waste will remain more diluted in the 55-gallon tank than in the 10-gallon tank. Eventually, the ammonia level would rise to toxic levels in both tanks, but it would take longer in the 55-gallon tank. The larger tank is simply more forgiving.

So how big is big enough? In the next section we discuss aquaria under 30 gallons. These aquaria are commonly known as nano tanks, so for the purposes of this chapter, we would recommend that beginners go no smaller than 30 gallons unless they are prepared to immerse themselves into nano reefing. We would prefer to see you with a 55-gallon tank or larger, but we'll first briefly touch on nano systems.

Nano Reefs

A nano tank is generally any tank that is under 30 gallons. If bigger is better in the saltwater aquarium world, then the converse should also be true, right? Generally, yes. But that's not to say that nano tanks don't have their place—even for the beginning aquarist. For example, if you're away at school, it's unlikely you are going to set up a 55-gallon reef tank in your dorm room, but you may just consider setting up a 10-gallon nano. Likewise, the office is another place where a large tank may not be an option, but a nano could be perfect.

We understand that the urge to have an aquarium might be stronger than our advice to start out with a 55-gallon or larger. We are here to tell you that you can successfully keep a nano tank as your first tank, but you are going to need to be very diligent. If you follow the advice we give throughout this book, you should be fine. Just remember, your nano tank is not very forgiving. Overstocking a little in a 135-gallon tank isn't good, but the system won't crash. Overstock your nano, and the system probably will crash. Letting your parameters slip a little one week is bad for any tank, but your 75-gallon tank can probably handle it. Elevated ammonia levels in your nano, on the other hand, may very well crash it within the week. If you decide to go with a nano as your first tank, we will offer three very strong pieces of advice in addition to everything else we say in this book:

- ◆ Stock with hardy species with a care level of "beginner"

- ◆ Understock your tank

- ◆ Be absolutely dogmatic about your maintenance

Acrylic vs. Glass

With any aquarium, you need to decide on the material out of which it is made. As we mentioned in Chapter 2, the first keepers of marine fish kept their livestock in ponds. At some point, however, somebody got the cool idea that it would be neat to look at the fish as if you, too, were underwater—especially if you didn't have to be underwater. Ta-da! Clear aquaria.

The first marine hobbyist, Anna Thynne, went from pie dishes to stone jars to glass bowls, and, for all intents and purposes, it has been glass from there on out … well, at least until everyone's favorite petroleum product entered the scene. Plastic is ubiquitous, so we should not be surprised to find plastic fish tanks—that's what acrylic is, after all. It's plastic.

Today, the aquarist must choose between glass and acrylic, and, like most things in this hobby, people feel very strongly about which is best. Our objective is not to tell you which is better, but rather to give you the information you need about both glass and acrylic so you can make your own informed decision.

Glass

Glass was first. It's the original. Is it better? Some people think so. They think it's better because it provides a better viewing experience. Is this true? Glass is harder to scratch than acrylic, and an aquarium with fewer scratches makes for better viewing. So, yes, this can be said to be true. Glass also traditionally ages better. Glass never loses its clarity as acrylic can due to chemical reactions caused by exposure to light. Some say acrylic is more prone to distortion, but this is only the case when acrylic bows. Then again, glass won't bow easily. But you know what? Acrylic of sufficient thickness won't either. Glass will start to leak at some point as a result of the silicone seals being compromised by organisms in your aquarium. Acrylic will never leak.

Some people prefer glass aquaria because glass tanks need less support. This is true. A glass tank can be positioned on a stand without a solid top because the glass bottom of the tank can support the weight of the water. Likewise, a glass tank requires less support structure and bracing at the top of the tank. This generally means that the top of a glass tank can be completely open, while the top of an acrylic tank will be at least partially obstructed by support braces.

Finally, and for some folks, this is all they need to hear, glass is cheaper when the tank is under 200 gallons. Acrylic is plastic, and as such, it is a petroleum product, and with the rising cost of oil ... well, we might be overstating this slightly (and we really don't want to get into politics), but suffice it to say that acrylic tanks are more expensive than glass tanks.

Warning

There is an important difference between tempered glass and plate glass. What you need to know is that you can't easily drill tempered glass. Plate glass can be drilled (although it is more difficult than drilling acrylic) and is therefore preferred by many marine hobbyists.

Acrylic

Acrylic tanks are newer technology. They are, it could be said, more advanced. Does that mean they are better? Some people think so. For one, people will tell you that acrylic is lighter than glass. True? You bet. In fact, it is so much lighter that most people getting into the 200-gallon-plus range choose acrylic for weight alone. Granted, you need to support the entire base of an acrylic tank so that the bottom does not collapse under the weight of the water, but that's not a big deal.

Some people will claim that acrylic is actually a better viewing experience than glass. They say this is because acrylic's index of refraction is remarkably similar to water, meaning that as you view Nemo, light is bent twice (as opposed to four times with glass). Less bending of light equals a less distorted image. Hence, some people say, Nemo looks better (more like he really looks) through acrylic than through glass. True? Well … maybe in a perfect world. As was mentioned previously, acrylic is more prone to bowing and scratching—both of which can certainly distort Nemo.

Conclusion

So, Mark and Ret, you ask, which is better? Well you could say acrylic is clearly better because it's more expensive, or glass is noticeably better because it's cheaper (and the original). The truth of the matter is that making a box to hold water is really not that challenging—heck, we've done it with plywood. Your decision will probably come down to size (if it's over 200 gallons, seriously consider acrylic because of weight), price (if it's under 200 gallons, and a standard rectangular tank is what you want, seriously consider glass), or shape (if you want an usually shaped aquarium, acrylic is your best bet). If you go glass, you'll want to be sure to avoid tempered glass, as tempered glass cannot be easily drilled for the type of plumbing most people want to run on a marine tank. If you go acrylic, make sure it is of sufficient thickness to support the size of the tank with minimum bowing.

Whoa! It Weighs How Much?

We've alluded to the weight of a fish tank several times, but let's take a moment to address it explicitly. A fish tank weighs a lot. Hang on, we're going to repeat that because it's really, really important. A fish tank weighs a lot. How much? Well, 1 U.S. gallon of freshwater weighs a little over 8 pounds at around 4°C. Saltwater, however, weighs 2.5 to 3 percent more than freshwater because of the dissolved salts contained in it (it also depends on temperature and the specific gravity of the saltwater). As such, it's fair to calculate that a gallon of saltwater in your tropical marine aquarium will weigh 8½ to 9 pounds.

At close to 9 pounds a gallon, a 75-gallon tank weighs almost 675 pounds, just counting the water. Consider now the weight of the aquarium itself (it will vary depending upon whether it's glass or acrylic), substrate/sand, 75 pounds of live rock (the minimum we would recommend), a sump of say 20 gallons (another 180 pounds), filtration equipment … well, you can see how it all begins to add up. What does this have to do with you? First, make sure your stand can support the weight of the full aquarium setup. Then, especially in older structures, make sure the floor can support the weight (especially a second floor in an old house). If in doubt, call on a professional.

Placement for You or the Animals?

When placing your saltwater aquarium, you should be primarily concerned with the animals. This may seem obvious, but you can't imagine how many tanks we've seen positioned primarily for the viewing pleasure of the aquarium owner. Ideally, a compromise can be reached where the needs of the animals and the desires of the humans are both met, but, if in doubt, needs should trump desire.

Fish are sensitive to light, noise, rapid movements, and temperature fluctuations. Your aquarium should therefore not be placed in an area of high traffic. It should not be near a window or a door. It should not be adjacent to a heating or cooling vent, a fireplace, or under a skylight. In short, your aquarium should be in a place where the inhabitants will have the least amount of disturbance.

Okay, but we're not completely unsympathetic to the fact that you just spent a pretty penny on this system, and you'd like to see it from time to time. Many fish and some invertebrates will become quite sociable—even downright personable. We've both seen triggerfishes that are better beggars than your worst behaved dog. Putting your aquarium in the living room away from direct sunlight and out of drafts is perfectly

acceptable so long as your neighbor's kid, Dennis the Menace,
doesn't constantly bang on the
glass.

In addition, you will want your
aquarium to have relatively easy
access to water and electricity.
You will be doing regular water
changes, and you will need to run
upwards of six different pieces
of equipment (even 16 in some

 Warning _____

You will need to employ
a number of hoses and
buckets to maintain your
aquarium, especially if source
water and drain facilities are
not adjacent to the tank. It's
best to use dedicated aquarium hoses and buckets safe
for marine aquarium use.

cases!) with power cords attached. Make it easy on yourself by thinking
through how you are going to handle those water changes and where
you are going to plug in all of those wires before you decide on where
the aquarium is going to live. Believe us: you'll be glad you did.

Aquarium Furniture

Should you spend the money on a manufactured aquarium stand? Well,
that depends. Remember that your aquarium is going to weigh a lot.
Do you know anything about building? What do you know about the
relative strength of dimensional lumber? If you're handy with wood and
have built structures in the past that have not killed anyone (a bridge,
tree house, cabin, etc.) then maybe you're up for the task of building
your own stand. If, on the other hand, you don't know that a two-by-
four doesn't actually measure 2 inches by 4 inches, then maybe you
should buy a manufactured stand or pay a professional to build it for
you.

If you opt for the manufactured stand, wrought iron is your cheapest
option but probably not the best for a marine aquarium. Wrought iron
stands are open, so it's difficult to hide all the "stuff" that it usually
takes to effectively run a saltwater tank. That's why you probably will
want to go with a wood stand. The plug-and-play kit we discussed at
the beginning of this chapter comes with a wooden stand and maybe
a wooden canopy (a canopy hides the lights necessary to sustain a reef
tank while providing a means for them to not generate too much heat).
Wooden aquarium stands can be quite elaborate and tailored to match
the design scheme of the room in which the aquarium is situated. They

can also be very expensive. Don't underestimate this component when creating a budget for your system, and don't plan on using existing furniture for a tank over 55 gallons.

Rules for Renters

So let's say you rent your home or apartment. How does this affect your planning when it comes to having a marine aquarium? Even with renter's insurance (including liability), you may not be covered in the event of an aquarium disaster. The only truly safe thing to do is to get it in writing from the manager of your complex or the landlord that you have permission to have a fish tank. Even with permission in writing, be realistic about the cost of a disaster, and insure yourself for the worst-case scenario.

I Have to Drill Holes in It? You're Kidding Me!

So you just spent close to a grand on this tank, and now Mark and Ret are telling you to drill holes in it? You've got to be kidding! This is a major "know before you buy" point. If you have the choice, you want a marine tank with something called a predrilled built-in overflow. In other words, you would prefer to have your tank come to you predrilled from the manufacturer for the type of plumbing you are going to want.

In Chapter 8 we discuss the details, but for our present purposes, know that a marine aquarium works best when it's drilled. Otherwise, you need to pull the water over the back of the tank, which is possible, but can lead to major headaches (read: flood) in the event of a power outage or as the result of equipment malfunction.

At the very least, it is good to have a hole drilled in the tank to drain the water to the sump (that's the external reservoir we talked about), but you may also want to have holes for various intakes and returns. Ask if you can have the tank predrilled to suit your specific needs. Sometimes you can buy a predrilled tank, and other times you can ask the manufacturer to drill the tank for you before shipping it. Many local fish stores will also drill your tank for you for a fee.

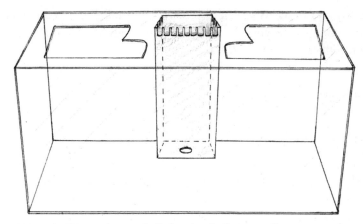

A predrilled tank. This tank is predrilled with a built-in overflow.

(Courtesy Karen Talbot.)

Keeping a Lid on the Action

It's a good idea to keep a lid on your marine aquarium. For one, this will help keep some things out of the tank (e.g., pollutants, pets) and some things in the tank (e.g., livestock). In addition, a lid will help limit evaporation, and it will protect your lights. Be careful, though. Too tight a lid can interfere with good oxygen exchange at the water's surface. Most systems will come with a lid of some sort. If yours does not, you can easily make one from acrylic purchased at the local hardware store. We suggest using inexpensive plastic eggcrate, which is available at most home supply stores.

Aesthetics

The last major point to consider is aesthetics. There are various options that may cost more, but may, in your opinion, be worth it. For example, you can usually have the back wall of the aquarium colored blue or black. Likewise, with an acrylic tank, you can have rounded corners. Bow-front aquaria are popular right now, although many other interesting shapes are available. Chances are these aesthetic decisions are more about you than the livestock, but you are going to spend a pretty penny on this setup, and you're probably going to be looking at it for a very long time.

The Least You Need to Know

♦ Seriously consider a DIY aquarium setup tailored to your specific needs and desires.

♦ In most cases, you should purchase the largest tank you can afford to set up and maintain.

♦ If your tank is large, seriously consider acrylic; if it's small, consider glass.

♦ Place your tank in a manner consistent with your livestock's needs.

♦ Consider the aesthetics your tank provides!

Chapter 6

Marine Aquarium Filtration

In This Chapter

- ◆ Learn the fundamentals of filtration
- ◆ Understand how to use sump-based filtration
- ◆ Become familiar with specific filters
- ◆ Decide what filter combination is right for you

An Internet search for "aquarium filtration" yields 52,400 web pages in less than one second. It was bad enough when the person just getting into the hobby had to contend with an aquarium supply catalog with page after page of filtration options all claiming to be "the best" filter for your saltwater system, but now ….

It's enough to turn even the most enthusiastic would-be marine aquarist back to freshwater.

The truth of the matter is that each saltwater system requires somewhat different behind-the-scenes components in order to provide the appropriate conditions for the tank's inhabitants. It doesn't, however, have to be all that complicated. By keeping the basics in mind and remembering what the end game is, you can easily put together an effective filtration system for whatever tank you are envisioning.

In this chapter, we examine the filtration components necessary for the health and stability of a marine aquarium so that you can decide what will work best for your individual needs. One final cautionary comment—filters are not magic. They do not replace other maintenance such as water changes, but used appropriately, filters are a critical component of any healthy saltwater system.

Filtration Fundamentals

The purpose of filtration, simply put, is to filter out (and ultimately remove) undesirable materials. In some cases, filtration devices convert waste products to less harmful substances as an intermediate step in the filtration process. Filtration is accomplished in the marine aquarium through three primary filtration mechanisms: mechanical, chemical, and biological.

There are many filtration devices designed to handle each of these filtration mechanisms, but as of yet, there is no truly effective all-in-one, plug-and-play filtration system that will work for every saltwater system. As a result, it is helpful if you understand how filtration works so that you can choose the appropriate combination of filtering equipment for your aquarium.

We begin with the basic principles of mechanical and chemical filtration and then deal with biological filtration later in the chapter. Specific filtration devices are described at the end of the chapter.

Mechanical and Chemical Filtration

You can think of the mechanical and chemical filtration in your aquarium like a point-of-use water filtration product such as a Brita filter. With such a filter installed, when you turn on the faucet the tap water enters a plastic housing and is pushed through a multistage filter before filling your glass. The end result is "cleaner water" for you to drink.

In the aquarium, filtration happens in much the same way. The purpose of aquarium filtration, however, is not to remove impurities from tap water (you already took care of this by using RO/DI filtered water). The purpose of marine aquarium filtration is to remove waste products created in the aquarium as a result of normal biological functions (e.g., digestion, respiration, decomposition, etc.).

A Sump-Based Mechanical and Chemical Filtration System

We recommend *sump*-based filtration—sometimes called an open system—for nearly all marine systems (yes, even nano tanks under 30 gallons). Sump-based filtration is simply the most effective configuration for capacity, overall system stability, and health. Tanks using sump-based filtration are also more aesthetically pleasing since most of the equipment can be placed in the sump instead of the display tank.

In a basic open system, water leaves the display tank via an overflow box and drains into a container called a sump. The sump, just like the Brita filter's plastic housing, is not a filter in and of itself. It simply holds the water while it is being filtered. It is what the aquarist puts in the sump (or adjacent to it) that matters.

def•i•ni•tion

A **sump** is a reservoir, often located beneath the display tank, which can hold sump-based filtration devices. Sumps increase the overall volume of the system, and, as a result, sump-based systems are more stable than non-sump-based systems.

Multistage Filtration

Before getting into the details of sump-based filtration, let's take a look inside a Brita filter cartridge to better understand the fundamentals. If you were to open the filter cartridge, you would see a multitiered filtration system involving fine mesh filters, ion exchange resin (small beads designed to simultaneously trap and release ions and commonly employed in water purification), and granulated activated carbon (for absorption of organic waste). At this point it is worth making a key distinction. Many filters, technically speaking, don't filter anything. It is the filter media housed in the filter that does the filtering. Filter media is designed to trap solid particles and separate them from the water either mechanically, chemically, or biologically. We will discuss all three, as most effective filters use a combination of all three.

Each tier in the Brita filter is responsible for a different filtration function—either mechanical or chemical. Tier one is a prefiltration tier where large particulate matter is captured in a mesh filter. Tier two involves ion exchange filtration intended to remove heavy metals and reduce carbonate hardness. In tier three, the water is filtered through activated carbon granules to absorb organic impurities. Finally, in tier four, the water passes through an ultrafine mesh filter to catch any remaining particulate matter.

The Brita filter uses a combination of mechanical filtration (tier one and four) and chemical filtration (tier two and three) to "clean" your tap water. Your sump, when properly configured, will do exactly the same thing for your aquarium water. Later in the chapter we will also add a biological filter to your sump.

Sump Basics

As Mark always tells customers, while there are many ways to handle the filtration of your saltwater tank, the best filtration is sump-based. A sump is often nothing more than a simple glass or acrylic box. It is generally positioned in the aquarium cabinet below the display tank. Manufactured sumps built for effective sump-based filtration can be purchased from most marine aquarium supply companies, although many do-it-yourself-inclined aquarists choose to make their own. The advantage of a purpose-built, manufactured sump is that it is precon-figured to support the most common sump-based filtration components without requiring a lot of modification work.

The most common configuration is a two-chambered sump. The two chambers are separated by an acrylic wall or baffle system that extends to about three-quarters height. Often a filter sponge can be positioned in the baffle to eliminate microbubbles, which can cause health prob-lems for your tank's inhabitants (not to mention they're unsightly). This filter also provides an additional layer of mechanical filtration. Once water in the first chamber fills to the top of the separating wall or baffle, it spills into the second chamber, where either a powerhead (sub-mersible pump) or an external pump returns the water from the sump to the display tank. Some two-chambered sump models also have a removable baffle included so that a special component called a refugium can be created in a third chamber (sump-based refugia are discussed in Chapter 7, where we discuss refugia in general). With this common, two-chambered sump configuration, it is easy to both install and maintain sump-based mechanical and chemical filtration devices.

> ### Pearls of Wisdom
>
> Although filter sponges are often included with a manufactured sump, it is not always advisable to use them. If you are using a filter sock, that should capture much of the particulate waste, and the danger is that the filter sponge will become a breeding ground for bacteria unless it is changed frequently. Microbubbles can and should be eliminated as a result of a well-designed baffling system.

Sump-Based Mechanical Filtration

Like the Brita filter, the first filtration mechanism in a sump is usually mechanical and is accomplished by a filter sock, which removes large particles from the water. Once in the sump, the water is often filtered— or skimmed—in the first chamber by a device called a protein skimmer (discussed in more detail later in this chapter). The protein skimmer's job is to take water from the first chamber (usually by way of a powerhead), remove dissolved organic nutrients from this water, and then return the water to the first chamber. Some protein skimmers can also be set up beside or in line with the sump if there is insufficient room in the sump.

Sump-Based Chemical Filtration

Chemical filtration can also occur in the first chamber of the sump. Commonly it takes the form of granular absorbent media like activated carbon or phosphate remover. This absorbent media is contained in a media bag, and may be placed directly in the sump. Chemical filtration removes dissolved organic waste in the same way that mechanical filtration removes particulate waste. For this reason, it might be claimed that chemical filtration is nothing more than mechanical filtration at the molecular level.

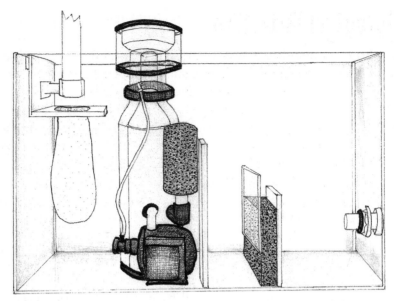

A common sump configuration with an in-sump protein skimmer installed.

(Courtesy Karen Talbot.)

Flexibility

Once the water has been filtered in the sump—mechanically filtered by the filter sock and protein skimmer, chemically filtered by activated carbon or other absorbent media, and again mechanically filtered by the filter sponge in the baffle separating the sump's first chamber from its second—it is now ready to be returned to the display tank.

While there are many variations and configurations for a sump, the setup just described is a fairly common and effective design that will handle the mechanical and chemical filtration needs of most saltwater systems. What's really nice about the sump is that it is extremely flexible and can accommodate a variety of additional or alternative filtration devices. Another perk of utilizing a sump is that all of the accessories many freshwater aquarists must put directly in the aquarium itself (heaters, thermometers, etc.) can be placed in a marine aquarium's sump. Overall, this makes the display tank better looking, less crowded, and safer for the tank inhabitants.

Biological Filtration

In addition to sump-based mechanical and chemical filtration, biological filtration is sometimes added to a multichambered sump through the addition of so-called biological filter media, often simply referred to as biomedia. This so-called biomedia may be natural (e.g., sand or rock) or artificial (e.g., round plastic balls or continuous plastic strips), and it is commonly housed in a sump-based biological filter. If biological filtration is not handled in the sump, then it needs to be handled in the display tank itself by utilizing sufficient quantities of live rock (discussed in Chapter 12) and, perhaps, a sandbed. Live rock is such an effective biological filter that it is often the *only* intentional biological filter in a healthy marine system.

We recommend that most saltwater systems use live rock in the display tank as their primary biological filtration mechanism. Nonetheless, there are situations where biological filtration in the form of a sump-based biological filter are recommended or even mandated. Before we discuss those situations, let's pause to briefly review what biological filtration is all about.

As you know from Chapter 2, the organisms in your aquarium excrete waste in the form of toxic ammonia (NH_3). Additional ammonia is generated in the tank through the process of decomposition of organic matter (dead organisms, uneaten food, etc.). Toxic ammonia, if present in sufficient quantities, will kill your livestock—that's why we need effective biological filtration. Unlike mechanical or chemical filters, biological filters don't actually filter the water. Instead, biological filters provide habitat for bacteria that convert the toxic ammonia to nitrite and then to relatively harmless nitrate. In short, promoting the conversion of toxic ammonia to a relatively harmless substance (the process of nitrification, which we discuss in Chapter 11) is the primary purpose of biological filtration.

Efficient nitrification in the marine aquarium requires lots of surface area upon which the nitrifying bacteria can grow. An entire book could be written on the various biological filtration methods and the arguments for and against each. Instead of writing that book, we are going to simply address biological filtration in terms of more efficient and less efficient methods and let you make up your own mind based on your system (although if you want more direction, you can always look to the sample systems shown at the end of the book). As you read through the options, remember that it's all about surface area.

Any habitat in your system that is colonized by nitrifying bacteria is, essentially, a biological filter. Having said that, we are only going to discuss purpose-built, sump-based biological filtration devices in the following section. The two most common sump-based biological filters are wet-dry trickle filters and fluidized bed filters. Both of these are efficient biological filters because they contain filter media (biomedia) rich in surface area, which provides good habitat for nitrifying bacteria. The location and operation of each is described below.

Specific Sump-Based Filtration Devices

The following filtration devices are all sump-based and are commonly used by aquarium hobbyists. Most of the manufacturers of these filters also make self-contained models that can be hung onto the back of the tank if the aquarium does not have a sump. In the next section, we will also mention other non-sump-based filters.

Filter Socks

Filter socks are mechanical filtration devices designed to capture particulate waste such as detritus, organic wastes, food, etc. Having all of your aquarium water flow into your sump through a filter sock is a good idea. Not only will it trap organic matter that you can then remove before it increases your tank's ammonia levels, but it will also protect your protein skimmer's powerhead (or any other submersible pump you have in the first chamber of your sump) from being damaged by large items that may otherwise make it from the display tank into your sump. Filter socks must be cleaned regularly and replaced periodically.

> **Pearls of Wisdom**
>
> Filter socks can be either soaked in a diluted bleach solution overnight, thoroughly rinsed and then reused, or you can wash them in the washing machine and hang dry.

Protein Skimmers

Many saltwater aquarists today would not think of setting up a system without a protein skimmer. In fact, many hobbyists employ a protein skimmer as their primary mechanism for nutrient export. A protein skimmer is a form of mechanical filtration whereby air bubbles produced inside the skimmer collect waste as they rise through the water column. Ultimately these waste-laden bubbles form a thick foam at the top of the skimmer, which is then skimmed off into a collection cup. The resulting residue—known as *skimmate*—is then emptied by the aquarist during regular maintenance. Protein skimmers allow the waste to be completely exported from the system.

When it comes to protein skimmers, bubbles are critical. More bubbles equal more skimming, and smaller bubbles are best because they have a higher surface area-to-volume ratio. In addition to bubble size and number, contact time is also very important. Other points to consider when choosing a protein skimmer include ease of maintenance and energy efficiency. Many different technologies are used to produce bubbles in skimmers, but the three most popular are venturi-driven skimmers, needle-wheel skimmers, and spray-injection skimmers.

Venturi-Driven and Needle-Wheel Skimmers

Most introductory-level skimmers are venturi driven and best for aquaria less than 50 gallons. Needle-wheel skimmers are really venturi skimmers with a twist, as they rely on a venturi valve. With needle-wheel skimmers, the air moves through a modified pump impeller designed to shred the air bubbles into a fine mist. The result is that needle-wheel skimmers produce more small bubbles than a straight venturi-driven skimmer. Venturi-driven skimmers can be placed in or beside a sump, or they can be hung on the back of the tank.

Be forewarned: most skimmers are overrated in terms of their skimming capacity. Having said this, if you power your skimmer with an appropriately sized powerhead, a venturi or needle-wheel skimmer can effectively skim a large tank.

Spray-Injection Skimmers

Jason Kim of AquaC invented a patented process in 1998 for inject-
ing air into a skimmer. The spray-injection method is mainly one of
brute force rather than finesse—lots of air and water flow yields good
performance. As Jason explains, "The best way to illustrate how spray
injection works is to imagine that you're washing your car—you've got
a bucket full of soapy water and a garden hose with a high-pressure
stream of water. If you direct the flow of water down into the bucket,
and use your thumb to force the water into a spray, you'll generate a ton
of air bubbles and foam. As the spray of water shoots into the bucket
below, the turbulence and force of the spray generates a tremendous
number of tiny air bubbles. When it comes to skimming, foam is a very,
very good thing!"

Spray-injection skimmers use a cloverleaf-shaped injector designed to
generate a powerful spray. The spray is directed downward into the
skimmer body, where it collides with the water inside (think of that
bucket of soapy water and the garden hose). From this point on, a
spray-injection skimmer works just like any other skimmer—the air
bubbles react with proteins and fish waste and eventually rise up and
form a foam, which is then collected inside a cup and discarded.

In addition to producing a massive amount of skimmate, spray-injection
skimmers generate the greatest amount of airflow for a given amount of
water. Generating a lot of air and water flow is particularly important
for large aquaria, and especially reef tanks, where oxygen exchange is
critical.

Spray-injection skimmers are somewhat more expensive (the least
expensive model is a hang-on skimmer for $165), but given the advan-
tages to your system, we believe this is one area where you don't want
to skimp.

In-Sump Wet-Dry Trickle Filters

When looking simply at efficiency, live rock is the least efficient biological filtration system. It has less surface area per pound than artificial
biomedia such as bioballs, and it is considerably more expensive. You
need at least 1 pound of quality live rock for each gallon of aquarium
water, but you only need a fraction of that weight and volume if you use

lightweight polyethylene bioballs. This is the primary reason why wet-dry trickle filters are used by many aquarists.

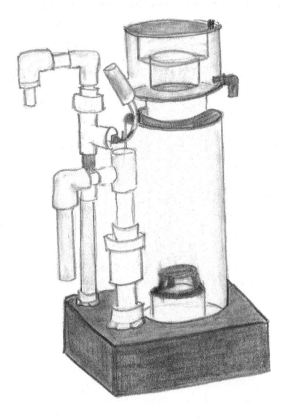

A protein skimmer is the workhorse of most saltwater filtration systems. The spray-injection model here is from AquaC.

(Courtesy Karen Talbot.)

A manufactured wet-dry trickle filter is essentially a sump like the one described above. In the first chamber there is a container, which suspends biomedia above the water. As water enters from the display tank, it drains down through this media in a random, cascading fashion, creating an ideal habitat for bacteria (oxygenated and wet). The typical wet-dry trickle filter provides, on average, up to 200 square feet of surface area per cubic foot of biomedia, making it a fairly efficient biological filter.

In addition to providing biological filtration, the wet-dry trickle filter can also provide chemical and mechanical filtration. Certain types of biomedia, like bioballs, can be filled (and refilled) with carbon and ceramic to promote additional chemical filtration, while filter sponges and mats trap particulate waste before it enters the sump. Overall, wet-dry trickle filters can provide adequate filtration for a marine system—especially a fish-only system. When it comes to a reef system, however, a wet-dry filter can lead to increased nitrates because of waste collecting in the biomedia, and this is why many reef aquarists steer clear.

In addition to the common sump-based wet-dry trickle filters, there are relatively new non-sump-based wet-dry filters integrated into canister filters (see below for a description of canister filters). Time will tell how these devices function.

A wet-dry trickle filter with an inline sump.

(Courtesy Karen Talbot.)

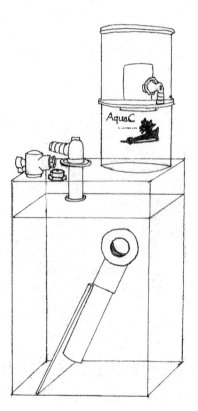

In-Sump Fluidized Bed Filters

A fluidized bed filter (FBF) is, in many ways, the most efficient biological filtration system available to the marine aquarist. A sump-based fluidized bed filter is either mounted in the sump itself, adjacent to the sump, or in-line with the sump. There are also FBFs that hang on the outside of the tank in systems without sumps.

Like all biological filtration, the object is surface area, and because the biomedia is "fluidized," it provides more surface area than any other commonly available filtration device. While individual models vary, the basic concept is that water is pumped into a chamber containing the biomedia and then flows out again. The biomedia is suspended in the water column by the flow of water moving through the chamber. This causes every surface of the biomedia to become excellent habitat for bacteria to colonize.

Because the biomedia is in constant motion, an FBF is said to be self-cleaning. As the biomedia collide in the chamber, detritus is knocked off and then filtered out of the water column by mechanical filtration elsewhere in the system. FBFs do need to have the media replenished periodically, and it is essential to disconnect the FBF from the system in the event of a power outage.

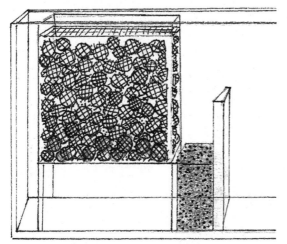

A fluidized bed filter is the most efficient biological filtration device available to the hobbyist.

(Courtesy Karen Talbot.)

Non-Sump-Based Filtration Devices

As we have already stated numerous times, we recommend sump-based filtration on almost all saltwater setups. Nonetheless, we realize there are times when the aquarist, for a variety of reasons, is not able or willing to employ a sump as a part of their system. There are also times when the aquarist with a sump-based system may want to set up a separate non-sump-based tank for use as a quarantine tank or a breeder. For these situations, there are models of the aforementioned filtration devices that can be hung on the back of the tank and do not rely on a sump. There are also the following non-sump-based filtration devices.

Undergravel Filters

While undergravel filters offer the promise of never changing a filter cartridge again, these inexpensive biological filters (they also offer a modicum of mechanical filtration) should not, in our opinion, be used in saltwater systems. Better, more efficient filter technologies exist, and there are some real risks with using an undergravel filter. The number-one problem with underground filters in a reef tank is that they are nearly impossible to effectively clean, given the large quantity of live rock in the tank. This leads to detritus buildup and reduced flow. While an undergravel filter (especially a reverse-flow undergravel filter) can work well if it is perfectly maintained and nothing goes wrong, in our experience, beginning hobbyists tend to have more problems with ammonia, nitrite, and pH when using undergravel filters.

Powerfilters

Powerfilters hang on the back of the tank and operate very much like the Brita filter described at the start of this chapter. Water is pulled into the powerfilter with an integral powerhead, and the water is then pumped through multiple tiers before returning to the tank. Inside the powerfilter housing, the aquarium water is filtered with a combination of mechanical filtration in the form of a filter sponge, chemical filtration in the form of activated carbon, and biological filtration in the form of ceramic biomedia. In addition to filtration, the powerfilter is responsible for turning over sufficient quantities of tank water and provides continuous aeration.

Some powerfilters are fitted with a device called a Biowheel. Biowheels provide excellent biological filtration because the biowheel itself provides habitat for bacteria, as it is constantly spinning in the current, remaining both wet and well oxygenated.

Despite all the advantages described above, powerfilters have their limits. They are generally only effective as the sole filtration mechanism on small systems with relatively light bioloads. Many powerfilters on the market also are not really designed for the saltwater environment, and so regular maintenance is an absolute must. Having said this, powerfilters are fairly inexpensive filtration options that can be effective on small marine systems—they wouldn't be our first choice, but we can understand why some aquarists use them in certain situations.

Canister Filters

Canister filters are inline filters that operate much like powerfilters. They generally sit on the floor under the tank instead of hanging on the back of the tank. Canister filters have several significant advantages over powerfilters, but the most significant is the canister filter's larger volume. When using a canister filter, water drains (or is siphoned) from the display tank into the canister where it is filtered with all the usual suspects. Some canister filters also now provide an integral wet-dry trickle filter as well.

If well maintained, canister filters can provide adequate filtration for a marine system. If they are not well maintained, they can become detritus traps leading to a multitude of water chemistry issues. Again, canister filters are not our first choice, but they do have their place in the saltwater hobby.

Sponge and Inside Box Filters

There are limited uses in the hobby today for sponge filters and inside box filters. While they do have their place in certain specialized situations, we do not recommend considering either of these options for a saltwater display tank.

Water Sterilization Devices

While not truly filters, there are some devices that do "clean" the water and, in our opinion, deserve mention in a chapter on saltwater aquarium filtration. While other books warn against the usage of these products because of the "problems" they can cause, we would encourage the forward-thinking aquarist to strongly consider these technologies, which are rapidly becoming the norm rather than the exception. Specifically we are speaking of ultraviolet (UV) sterilizers and ozonizers.

UV Sterilizers

Microorganisms in the system water, such as bacteria, algae spores, and protozoa, contribute to algae blooms in the tank and common parasitic illnesses from which marine fish suffer. There are many methods to combat potentially harmful microorganisms, but UV sterilization is, in our opinion, the best. That is why we recommend UV sterilization as a basic filtration device on all marine systems.

A UV sterilizer's effectiveness is based on several factors, including the UV bulb wattage, the age of the UV bulb, how clean the quartz sleeve is, and the flow rate through the sterilizer. Generally speaking, a higher-wattage bulb results in greater efficiency, although the wattage is typically rated to a particular tank size.

When using a UV sterilizer, flow rate through the quartz sleeve determines contact time (or dwell time) and, ultimately, what microorganisms are killed. Flow rate is often controlled with a ball valve and bypass system, and it is up to the aquarist to use the manufacturer's recommendations for appropriate flow rate and wattage combinations.

A UV sterilizer should be, in our opinion, standard on most saltwater systems.

(Courtesy Karen Talbot.)

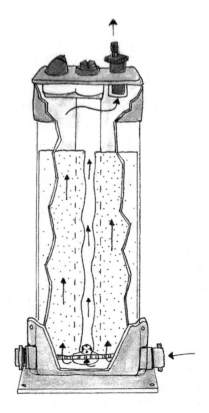

Ozonizers

Ozone can effectively destroy toxins and a variety of liquid wastes. As such, it has been used to sterilize water for drinking for a long time. In the marine aquarium, ozone has been shown to be very effective in sterilizing system water, but given its potential risk to humans, we suggest it only be used by the more experienced aquarist.

Warning

Ozone and its byproducts present a significant health risk to humans and aquarium inhabitants. For the safety of people, pass the effluent air over activated carbon as explained in the instructions to eliminate any ozone smell. Consider purchasing a test kit or meter for airborne ozone detection.

Which Filtration System Is Right for Your Tank?

As we said at the opening of this chapter, each saltwater system requires somewhat different behind-the-scenes components in order to provide the appropriate conditions for the tank's inhabitants. Without some form of filtration, the waste products produced by normal biological functions would eventually reach toxic levels, and your system would crash. For some in the hobby, the truly self-contained system (where no supplemental filtration is needed) has been the Holy Grail. This is the way the hobby began way back in mid-nineteenth-century England in the parlor of Anne Thynne (her story is told in Chapter 1) and the greenhouse belonging to Nathaniel Ward. Today most aquarists agree the truly self-contained home aquarium is not possible—at least not if you're going to have any sort of bioload at all in the tank.

Luckily, as you have seen, a whole range of filtration devices are available to the twenty-first-century hobbyist. Which filtration is best for you? The answer to this question is that a combination of filtration devices is what most aquarists use. As we have said time and again throughout this book, we recommend sump-based filtration (with sufficient quantities of live rock in all tanks). In our way of thinking, a sump-based protein skimmer and a UV sterilizer should be standard equipment. For smaller setups or setups with no sump, we recommend a hang-on protein skimmer and a hang-on UV sterilizer. For additional system configurations, be sure to check out the sample systems at the end of the book.

The Least You Need to Know

♦ Every saltwater system requires somewhat different filtration based on what livestock you plan to keep.

♦ There are three primary kinds of filtration: mechanical, biological, and chemical.

♦ If at all possible, plan on utilizing a sump.

♦ Don't skimp on skimming; buy a good protein skimmer.

♦ Seriously consider using an UV sterilizer on most marine tanks.

7

Other Components to Consider Before Plumbing the System

In This Chapter

- ◆ Increasing and maintaining calcium levels
- ◆ Phosphate reactors
- ◆ Heaters and chillers
- ◆ Aquarium controllers
- ◆ The refugium

In the last chapter we covered the basics of filtration, and in this chapter we're going to discuss some other equipment that can promote the health of your marine aquarium. While you can run a successful marine aquarium with just the equipment we mentioned in the last chapter, some of the equipment we mention here makes it even easier.

Calcium

We discuss calcium as an important component of seawater in Chapter 11, but we're also going to talk about it briefly here because the first additional piece of equipment we are going to discuss is designed to maintain high calcium levels.

If you have a reef or invertebrate aquarium, you will need to keep your calcium levels elevated to the level of natural seawater (or higher). Natural seawater has a concentration of calcium of around 420 parts per million (ppm), and you should try to keep your reef aquarium's calcium level somewhere between 420 and 500 ppm. Many reef inhabitants— from stony corals to coralline algae—need calcium in order to thrive.

When you mix up a new batch of synthetic saltwater, the calcium levels are probably sufficient, but, over time, the calcium is used by those organisms in your system that need it. The more calcium-hungry organisms you have, the more aggressive you will need to be about replacing and then maintaining calcium in the system. There are several ways to replace and maintain calcium levels in the aquarium:

- ♦ Use of a calcium reactor
- ♦ Use of Kalkwasser (calcareous water or "lime water")
- ♦ Use of a two-part solution (calcium and buffer)

We prefer and recommend the use of a calcium reactor in a reef system.

Calcium Reactor

One excellent way to replace and maintain calcium in the aquarium is with the use of a calcium reactor. A calcium reactor also maintains alkalinity (also discussed in Chapter 11). Calcium reactors maintain calcium levels in the aquarium by adding a steady dosage of calcium and bicarbonate ions into the water, usually in the form of a drip going directly into the sump or, in some cases, the protein skimmer.

In very general terms, a calcium reactor has a reactor chamber in which appropriate media (calcareous gravel) is placed. System water is then pumped through this media while CO_2 is injected into the reactor chamber. The injection of CO_2 into the reaction chamber lowers the pH (to around 6.5), making the water acidic. This acidic water is then responsible for dissolving the media and producing calcium and bicarbonate effluent, which is dosed back into the system.

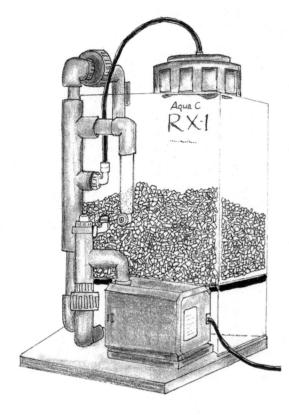

An AquaC calcium reactor is easy to use and almost maintenance-free.

(Courtesy Karen Talbot.)

When you buy a calcium reactor, either buy an entire package (many retailers sell calcium reactors this way), or make sure you have all the individual components to run it. You will need the following components: calcium reactor, CO_2 regulator with a needle valve, CO_2 tank, and media (calcareous gravel).

You will probably also want a pH probe to monitor the pH level in the calcium reactor and in the tank itself. Many aquarists use a pH probe with an aquarium controller (which we discuss later in this chapter) to control the amount of CO_2 being injected into the reactor chamber. This way, if the pH falls off too much, which could be disastrous to your system, the controller stops the flow of CO_2 until the pH moves back into the preset range.

The calcium reactor can be a little tricky to set up and dial in, but once you have it adjusted, with the exception of replacing media and refilling the CO_2 canister, there is very little maintenance. The calcium reactor is one of the safest methods for adding and maintaining calcium in your system.

> **Warning**
>
> CO_2 is dangerous, and you should carefully follow the CO_2 tank manufacturer's instructions for safe operation. In general, do not let your CO_2 tank get too hot by storing it in direct sunlight, leaving it in your car, or keeping it in a hot, unventilated aquarium cabinet. Don't fill your own CO_2 tank unless you are qualified to do so. Make sure your CO_2 tank is secure and will not be knocked over—it can become a projectile should the valve be sheared off!

Kalkwasser

Kalkwasser is German for lime water—at least that's what we have been told (neither of us speak German). Regardless, adding Kalkwasser to your system is another common way to replace and maintain calcium levels in your reef or invertebrate tank.

Kalkwasser is a solution of calcium hydroxide or calcium oxide, and it is actually quite unstable and caustic (its pH is 12.45). Kalkwasser is about 10,000 times more basic than the synthetic saltwater you initially mixed up, and this could obviously have dire consequences on your aquarium if it is not used correctly.

Thankfully, it is not difficult to dose your system with Kalkwasser by setting up a simple drip system that adds the Kalkwasser slowly to the sump. Again, it is a good idea to have a pH probe monitor the pH level in the sump—in this case to ensure it doesn't go too high (remember, with the calcium reactor, we were worried about it dropping too low).

To make Kalkwasser, simply buy one of the commonly available commercial brands and follow the instructions carefully.

Two-Part Solutions

The third and last means we will discuss to replace and maintain calcium levels is our least favorite, but it does work. It calls for using a two-part solution. With this approach, you are going to add a calcium additive, which probably contains calcium chloride. Calcium additives are a good way to quickly raise calcium levels in the tank, but they do have their downsides—especially when it comes to maintaining appropriate calcium and alkalinity levels. Most calcium additives will lower your alkalinity, and therefore, you need a buffer (part two) to bring the alkalinity back up. Unfortunately, these additives are generally expensive, and many two-part solutions actually increase nondesirable algae growth.

If you do use a calcium additive to bring your calcium levels up to the 420 to 500 range, consider then maintaining that calcium level with either Kalkwasser or, our favorite, a calcium reactor.

Phosphate Reactors

In theory, phosphate levels in an aquarium that utilizes an appropriate-sized protein skimmer and is slightly understocked should be at or close to zero. If, however, you are not religious about your maintenance, you skimped on your skimmer, or you have overstocked your tank, you may well see phosphate levels rising leading to a nuisance algae bloom. A phosphate reactor is designed to absorb phosphates so they can be removed from the system, but a phosphate reactor is not a means to doing less maintenance, nor is it an excuse to overstock your aquarium. Okay, we'll get off the soapbox now.

In any tank, low phosphate levels are a good thing. In a fish-only tank, phosphates are going to cause algae outbreaks at worst, but in a tank with calcareous corals, the phosphates act as a calcium-crystallizing inhibitor, which will stunt the growth of corals and put lots of stress on the organism. As a result, having a strategy for removing phosphates is a very good idea with most tanks containing stony corals.

A phosphate reactor suspends filter media in a reactor chamber (like the fluidized bed filter we discussed in Chapter 6) and provides specialized chemical filtration for your aquarium. While it's common to use a commercial chemical filter media like PhosBan in the reactor to absorb phosphate from system water, you may also use a variety of chemical filtration media in the phosphate reactor's reaction chamber (e.g., activated carbon).

Some aquarists will say that a phosphate reactor is not really necessary and is a waste of money since phosphate filtering/removal media can be placed in a media bag and go directly in the sump (as we discuss in Chapter 6). This is true (in fact, PhosBan comes packaged with a media bag for exactly that purpose). It is also true, however, that phosphate filtering/removal media works more efficiently in a phosphate reactor. In addition, iron-based phosphate-removing resins must be used in a reverse-flow phosphate reactor to avoid instant channeling. This gives the media the best chance of being completely utilized. Like the protein skimmer and fluidized bed filter, you will need a small pump to push water through the reactor chamber.

In conclusion, there is nothing wrong with running a phosphate reactor as part of your system, and it's quite convenient to have a reaction chamber plumbed to the system in which to add chemical filtration media (whether it's phosphate filtering/removal media or not). Is it necessary? No, although it's a really good idea to have some phosphate-removal strategy for a reef tank. Let us finish where we began—a phosphate reactor is not the solution to your algae problem. If your phosphates are high, we suggest you review your husbandry practices first rather than turning to technology as a quick fix.

Temperature Control

Chances are you will need a means to stabilize the temperature of your aquarium within a range somewhere between 24 and 27°C (about 76–82°F). Stability (within that range) is much more important than hitting a specific target temperature. Some aquarists keep a temperate-water tank, and their temperature needs will be very different, but most tropical species do well in the above temperature range.

Heating is simpler and less expensive than chilling. Heaters for the marine aquarium are similar to those used in the freshwater aquarium. Generally a submersible heater with a built-in thermostat is placed in the last compartment of the sump from where water is returned directly to the aquarium. Heaters are sold based on wattage, and a minimum of 3 to 5 watts per gallon is recommended for keeping your aquarium at optimal temperatures.

Even without a heater, a reef aquarium can easily become too warm as a result of submersible pumps or powerheads and high-intensity reef lighting. As a result, you may need a chiller to keep your tank under 27°C (80°F). A chiller works either as a "drop-in chiller" or an "in-line chiller." The former works by placing a cooling coil into the sump, while the latter requires water to be pumped into the chiller, cooled, and then returned back to the tank or sump.

Reverse Osmosis/Deionization Units

Reverse osmosis/deionization units (often simply referred to as RO/DI) remove impurities from your tap water. Even if you have great tap water (whatever that means to you), chances are some of the stuff in your tap water is not so great for your aquarium. In fact, not using RO/DI water is one of the leading causes of nuisance algae blooms in marine aquaria. We can't tell you how many times we've seen someone battle nuisance algae using every trick in the book before finally switching over to RO/DI water and—voilà!—the algae is under control. Some of the "impurities" that really pose no harm to us (e.g., phosphates and nitrates) are like fuel for nuisance algae, and deionization removes these impurities with surgical efficiency.

In addition to the natural "impurities" in your tap water, you may also have to contend with chlorine and chloramines, heavy metals, and even pesticides. Yikes! You don't want to be drinking that stuff either, which is why you may as well go ahead and just install an RO/DI filter in your home. Although it can be dedicated to the aquarium, relatively inexpensive home models can produce in excess of 100 gallons of RO/DI water per day! Plenty for your tank and your family. Who said this hobby wasn't good for the whole family?

Aquarium Controllers

An aquarium controller is a device that (you're not going to believe this) controls various functions in your aquarium. It does this by being connected to sensors or probes that are constantly monitoring your system's parameters. In addition, most controllers allow you to set a complex matrix of timers to turn various pieces of equipment on and off.

The big story in controllers today is the fact that most either come web-enabled or have a web-enabling option. In other words, you can monitor and, in some cases, control your aquarium remotely. You can also log a massive quantity of data and then display it on your computer in nifty graphs and charts. Wow!

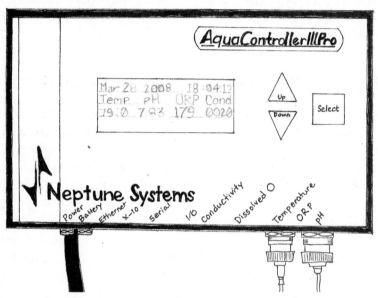

A web-enabled aquarium controller by Neptune Systems.

(Courtesy Karen Talbot.)

Is this all just one colossal bell and whistle? Some would say so, but not us. We like technology, especially when the needs of the livestock drive the technology. The top controller manufacturers out there make a product that truly can be used to improve the health of your livestock and your skills as a marine aquarist. Charting trends in your tank over an extended period, and then adjusting your approach to husbandry in order to try to change certain parameters, will teach you an awful lot about your system and the hobby in general.

On the road a lot? Then why do you have a 240-gallon reef tank in your living room, for crying out loud! Seriously, if you are away a lot, think of the peace of mind you'll get by being able to check in (online or even on your phone) on your tank while you're away. Also, imagine how much better you'll sleep knowing that the controller is equipped to handle many potential emergencies. A controller can do everything from stopping a flood to turning off a possessed piece of dosing equipment (imagine CO_2 from a needle valve gone bad streaming into your system while you're 300 miles away).

Do you need an aquarium controller? Absolutely not. Will it make your life easier? Possibly—if you actually take the time to learn how to use it. The bottom line is that the more complex your system is and the more difficult the livestock are to keep, the more potentially valuable a good controller becomes.

Refugia

A refugium, at the most basic level, is a separate tank (or even just a container) that shares your system water, but, as the name implies, acts as a refuge for the life living in it. Why would you want one of these, you ask? There are many reasons, but the big ones are as follows:

◆ Live food source

◆ Filtration/nutrient cycling

◆ pH stabilization

◆ Increased system volume

◆ Refuge for unusual/incompatible display species

◆ Experimentation with interconnected biotopes

Before we discuss each, let's talk briefly about plumbing a refugium to your system. Many people include their refugium in their sump, and, as discussed in Chapter 6, some manufactured sumps are set up to simply add a refugium. The sump-based refugium works well, but it is only one of many ways to set up your refugium. We're just going to discuss one way here. We call it "the display refugium."

The display refugium is unusual for a refugium because it is intended for display. In other words, while most aquarists keep their refugium "off stage" (sometimes in the sump, sometimes just in the aquarium cabinet), we're suggesting you place your refugium in a place where you can enjoy it.

To plumb this system, the overflow from the main display tank splits with a wye (see Chapter 8 for more information on PVC fittings). A ball valve (again see Chapter 8) is located on one side of the wye, and this side drains into the refugium, while the other side of the wye drains directly into the sump. The refugium, just like the main display tank, has a built-in overflow which drains into the last chamber (or "clean water chamber") of the sump (we discuss this more in Chapter 18, but this allows tiny organisms to make their way into the display tank without being filtered out of the water first). Finally, the return pump is plumbed, as usual, to return water to the main display tank from the sump.

Plumbing the overflow from the display tank to a refugium using a wye and a ball valve.

(Courtesy Karen Talbot.)

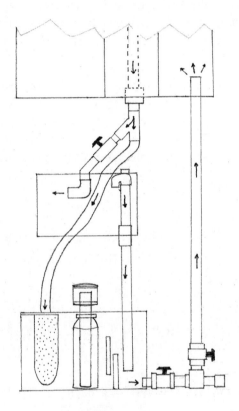

The purpose of the ball valve on the side of the wye going to the refugium is to limit the amount of flow moving through the refugium. The refugium will have a deep sand bed (actually, it's a mud bed in the case of the sample system), and we want to keep the current velocity slow enough that the sediment will not be blown into suspension. You adjust the flow of water entering the sump by simply adjusting the ball valve.

Now that you know how to plumb the refugium so that it shares your system's water, let's talk about why you may want to go to all that trouble.

Live Food Source

One of the most useful functions of a refugium is its ability to produce a constant source of live food for the animals in your display tank. Over time, the conditions in the refugium will be ideal for tiny organisms like copepods and amphipods. Without any predators, these organisms will thrive. From where do they initially come? Natural colonies will emerge from live rock and live sand over time, but you can get the process moving even faster by "seeding" the refugium with a commercially available culture.

"Pods," as they are frequently called, are small crustaceans that eat phytoplankton, bacteria, and detritus. Because of this diet, copepods are the largest source of protein for marine species to snack on in the wild, and pods make excellent food for many species of fishes in captivity. In fact, some fishes will only eat live food in captivity (at least at first), and pods (in addition to other live foods such as mysids) work great (we discuss this in more detail in Chapter 18).

Having a mature refugium connected to your system goes a long way toward successfully keeping certain hard-to-keep species like a green Mandarin dragonet *(Synchiropus splendidus)*. While you can collect pods from the refugium using a turkey baster, if you plumb your refugium the way we suggested previously (with the refugium overflow going straight to the "clean water" section of the sump), then a certain number of pods will naturally make their way into the display tank and bolster the populations already living in your display tank's live rock.

Filtration/Nutrient Cycling

Marine plants, like macroalgae, can help export phosphates and nitrates from the system. These nutrients are taken up and stored in the macroalgae, which you then prune regularly. Mangroves can also be grown in the refugium, although they grow very slowly. They are even better than macroalgae at storing nutrients, but slow growth and low biomass makes them an inefficient nutrient exportation strategy in and of themselves. Sea grasses are one of the most important marine plants in terms of nutrient cycling, and you can grow several species in a refugium.

Also, a refugium can have a deep sand bed (sometimes referred to in the hobby as simply a DSB). DSBs are very controversial because, while they can provide excellent biological filtration, they can also release toxins into the tank if they are disturbed. This is why some aquarists put their DSB in the refugium, where it can act as a filter, but where it won't be disturbed. You can also use commercially available marine mud products instead of sand in your refugium.

While a refugium will not handle all of your filtration needs—and in no way is it a substitute for the other filtration methods we discuss—it does contribute to system health and moves us a little closer to a truly self-contained system.

pH Stabilization

If you were to monitor your pH level over a 24-hour period, you would notice a dip in pH at night (we discuss why this happens in Chapter 11). Running your refugium lights on a reverse cycle with your main system, or keeping the refugium illuminated at all times, has been shown to stabilize daily pH fluctuations, and, as we have discussed many times, stability in the marine aquarium is a very good thing.

Increased System Volume

A refugium adds volume to your overall system, and more volume leads to greater system stability. Whether you use a 10-gallon refugium on a 30-gallon tank or a 55-gallon refugium on a 135-gallon tank, you are adding volume to your overall system.

Refuge for Unusual/Incompatible Species

At the beginning of this section, we commented on the fact that a refugium is a refuge. What aquarists generally mean is that the refugium is a refuge for small animals and marine plants that would be consumed in the display aquarium, but you can take it a step further.

Your refugium is an excellent place for you to experiment with keeping unusual species and species that are not compatible with your display tank's livestock. Obviously you don't want to have species in your refugium that consume massive amounts of algae or pods, but adding some brittle stars, feather dusters, sponges, and sea cucumbers can really make your refugium come alive. In some larger, well-established refugia, you could even introduce seahorses *(Hippocampus spp.)*, blue striped pipefish *(Doryrhamphus excisus)*, or other species you could not keep in your display tank.

The display refugium is, in our opinion, one of the most interesting frontiers in the marine hobby. For example, what if you set up several interconnected, biotope-specific refugia, each representing a biotope connected in the natural ecosystem. A main display reef tank, for example, could be connected to a sea grass refugium and a separate mangrove refugium. Each of these biotope-specific refugia could be populated with naturally occurring species (see Chapter 3 on the biotope approach to stocking). The aquarist would no doubt gain invaluable insight into the interactions between these biotopes that may prove invaluable to the hobby and even the ecosystems at large.

The Least You Need to Know

◆ Maintain calcium levels between 420 and 500 ppm.

◆ Don't rely on a phosphate reactor to make up for a poor maintenance regiment, but do consider adding a phosphate reactor on a reef tank.

◆ An aquarium controller can make caring for your system easier— even when you are away!

◆ Consider adding a display refugium to your system for the health of your livestock.

Chapter 8

Putting It All Together–Plumbing

In This Chapter

- ◆ Choosing a return pump
- ◆ Working with PVC
- ◆ Building a closed-loop system (CLS)

In this chapter, we will look at how to put all of the pieces of equipment we have discussed so far into a functioning, sump-based marine system. If you went with a plug-and-play system (not our favorite way to go), you may not need to read this chapter, although we suggest you do anyway. Chances are, with a plug-and-play kit (like the one discussed in Chapter 5) you will want to start modifying and upgrading right away, so you'll have to understand how all that plumbing works.

If you did as we suggested and purchased individual components specific to the aquarium you designed and the species you intend to keep, then this chapter will be invaluable to you. While it is not always the case in this hobby, it is not infrequent that a piece of equipment will arrive with either no instructions or very limited instructions. It is even rarer that a piece of equipment will give you instructions on how to attach it to other pieces of equipment made by different manufacturers (and chances are you will have equipment made by many different manufacturers). To be honest, this can be quite over-whelming to the beginning aquarist.

Our goal here is to walk you logically through what you need to know about pumps, pipes, and PVC. We'll start with the return pump (some-times called the circulation or recirculation pump) that returns water from your sump to the aquarium. Then we'll move on to the intrica-cies and joys of working with PVC. We will finish up the chapter by discussing something called a closed-loop system (or CLS for short) that we recommend be a part of every marine system, but especially an invertebrate or reef system.

Return Pumps

A return pump, as the name implies, returns water from the sump to the aquarium and is in continuous operation. Remember our discussion from Chapter 6 about how water moves through the system? It first drains from the aquarium by way of a built-in overflow box or a hang-on siphon overflow box (we prefer the former). The drain then directs the water to the sump (or to the sump and refugium, if you are running a refugium as discussed in Chapter 7). The water is filtered in the sump (discussed in Chapter 6), and then it is returned to the aquarium by way of the return pump.

The first decision you need to make about your return pump is whether you want a submersible pump (often referred to as a powerhead) or an external pump.

Powerheads vs. External Pumps

Powerheads (submersible pumps) and external pumps can be used to return water from the sump to your tank. There are several advantages and disadvantages with each, and so you need to decide what works best for you given your system and budget. We will try to give you a broad overview here so you can make an informed choice, but ultimately, it's up to you.

Powerheads, like most pumps, come in a range of sizes to pump as little as 50 gallons per hour (gph) to more than 3,000 gph. Powerheads used as return pumps are generally placed in the second chamber (or "clean water" chamber) of the sump. While they offer the advantage of not having to have a predrilled sump, powerheads do take up space in the sump and increase the water temperature (a major issue for reef and invertebrate tanks that are already getting lots of heat from high-intensity lighting). Although they take up space in the sump, power-heads take up less space overall because they are in the sump, not beside it. In general, powerheads are not as powerful as external pumps.

External pumps are the workhorses of the marine aquarium hobby. A large system will almost certainly need to employ an external pump. Like powerheads, external pumps can pump a wide range of gph, depending on the model. Some commonly available external pumps are capable of pumping well over 5,000 gph. External pumps are situated adjacent to your sump and draw water through a hole in the sump wall (many sumps come predrilled, or you can drill the hole yourself). Although external pumps require more space than powerheads, they generally add less heat to the aquarium water and make cleaning the sump easier.

If you have a small system and space is limited, you may want to consider a powerhead as your return pump. If you have a large system, you probably want to utilize an external pump.

Which Model?

Before going any further with your return pump selection, you will need to decide how many gph of system water your pump needs to move. In general, you will want to turn over your system water between 7 and 10 times an hour using your return pump. In an invertebrate or reef tank, you'll want to definitely have it be 10 to 20 (or more) times per hour, as many reef organisms only flourish with strong current. As an example, a 75-gallon reef tank should have a return pump rated to at least 750 gph. Later in this chapter, we discuss additional circulation strategies to bring a reef tank's circulation up to three, four, or five times that amount.

In a perfect world, a pump rated to 750 gph would pump 750 gph—if only it were that easy. It's not a perfect world, especially seeing that we have to contend with gravity, resistance, and overzealous marketing folks. The reality is that a 750-gph pump will not pump 750 gph through your system because it will be fighting gravity and plumbing resistance. In addition, it's just a sad fact that some pump manufacturers pump up their own egos in their marketing material and cannot practically pump the volume of water advertised.

Chances are you will need to pump the water up at least several feet from the sump to the display tank. Because of gravity, the water will face resistance as it is pushed up the pipe between the sump and the display tank. This is called head or lift. In addition to head or lift, the water is being forced through a pipe with a fixed diameter, and this diameter can have a significant effect on how much resistance the return pump experiences (keep the return pipe the same diameter as the pump outlet). You will also need to take into account the resistance created by any angles in the return line (usually right angles and 45-degree angles). Finally, you will need to calculate the resistance created by submerged returns inside the aquarium.

What!? You don't have an engineering degree? Thankfully, you don't need an engineering degree since you are only interested in getting a rough estimate of the resistance (often called back pressure or head pressure) that your pump will experience. Here's how you do that:

1. Measure the head or lift (the distance between the return pump and the top of the tank).

2. If the tank has multiple returns, measure the length of any horizontal plumbing used to feed those multiple returns. One foot of horizontal pipe equals 10 feet of vertical pipe.

3. Calculate the resistance caused by the return line's plumbing configuration by adding 1.5 feet for every 90-degree turn (this is only an estimate, as the resistance varies with pipe diameter). Then add 1 foot for every 45-degree angle. This is most likely overkill, but it will ensure you don't encounter unexpected resistance.

4. Calculate the back pressure caused by submersed returns in the tank by adding an additional foot for each return located no more than 2 inches beneath the surface.

5. Add all this up.

You now have a general idea of how much head pressure (measured in feet) your return pump is up against. That wasn't that hard, was it? Okay. We're almost finished.

Using the head pressure you just calculated and the flow rate you decided you wanted from your return pump, consult the pump manufacturer's flow curve charts to determine what pump is best for your system.

HEAD FEET	DART FLOW GPH	WATT DRAW	HEAD FEET	SNAPPER FLOW GPH	WATT DRAW
0	3600	145	0	2,500	105
4.0	3,035	152	4.0	1,900	110
7.0	2,428	155	7.0	1,500	108
10.0	1,520	146	9.0	900	97
12.0	630	125	10.5	300	75

HEAD FEET	BARRACUDA FLOW GPH	WATT DRAW	HEAD FEET	HAMMERHEAD FLOW GPH	WATT DRAW
0	4,300	225	0	5,800	350
4.0	3,843	236	4.0	5,500	360
8.0	3,333	248	9.0	4,880	375
10.0	3,018	251	14.0	4,200	360
12.0	2,730	253	16.8	3,600	345
16.0	1,810	237	19.5	3,000	325
19.3	603	189	24.0	600	265

You will want to consult the pump's flow curve chart to determine which return pump is right for your system.

(Courtesy Sequence Pumps.)

There are many, many other factors you could consider when choosing a return pump, but this simple approach should get you in the ballpark. Here are a few closing thoughts and tips regarding return pumps.

◆ Return pumps are made to push water (not pull it), so mount the return pump as close to the sump as possible and below the water level.

◆ Install a ball valve and a union (discussed below) on your return line between the return pump and the aquarium so you can easily regulate the flow rate in your return line and easily isolate the pump for maintenance, repair, or replacement.

◆ Never limit the intake flow—this can damage the pump. Use a union and a ball valve on the line between the sump and the return pump so you can isolate the pump for maintenance, repair, or replacement, but only shut the ball valve when the pump is unplugged.

◆ Make sure your inlet pipe diameter is the same as (or larger than) the outlet pipe diameter.

◆ Mount your returns high in the tank. In the event of a power outage or pump failure, aquarium water will back-drain through the returns into the sump. By placing all your return pump's returns high in the tank, you limit the amount of water that will drain back into the sump.

A PVC Primer

PVC, or polyvinyl chloride, pipe is made from, as the name suggests, plastic and vinyl, and it is your very good friend when plumbing a marine system. PVC pipe is cheap, lasts forever, and is remarkably durable. PVC is commonly available in either schedule 40 or schedule 80. All this basically means is the amount of pressure to which the pipe is rated. For example, a 1-inch schedule 40 pipe is rated to 450 psi, while schedule 80 pipe is rated to 630 psi. It's best to use schedule 40 pipe for your aquarium plumbing, as it has a larger interior diameter (ID) and is more than sufficient for the pressure.

Pipe Diameter

A 1-inch schedule 40 PVC pipe has an outside diameter (OD) of 1.315 inches and an inside ID of 1.049 inches. Now, as you can probably guess, the thickness of the pipe wall is what makes the difference between schedule 40 and schedule 80. One-inch schedule 40 PVC pipe has a pipe-wall thickness of .133, while schedule 80's wall thickness is .179. (Pretty logical, eh?) The thicker pipe wall can handle higher pressure.

PVC Fittings

PVC fittings are the pieces that join or terminate PVC pipes. PVC fittings commonly come in 90° elbows, 45° elbows, tees, crosses, and wyes. You can also get caps, plugs, couplings, bushings, unions, and adapters (and more!). When choosing fittings for your aquarium plumbing, you will need to choose between a threaded fitting and a nonthreaded fitting (called a slip fitting). If you are using threaded fittings, you need to match up male fittings with female fittings (a male fitting is a fitting with external threads that can be screwed into a female fitting with internal threads). If you are using slip fittings, you will be solventing them (we discuss gluing PVC next). Threaded fittings are not solvented. Instead, you wrap threaded fittings with Teflon tape to form a watertight seal that can be unscrewed at a later point in time. It's better to use schedule 80 fittings for ball valves and other places where leaks are common (e.g., adjacent to pumps).

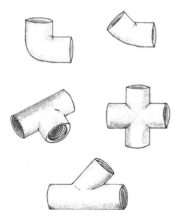

Clockwise: 90° elbow, 45° elbow, tee, cross, and wye.

(Courtesy Karen Talbot.)

Here's a quick example. Walk into your local hardware store and tell the helpful employee that you are looking for 1-inch schedule 40 PVC pipe with a 1-inch schedule 40 female adapter (this will join the 1-inch outlet on your return pump to the 1-inch return pipe) and two 1-inch, slip schedule 40 90° elbows (this will allow you to "bend" the return line horizontal to the top of the aquarium and then "bend" it again so the return flow is directed down into the aquarium). Got it?

A simple return configuration. This return configuration uses 1½ inch schedule 40 PVC pipe with a 1½ inch schedule 40 female adapter to join the return pump (in this case a ReeFlow Dart outlet (FNPT) to the return pipe, two 1½ inch, slip schedule 40 90° elbows to "bend" the return line horizontal at the top of the aquarium and then "bend" it again so the return flow is directed down into the aquarium. A siphon break used in conjunction with a check valve may be employed to avoid a flood.

(Courtesy Karen Talbot.)

You may also hear or see the following PVC acronyms:

NPS: national pipe straight

NPT: national pipe taper

FNPT/Fips: female national pipe taper

MNPT/Mips: male national pipe taper

GHT: garden hose thread

FHT: female garden hose thread

MHT: male garden hose thread

Pearls of Wisdom

NPT is the most common thread you will run into when working with PVC. There is also GHT, and a GHT and NPT are not compatible. Stick with the NPT.

Cutting PVC

To cut PVC, use a PVC handsaw (cheapest), a circular saw with a plastic cutting blade (next cheapest if you already own a circular saw), or a pair of specially designed PVC shears (most expensive). It doesn't really matter which you use, so long as you get a good, straight cut. One key to a leakproof joint is to have the pipe fully seated in the fitting, and to do this, the pipe needs to be flush inside the fitting.

Joining PVC

When joining slip fittings to pipes, it is absolutely essential to make sure the connection is leakproof. To do this, you use a solvent cement that causes the PVC to swell, making a watertight connection. To get a good, watertight connection on the first attempt, be sure to deburr the pipe after cutting and dry fit the joint to make sure you are dealing with compatible components. Then clean the pipe and fitting joints with a pipe cleaner and pipe primer. Finally, apply the solvent cement with the included brush, fit the joint together, and allow it to cure. Solvent cement, cleaners, and primers will usually be located next to the PVC fittings in the store. Read the directions carefully before use.

Threaded fittings are joined by screwing the male fitting into the female fitting. Wrapping the male fitting with Teflon tape first is essential. To join a pipe to a threaded fitting, first glue an adapter onto the end of the pipe.

Special Fittings

There are several special fittings beyond the ones mentioned above. In particular, we want to introduce you to bulkhead fittings, union fittings, ball-valve fittings, and check-valve fittings. Chances are you will hear people in the hobby talking about all four of these fittings, and you may have occasion to use them all when plumbing your system.

Bulkhead Fittings

A bulkhead is the fitting you use when you need to run a pipe through the aquarium or sump. We recommend that you purchase a predrilled tank, and you can even ask for the bulkheads to be installed (or at least included—they are easy to install yourself).

If your tank is not predrilled, it is not difficult to drill acrylic tanks, but do not drill glass tanks if you don't know the difference between tempered and plate glass. While it's not difficult to drill an acrylic tank, it can be pretty scary given how much money you just spent on it. We'll admit that it does seem counterintuitive to drill a hole in a watertight box. Many local fish stores will drill your tank for you, especially if you bought the tank from them.

Unlike PVC pipe, bulkhead fittings may not have the same OD. It is critical that you remember this if you intend to drill so that you make sure to drill the right size hole. That's why we think it's best to have the bulkhead in hand before you start drilling (just to be safe).

You can read up on drilling acrylic online, or ask another hobbyist. In general, however, use a quality hole saw, go slow, and use a spray bottle to keep the bit cool.

Schedule 80 bulkheads are highly superior to schedule 40 in a place where it really counts.

A standard threaded bulkhead.

(Courtesy Karen Talbot.)

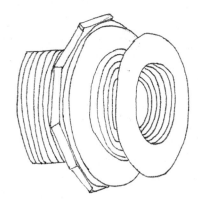

Ball Valves, Check Valves, and Unions

Ball valves allow you to limit or stop flow through a pipe by simply turning a handle. Check valves allow water to only move one way through a pipe, but, in our experience, using the cheap ones in saltwater is dubious at best. At least purchase the clear check valves if you are going to use them in your system, and check them regularly. A union is a fitting that joins two pipes so that they can be easily separated at a later point simply by unscrewing the union.

The combination of a union and a ball valve are worth their weight in gold in a saltwater system. With a union and a ball valve installed, you can shut off water to a particular portion of pipe and then separate the pipe at the union. This is critical for maintenance.

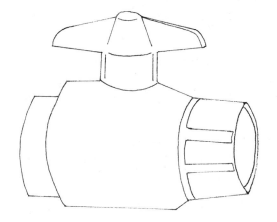

A ball valve and union fitting.

(Courtesy Karen Talbot.)

For example, having a ball valve and union on either side of your external return pump allows you to unplug the pump, shut off the ball valve on the return line (otherwise water will back-flow into the sump from the aquarium), shut off the ball valve between the pump intake and the sump, and then separate the unions to remove the pump. There is a nifty (albeit expensive) fitting called a true union ball valve that incorporates both a union and a ball valve in the same fitting.

Like other fittings, you can purchase threaded or slip ball valves and unions. They are joined to other fittings and pipes in the same way described previously.

Closed-Loop Systems

The return pump configuration we described at the start of this chapter may accurately be termed an open-loop system. We are now going to discuss a closed-loop system. A closed-loop system (or CLS) is separate from your sump and provides additional flow in the aquarium. You might ask why we can't just get a bigger return pump if we want more flow. There are two very good reasons why you would rather have a whole separate system.

Why Have a CLS?

First, conventional wisdom says that you should attempt to match your protein skimmer's pump to your return pump so that you are not returning unskimmed water to the aquarium. The reality is that you probably will return some unskimmed water to your aquarium, and, in truth, that's not the end of the world. In fact, an argument could be made that you can overskim your system. This is not a debate with which the beginning aquarist need concern him- or herself. At this point, just know that running too powerful a return pump will seriously detract from the efficiency of your protein skimmer. When you're starting out, you'll be fine as long as you return no more than 10 times your system volume per hour.

Pearls of Wisdom

It's recommended, for example, that an AquaC EV-180 protein skimmer use a Mag Drive 7 pump on a 75-gallon tank. The Mag Drive 7 pump is rated to a maximum flow of 700 GPH, meaning that you would like to use a return pump rated to not much more than 700 GPH for your given head pressure.

So if you're not going to get your 20, 30 or 40+ times per hour turnover from your return pump, then where will you get it? This is where the CLS comes into play; it is how you increase the flow in your tank without increasing the flow in your sump.

The second good reason to have a CLS is for the redundancy it provides. If your main return pump fails for some reason, you could lose most (if not all) of your livestock within about 8 to 10 hours due to no circulation in the tank. With a CLS installed, you buy yourself a lot of time, because although the filtration will not be working, the water will still be circulating in the aquarium.

Installing a CLS

To install a CLS, you need a dedicated CLS pump, PVC pipe, PVC fittings, solvent cement, at least one bulkhead, and some true union ball valves. The pump is the heart of your CLS system, and you will probably want a powerful one. There is no concern here about moving too much water, unless the current is blowing your sand around and knocking your aquascaping over. As mentioned above, some aquarists have their reef tanks turning over 40+ times per hour (that's the return pump and the CLS combined). Many reef species appreciate this brisk flow.

Your CLS pump will most likely go under your aquarium. It will be an external pump that pulls water from the aquarium by way of an intake drilled in the back wall of the tank. While it's possible to run your CLS intake line over the top of the tank, it's better to drill a hole (or holes) for the intake(s) at about midheight. You are already pulling water off the surface with your overflow, so it increases flow in the tank by also pulling water from the midlevel. The CLS intake line is plumbed to the CLS pump's intake and then the return line(s) is directed back to the tank. It is very common to divide the return line into four or more separate returns and then run these returns to different corners of the tank. The goal here is to avoid dead spots where detritus can build up. We discuss the CLS more in Chapter 10, especially when it comes to using the CLS to create random flow patterns in the tank.

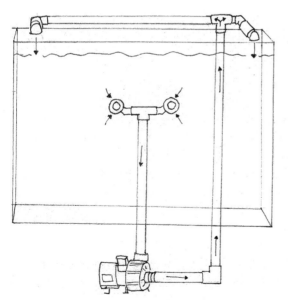

A simple closed-loop system for a reef aquarium.

(Courtesy Karen Talbot.)

If you choose not to employ a CLS on your system, you can still increase circulation in the tank without increasing the size of your main return pump. You do this by adding powerheads in the tank itself. While not aesthetically pleasing, these powerheads can do an excellent job creating supplemental flow patterns in which reef species can thrive. We discuss the use of these powerheads in Chapter 10.

The Least You Need to Know

♦ On large systems, use an external pump.

♦ Calculate your system's head pressure before choosing a pump.

♦ Use schedule 40 PVC with a combination of schedule 40 and 80 fittings for plumbing your system.

♦ Seriously consider including a CLS on your tank (especially on a reef tank).

9

Shedding Some Light on Lighting

In This Chapter

- ◆ Natural lighting
- ◆ Fluorescent lighting
- ◆ Metal halide lighting
- ◆ LED lighting
- ◆ Timers

While tanks and chillers and protein skimmers are expensive, it is the lighting that can really add up, especially in a reef tank. In this chapter, we'll discuss the major options and make some recommendations for the system you are planning.

Going au Naturale

Isn't the sun's light sufficient to support reef life in the wild? Then why can't I simply use the sun's light for my reef aquarium? This is a common question with a common answer: don't do it.

If you live in the Tropics, are not interested in viewing your tanks at night, and have an effective strategy for cooling the tank, maybe you could safely rely on the sun for your livestock's lighting needs. For the rest of us, the days are too short, our desire to view our aquaria when we are home in the evening is too strong, and our pockets are simply not deep enough to purchase and run the size chiller we would need to keep the aquarium temperature low enough to sustain life. So we turn to artificial lighting.

Beaming Fluorescent Light

Fluorescent lights are the most commonly used lights in the aquarium hobby. They use electricity to produce a short-wave ultraviolet light that causes a phosphor to fluoresce. The result is visible light. Fluorescent lights have the advantage of being less expensive than other types of lighting. They also have a low operating cost and do not emit as much heat as other bulbs. Having said that, most fluorescent lights alone are not appropriate for a marine aquarium. The only florescent bulbs that can provide the necessary light for the health of your animals are full-spectrum fluorescent lights (not broad spectrum and not wide spectrum—full spectrum) that are also high-intensity fluorescent lights.

When purchasing a full-spectrum fluorescent bulb for your marine aquarium, you will have several options to consider. Full-spectrum fluorescent lights are rated with color temperature in Kelvin (K), luminosity in lumens, and a color rendering index or CRI. A decent, full-spectrum (daylight) fluorescent bulb will be at least 5,500 K (preferably between 6,000 K and 7000 K), 2,000 lumens, and have a CRI over 80 (better if it's over 90). A high Kelvin-rated fluorescent bulb will be between 10,000 and 20,000 K.

Pearls of Wisdom

Color temperature is measured in Kelvin. The higher the Kelvin, the whiter the light is. Higher-temperature lights are said to be "cooler," while lower-temperature lights are said to be "warmer." Cooler light is dominated by violet blue and green, while warmer light is dominated by orange and red. The color temperature of dawn and dusk may be as low as 2,500 K, while the color temperature of sunlight is around 5,800 K.

In addition to Kelvin, CRI, and lumens, fluorescent lights are sold in a variety of lengths. These lengths correspond to the light's wattage. All florescent lights require a ballast, which is either built into the housing or is separate. The ballast starts the lights and regulates the flow of power through the bulb while it is operating.

Most retailers simplify the process of choosing fluorescent lights by offering some variation on two general categories:

- Normal output fluorescent lighting
- Compact fluorescent lighting or power compact lighting

Normal Output Fluorescent Lighting

Normal output fluorescent lights include the full-spectrum and high-intensity lights mentioned above. It is quite common, however, to augment these full-spectrum lights with another normal output fluorescent bulb(s) that is not full spectrum. For example, you may use both a full-spectrum bulb(s) and an actinic bulb(s). Actinic bulbs look bluish in color and are great for adding a natural-looking underwater hue that really brings out the colors in some fishes and corals. Combining a high-intensity fluorescent bulb(s) with an actinic bulb(s) will also assist with photosynthetic coral growth in a reef tank.

In addition, you will see high output (HO) fluorescent lights and very high output (VHO) fluorescent lights. HO and VHO lights require a specialized ballast, but they produce a much higher luminosity. Both HO and VHO can be used on reef systems with reef species requiring moderate lighting (check the CD-ROM).

Power Compact Fluorescent Lighting

Power compact fluorescent lights (CF or PC) are a great upgrade from normal output fluorescent lighting. These are high output lights that come in a very compact package. A single PC light fixture is easily twice as powerful as a single normal output fluorescent light fixture. The reason for this is that compact fluorescent bulbs combine multiple bulbs in a single fixture. Like other fluorescent bulbs, they are efficient to operate, and do not produce excessive heat.

Metal Halide (MH) and Hydrargyrum Quartz Iodide (HQI) Lighting

Metal halide (MH) lights work on a completely different principle than fluorescent lights and provide some of the strongest possible lighting for a marine aquarium. Hydrargyrum quartz iodide (HQI) lighting is a variety of MH lighting. If you intend to keep corals with very high lighting requirements, metal halides are probably going to be your first choice, especially when combined with actinic or other fluorescent lighting.

MH lights are also ideal (even necessary) for deep tanks, as they are one of the few lighting options that can penetrate to 60 centimeters (24 inches) or more in depth. Some reef aquarists not only consider MH/HQI lighting the gold standard in reef keeping, but even required equipment. Unlike fluorescent lights, metal halides do produce a lot of heat (so much so that most reef tanks using metal halide lights often need to use a chiller). Appropriate ventilation, however, can go a long way to dissipating the heat. MH/HQI lights are also expensive to purchase and, at least on the surface, costly to operate. In reality, MH/HQI lights are more cost-effective than many other lights considering the life expectancy of the bulbs and the useful light per watt. An entire book could be written on aquarium lighting, so we suggest you use our comments as a jumping-off point for doing your own research.

LED Lighting

LED lighting may be one of the most exciting new frontiers in aquarium equipment. These lights don't produce the same heat, and they cost significantly less to operate. In addition, the bulbs last much longer than metal halide bulbs or fluorescent bulbs. Unfortunately, LED lighting is still cost-prohibitive for many people, but as the technology advances, the cost is coming down and the quality is going up. LED lights are something to keep your eye on.

Lunar Lights

LED lights are frequently used for moon lights or lunar lights that can simply create a cool nighttime effect or actually stimulate various behaviors in certain species. They can either be set up to simply turn on and then turn off, or they can be run by a controller to simulate actual lunar cycles.

Popular Light Pairings

There are a lot of strongly held opinions about which lights should go with which system. Each system is so unique that we tend to not believe in "best" pairings between lights and tank type. Having said that, in our experience the following pairings can work well.

Fish-only systems can be paired with full-spectrum fluorescent lights or PC lights. PCs are more expensive to buy, but they last longer and provide a higher intensity per fixture. PC lights are also more expensive to operate, and they do produce additional heat in the aquarium (possibly necessitating a chiller). Nonetheless, we recommend PC lights for a fish-only system, especially since they give you more flexibility if you decide to add coral down the road.

Invertebrate and reef tanks can be paired with VHO or PC fluorescent lighting, but only if you plan to keep corals with moderate to low lighting requirements (check the CD-ROM for individual species' lighting needs). If you decide to keep corals and invertebrates with high lighting requirements, it's best to go with metal halides combined with fluorescent bulbs. MH lights of 6,500 K to 10,000 K are ideal, especially when combined with actinic bulbs.

Plug-and-Play Lights

While we tend to not like plug-and-play reef kits, we are more supportive of some plug-and-play lighting systems. There are many of these on the market these days, and they allow you to purchase a single unit that will cover all of your bases without needing to be an electrician. While you can certainly build your own lighting system from the ground up, commercially available units can provide you with the true 24-hour lighting experience with almost no hassle. Many of these systems incorporate metal halide lights, various fluorescent lights, and LED lunar lights all packaged in a neat housing with built-in ballast, on-off switches for each light, and integral cooling fans. These lighting systems are not cheap, but they do take the headache out of piecing a lighting system together.

Pearls of Wisdom
When discussing lighting, you will often hear people speak of the reflectors as being at least as important as the bulbs themselves. This is very true, as a bulb is only as good as its reflector. Be aware that while many of the plug-and-play lights make lighting easier, usually these systems have reflectors that do not maximize the bulb's intensity.

Perfect Timing

We strongly recommend you run your lights on a timer(s). The plug-and-play kits we described above sometimes come with an integral timer, or they ship with external timers. If your lights don't come with timers, get them. An alternative is to use an aquarium controller (discussed in Chapter 7) to control your lights. However you do it, you will want to have your lights on between 12 and 14 hours per day.

If you use a combination of lights, you could program your actinics to come on for an hour or so before the full spectrum fluorescents or metal halides come on, and then have the full spectrum fluorescents or metal halides go off about an hour before the actinics go off. In this way, you mimic dawn and dusk. If you have LED lunar lights, you can also set these up to simply come on at night or to mimic the phases of the moon. Regardless of how you set up your system, remember that lighting is critical, and so is consistency from day to day.

Wattage

There are many people who talk about a watt-per-gallon ratio when purchasing lights. We personally don't put a whole lot of credence in the watt-per-gallon equation—again, there are simply too many variables. Nonetheless, you will hear people mention it, so we'll briefly explain what they mean.

It has been said that you should provide 2 to 5 watts of light per gallon, and in a cookie-cutter world, that may work. There are, however, many variables that get in the way of using this simple formula. For example, what really matters is the lighting requirements of the livestock, the depth of tank, and the placement of the sessile photosynthetic invertebrates in the tank. It also matters which type of light you use, as a PC bulb is going to kick out more light per watt than a normal output fluorescent light.

Lighting and placement of photosynthetic sessile invertebrates including non-photosynthetic orange cup coral (Tubastraea coccinea) *on the sand bed in cave mouth (lowest light), trumpet coral* (Caulastrea curvata) *at mid-depth (moderate light), and acropora* (Acropora *spp.*) *high in the tank (highest lighting).*

(Courtesy Karen Talbot.)

The Risks of Getting It Wrong

Don't underestimate the importance of lighting in the marine aquarium. Using the wrong lights can have disastrous ramifications for your tank and its inhabitants. The wrong spectrum of lighting can starve photosynthetic invertebrates or cause massive algae outbreaks. Lights that are too powerful can shock, "bleach," and even kill certain corals.

Our recommendation to the beginner is to spend good money on your lights, and it wouldn't surprise us at all if your lights are the single most expensive piece of equipment you purchase—they are that important.

Pearls of Wisdom

If you do decide to go with fluorescent lights initially and then upgrade later to metal halides, make sure to take the time to acclimate your sessile invertebrates to the new lights by moving them temporarily lower in the tank or by shading them from above. This is also the case when acclimating new animals.

The Least You Need to Know

- ◆ Invest in the right lights for your system even if they are the single most expensive piece of equipment.

- ◆ If you are planning a reef tank, seriously consider using metal halides as part of your lighting system.

- ◆ Look into all-in-one, plug-and-play lighting systems—many are quite good for the beginner.

- ◆ Be sure to connect your lighting to either a timer(s) or controller for consistency.

Chapter 10

The Motion of the Ocean

In This Chapter

- ♦ What is ocean current all about?
- ♦ Wavemakers and powerheads
- ♦ Aquarium controllers
- ♦ Emulating natural water flow

Flow is critical to successfully keeping many saltwater species, especially sessile invertebrates. In fact, most serious reefers would agree flow is *more important* than light. The ocean is a dynamic environment where tides and currents are constantly moving massive volumes of water back and forth, up and down, in and out. Surface storms create chaotic wave action, while structures such as reefs cause their own internal waves and currents. Marine species have adapted to this environment to the point that many will only thrive if you replicate it in the aquarium. In this chapter, we talk about how to create alternating flow and strong currents in your aquarium.

Water movement is particularly important for an invertebrate or reef tank where many sessile invertebrates rely on the flow of water to bring them food and clean off waste. Water movement can also assist with the maintenance and health of a FOWLR tank, although it is not as critical for most fishes. While some biotope-specific tanks require minimal water movement, they are most certainly the exception to the rule. You'll hear some experienced marine aquarists say that too much flow is impossible, but more on that later.

Why Current Is Good

If you have ever been snorkeling or diving on a coral reef, you may have noticed tiny particulate matter moving about in the current. This particulate matter is sometimes called *reef snow*, and studies have shown that it is critical to the health of many reef species, especially coral. Due to the fact that most corals are fixed in place, they are forced to rely on food coming to them in the form of reef snow moving with the current.

def•i•ni•tion

> **Reef snow** is organic particulate matter, plankton, and detritus that is visible to the naked eye and is moved about the reef by ocean currents. It is a critical source of nutrition for nearly all reef species. Several commercial products are made that mimic this crucial food source, including the aptly named Marine Snow made by Two Little Fishies.

What's in reef snow? The short answer is a lot. Plankton, detritus, algae, bacteria ... basically whatever is small enough to be blown into suspension or carried by water movement. Without current to carry reef snow, many sessile invertebrates would not thrive (or in some cases, even survive).

In the aquarium, water flow that mimics the flow patterns found in the wild lifts reef snow into suspension from the substrate and live rock and makes it available to sessile invertebrates (and other animals in your system). In addition to providing a constant source of food and oxygen, strong flow also brings essential dissolved nutrients and trace elements to the coral. Obviously, a more mature tank (at least six months old) has more of this reef snow available than a brand-new tank. This is one reason you'll hear some aquarists say certain species (e.g., dragonets) should not be introduced into a new tank—there simply is not enough food in the system to provide the type of constant forage they require.

Both in the wild and in the aquarium, strong flow is critical for removing sedimentation—detritus and other particulate matter—that has settled on the substrate, rocks, and, worse, on corals themselves. Accumulated sediment on a coral can easily choke and even suffocate that coral. Conversely, strong flow constantly rids corals of this detritus, as well as the waste produced by the coral itself.

How Much Current Is Enough Current?

For many reef aquarists, water movement is said to be too strong only if the substrate itself is being blown into suspension and rocks are being moved by the current. Many an experienced aquarist might say that anything just shy of that is appropriate. We agree that it is hard to have too much flow in a marine aquarium; most water movement problems are the result of not enough flow instead of too much. Nonetheless, you can't simply add tons of flow and be done with it. There are many different types of flow, and too much flow of the wrong sort can easily kill a coral. In addition to creating flow, you need to create the right kind of flow.

Oscillatory Flow   Not all water movement is the same. There is water movement caused by waves, for example, which is called oscillatory flow. This type of flow is an uninterrupted back-and-forth motion between two extremes. Oscillatory flow is often most pronounced as wave action affecting water movement at the surface of the ocean, but it is also present in deeper water where surface wave action creates deep, rhythmic undulations.

Laminar Flow   In addition to wave action, there are currents that are the result of winds and tides. These currents cause large masses of water to move, usually in a unidirectional pattern known as *laminar* flow. This laminar flow caused by currents is unlike the oscillatory flow produced by waves. Some laminar flow reverses direction with tides or seasonal changes in wind patterns.

Variable or Chaotic Flow   There are other currents caused by a variety of environmental factors. Most of the time, some or all of these forces are at work at once on a particular section of reef resulting in chaotic, variable flow. This is the opposite of what you find in a river, where organisms have adapted to a laminar flow. In the ocean (and in the aquarium), strong variable flow is what many species need to thrive.

Various flow patterns represented graphically.

(Courtesy Karen Talbot.)

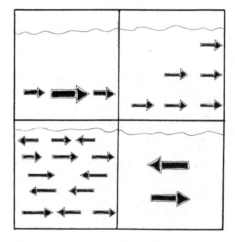

Measuring flow rate with a stopwatch.

(Courtesy Karen Talbot.)

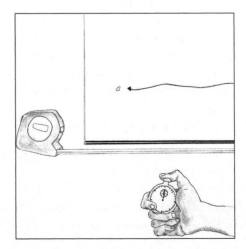

Creating Flow in the Aquarium

There are many ways to create strong, variable flow in the aquarium. We discuss creating flow with the main return pump in Chapter 8, but we also point out that most people will not want their return pump to be the only source of water movement in their system. We also discuss closed-loop systems (CLS) in Chapter 8 and suggest that a CLS, in combination with the return pump, can produce the water movement necessary. Later in this chapter, we look at alternatives to installing a CLS such as powerheads and wavemakers, but first let's take a look at how to maximize your CLS.

Creating Alternating Currents with a CLS

Laminar current alone can be detrimental to coral in the aquarium. As we discussed above, there are many types of water movement occurring in the ocean at any given time, and it is best to try to replicate this type of water movement in your aquarium. Luckily, a closed-loop system can easily create alternating and random flow in a marine aquarium.

The best way to get alternating, variable current from your CLS is to have a device between the CLS pump and the returns in the tank. This device—which may be broadly termed a wavemaker—will cause the flow to alternate between the returns. There are several devices that do this job well. We have had good experiences with both SCWDs (pronounced *squids*) and Oceans Motions alternating current units.

SCWDs are simple devices that are mounted inline between the CLS pump and two tank returns. SCWD stands for Switching Current Water Director. Water is forced into the bottom port of the SCWD by the CLS pump, and the two side ports alternate the output. We recommend you use a powerful CLS pump to get the most out of these units (up to 1,400 gallons per hour). SCWDs are relatively inexpensive (especially as they use no electricity), and they do a nice job of creating alternating flow, especially in a small aquarium.

One major limitation of SCWDs is that they are restricted to feeding only two returns, meaning that the flow would end up being little more than alternating laminar flow instead of truly variable flow. You could increase the variable nature of the flow by bouncing it off the aquarium glass, but you would have to use several SCWDS (and several pumps) to create enough alternating flow to be truly effective in all but the smallest tanks. These additional pumps, in turn, would further increase the temperature of your tank and its operating cost due to power consumption. As a result, the SCWD is probably best for smaller systems.

The SCWD is a simple, inexpensive device that can be used to create alternating current in a marine aquarium.

(Courtesy Karen Talbot.)

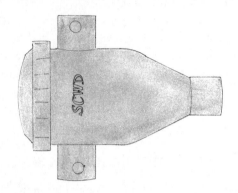

In a large system, the Oceans Motions units are clearly the best choice (albeit a relatively expensive choice) for creating variable currents with your CLS. The Oceans Motions devices can handle up to eight returns, alternating output to these returns in a variety of patterns from which you can choose. Oceans Motions units (the OM-4 provides four returns and the OM-8 provides eight returns) is plumbed, like the SCWD, inline between the CLS pump and the returns. Based on which model you purchase, you can select a variable pattern where water is forced out of different returns at different times. As such, it is possible to create barreling effects and truly chaotic flow where two returns send water colliding into itself.

The Oceans Motions OM-4 is a popular (albeit expensive) solution to creating alternating currents in a marine aquarium.

(Courtesy Karen Talbot.)

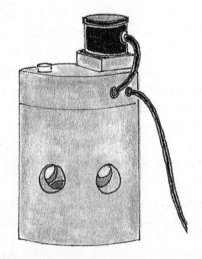

Creating Alternating Currents with Pumps and Powerheads

While a CLS with either a SCWD or an Oceans Motions unit is a good way to go in our opinion, there are other effective alternatives that do not require a separate CLS. We prefer the CLS because usually the tank returns are drilled, and, as such, there are minimal devices in the tank itself beyond the intake(s) and returns. Drilling your tank also allows you to place the returns where they will be most effective (such as on the bottom of the tank). If, for whatever reason, you decide not to have a CLS, current can be created using submersible pumps called powerheads.

Placing small powerheads in the tank itself can provide flow, but as you might imagine, a single powerhead mounted on the side wall of a tank will usually produce nothing more than laminar flow and, given the size of the pump, not very much of it. You could, of course, add a second powerhead and put it on the opposite wall of the tank so that the two currents meet in the middle. This is better, but it still only provides a limited space in the tank where there is variable flow. You could keep adding more powerheads at different angles, but now you are seriously cluttering the tank, probably increasing the temperature of the water, and increasing your operating costs due to power consumption. What to do?

The solution to this problem is to use fewer, more advanced power-heads and have them controlled by a dedicated controller (this is also sometimes called a wavemaker) or a master aquarium controller such as the ones we discussed in Chapter 7. By a "more advanced" power-head we mean a powerhead that doesn't simply shoot a jet of high flow directly at a specific point. You want a powerhead that produces more marginal flow and that is even scalable in terms of its output based on how you set the controller.

A powerhead such as the Turbelle Stream made by Tunze is an excellent example of a quality, advanced powerhead. It delivers gentle parallel flow lines with lower flow rates and unrivaled energy conservation. Using one or two of these powerheads (each rated to over 3,000 gph) connected to a dedicated controller (Tunze sells them as sets, so it's truly plumb-and-play) can be a highly effective and relatively affordable solution to your flow needs.

The dedicated controllers made by Tunze are capable of creating a variety of flow patterns. With programmable capacity and pulse control of a single powerhead, the controller can easily simulate large and small waves washing in sequence over a reef. With multiple powerheads and the more configurable controller, you can create everything from surging pulses to tidal currents and even random flow patterns. Tunze also offers photoelectric cells and moon simulation accessories that can give your water movement a truly 24/7 quality.

If you are thinking of using a master aquarium controller such as the Neptune System's industry-standard AquaController series, you can easily create similar effects without needing the dedicated wavemaker controller (although you should be aware that using one company's powerhead with another company's controller may void your warranty). In fact, a controller such as the AquaController III Pro can control an almost limitless number of devices and allow you full web integration—a nice bonus for many.

Flow Patterns to Emulate

Whichever option you choose to create flow in your aquarium—a CLS with a wavemaker or one or more powerheads connected to a controller—you will want to get back to the basics and look at the natural ecosystem. If you are using the biotope stocking method explained in Chapter 3, then you simply need to consider the physical characteristics of the biotope being replicated. If, however, you chose the habitat approach, you will probably want to create many different flow patterns and strengths within the aquarium so that you can position a variety of sessile invertebrates in locations where they are exposed to the flow they prefer.

Rest assured that, with a little creativity, you can create effective flow patterns in your aquarium using any of the methods explained so far in this chapter. In other words, it is not necessary to run out and spend a lot of money on fancy wavemakers and controllers. The more high-tech devices described, such as the Ocean Motions, Tunze, and EcoTech systems, may make it easier to grow many types of corals and to make them grow faster. In addition, the more advanced wavemakers have the advantage of being plumb-and-play, if that's important to you.

Chaotic Flow

Remember how we said earlier in the chapter that laminar flow is not good for most sessile invertebrates? While that was indeed true, a chaotic flow pattern can easily be created by having at least two linear flows intersect in midwater. This could be as simple as having your return line's effluent face off against a powerhead mounted on the opposite side of the tank. The area of true chaotic flow will be limited, and strong laminar flow at the return and powerhead will prevent you from placing most species of sessile invertebrates in the jet of water, but good results can be achieved for minimal money.

Better results can be achieved with more returns and more power-heads. By splitting the return line with a PVC tee pipe, you can have two return lines directing two constant laminar flow patterns into the tank. Then you can use two powerheads to oppose those two returns. This can achieve a chaotic flow pattern in the tank. If your power-heads create a far more powerful stream of water than your returns, consider having the powerheads oppose each other while the returns are directed to collide with the chaotic flow created by the opposing powerheads. Obviously, adding more powerheads to the mix will create more turbulent flow. Just be mindful of the heat generated by multiple returns in the aquarium.

Random Chaotic Flow

Using a timer, wavemaker, or aquarium controller to turn multiple powerheads on and off at various intervals can create a truly random, chaotic flow pattern in the aquarium. You can use the above logic of opposing powerheads, but now you can turn them on and off in various preset or random sequences. Some powerheads (like those by EcoTech) even have the ability to wirelessly sync with one another to create and maintain the most exact wave pattern possible.

Alternatively, you can set up an Oceans Motions wavemaker device on a closed-loop system with four or eight (or more) returns switching on in various patterns. When purchasing an Oceans Motions unit, you select an insert called a drum that causes the device to pump system water to various returns in a preset order.

Surge and Swell

The absolute best flow pattern for most reef tanks is a surge or swell pattern that mimics the massive volume of water that surges over a reef in one direction and then empties back out in the other. This is also the most difficult flow pattern for the home aquarist to set up. There are plenty of products and DIY projects that can create a surge-and-swell effect, but most are large, noisy, and messy. If you want to attempt this type of flow, your animals will definitely appreciate it (although your spouse might not).

The easiest way to create a surge and swell is to mount a bank of powerheads on one side wall of the aquarium. Then, with a wavemaker or controller, have the powerheads start up in sequence, one after the other. This creates a building swell and can then be repeated at whatever interval you choose (or it can even be set up for random intervals with most wavemakers and controllers). This approach is very good in theory, but it tends to fall short in many smaller home aquaria. The reason for this is that, in most cases, the length of the aquarium will not be long enough, causing the building swell to hit the far wall of the aquarium and "bounce back" far too quickly to replicate a true surge-and-swell flow. Having said that, this is the best surge and swell the home aquarist with a modestly sized aquarium can achieve. Note that you will need to leave room at the top of the aquarium for the swell.

One of the most exciting advances in water movement is the VorTech aquarium powerhead line from EcoTech. Some of these powerheads feature wireless coordination between multiple powerheads with sync and anti-sync slave modes. Why is this good? Because in a multi-pump setup, slave pumps will operate in sync or inverse (anti-sync) to the master pump to create some of the most realistic tidal currents possible in a home aquarium. In addition, the VorTech powerheads' motor is outside the aquarium, which gives these powerheads a very small in-tank footprint and less heat generation in the system.

The other methods for creating a true surge and swell involve large mechanical wavemakers such as the Tunze Wavebox. This is the only commercially available wavemaker that, in our opinion, generates truly oscillating current such as that found on a shallow reef top, but it only starts making sense in an aquarium over 500 gallons. The Borneman Flush Device and the Carlson Surge Device are two DIY surge-and-swell devices the intrepid aquarist might consider. Plenty of information is available on both Borneman's and Carlson's devices online and in various books, but they are beyond the realm of our present discussion. For most beginning and intermediate hobbyists, random chaotic flow created with either a closed-loop system and a wavemaker such as a

SCWD or Oceans Motions unit, or powerheads run by a wavemaker or controller will more than suffice.

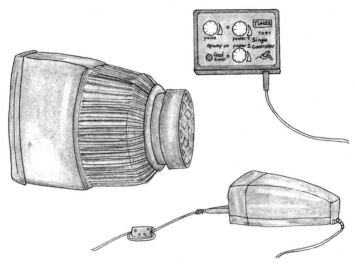

A surge-and-swell wavemaker setup utilizing a Tunze Turbelle Stream powerhead Tunze Multicontroller.

(Courtesy Karen Talbot.)

Pearls of Wisdom

In addition to daily and monthly cycles, ocean currents shift seasonally as well. The El Niño climate phenomenon is so named because "El Niño" translates as "Christ Child," and the seasonal change for which it is named occurs in December or January (around Christmas). El Niño is caused by seasonal changes in prevailing winds that affect ocean currents in the Pacific and, ultimately, affect Peruvian fisheries and the fisherman who fish there. These fishermen were the ones to name El Niño.

Changing and Interrupting Currents

There are times when you may want to change the flow patterns in your tank. This is easily accomplished using any of the previous methods. Simply use a nozzle such as a Loc-Line nozzle or an Oceans Motions Omniflex dual nozzle on all your returns. These devices cost a little more, but the benefit of being able to direct flow is well worth it. While the CD-ROM included with this book will tell you about a sessile invertebrate's lighting and placement needs, the reality is that it takes some trial and error to find the optimum location for an animal that cannot move itself. Often moving a coral a few inches, or simply directing a different angle of flow toward that coral, can make the difference between a stressed-out, unhealthy specimen and a show specimen.

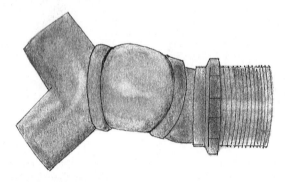

An Omniflex nozzle (Oceans Motions) makes directing water a breeze.

(Courtesy Karen Talbot.)

Finally, there are times when you will want to be able to interrupt your water movement altogether. For example, in a particularly turbulent tank, you may want to stop the bulk of the water circulation while you affix a new coral specimen and allow the epoxy to harden. Alternatively, you will use less fish food if you stop the current while you feed (less food will be pushed into the overflow). Most controllers have a dedicated "feed" cycle where you simply push a button and the bulk of the water movement stops.

The Least You Need to Know

- Most sessile invertebrates need strong and variable flow to thrive in the aquarium.

- Strong variable flow can be created with either a CLS plumbed to a wavemaker or by employing powerheads in the tank.

- High-tech aquarium controllers and wavemakers are not necessary, but they can make controlling water flow easier and more effective.

- Replicating natural cycles of water movement may have unanticipated beneficial results for your livestock.

Part 3

Putting It All Together

It's time to put it all together and add some water. In this part of the book, we'll take a look at exactly what saltwater is, how to make it, and how to keep it within the proper parameters. We'll also talk about aquascaping your aquarium and the multitude of different aquascaping alternatives. From bare-bottom tanks to shallow and deep sand beds, we'll show you how to set up the right system for the stocking list you developed in Part 1. Finally, we'll cover the fundamentals of cycling your tank and testing the water, so that by the time you finish this part of the text, you'll be ready to start adding animals.

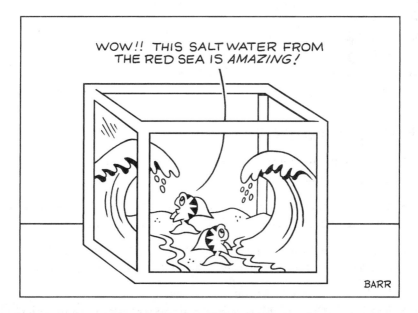

Chapter 11

Just Add Water–Water Quality

In This Chapter

- ◆ Finding out what's in natural saltwater
- ◆ Using salt mixes to make synthetic saltwater
- ◆ Identifying the major water parameters

If it were only as easy as just adding water. Achieving and maintaining the quality of marine aquarium water is often one of the most difficult hurdles for beginning marine aquarists to overcome, but it really doesn't have to be that complicated. There are many excellent products and technologies available that make managing water quality relatively easy.

While managing your water quality can be fairly simple, it is important to understand the fundamentals, and that's what we are going to cover here. We will discuss natural versus artificial saltwater and the various water parameters that are important to the health of your marine aquarium. We will also give you the target ranges for each parameter in this chapter, although we do not discuss testing here (we cover it in Chapter 13).

Natural Seawater

Natural seawater is made up of, well, just about everything. That's right, choose any old element (or ion—marine aquarists often use the terms interchangeably) from the periodic table, and it has probably been measured in seawater. Having said that, a very few elements make up the vast majority of natural seawater. Common salt (the kind on your kitchen table next to the pepper) is made up of two atoms—sodium and chloride. These two ionic solids, not surprisingly, are the major players in seawater. No other ion makes up more than 10 percent of the total weight of ions in seawater. When we add sulfate ions and magnesium ions to the equation, we have identified upwards of 97 percent of the weight of ions in naturally occurring saltwater.

Major Ions

Add calcium, potassium, bicarbonate, bromide, carbonate, strontium, borate (boron), and fluoride, and you now have the very great majority—upwards of 99 percent—of seawater's ionic weight. These ions listed are what are commonly referred to as the *major ions* (if we were to calculate major ions strictly on ions present instead of the weight of those ions, lithium joins the party) in naturally occurring saltwater. Making up far less than 1 percent of the weight of ions in seawater are the minor ions and the trace ions.

Minor Ions

While major ions remain remarkably consistent in a sample of saltwater regardless of where that sample is taken, *minor ions* can vary dramatically from one location to the next. Common minor ions with which the marine aquarist should be familiar are phosphate, iodine, and iron. Depending on who you talk to, some minor ions (like iodine) are considered trace elements.

Trace Ions

In addition to major and minor ions, there are *trace ions* in saltwater. Many of these trace ions are metals (e.g., copper), but just about every element known to man has been recorded in seawater. In the aquarium hobby, we further divide trace ions into essential and nonessential trace ions. It turns out that many of the trace ions in naturally occurring saltwater are nonessential for successful marine aquarium keeping. The exceptions to this rule make up the so-called essential trace ions, and, interestingly enough, some of the trace ions that are present in far lower concentrations are essential trace ions (e.g., iodine), while others that occur in exponentially larger concentrations are unimportant to the marine hobbyist.

def•i•ni•tion

As far as the marine aquarist is concerned, there are three types of ions (more accurately termed elements) in seawater: **major ions, minor ions,** and **trace ions.** Major ions are ions like calcium that are concentrated at one part per million (ppm) or more. Minor ions are ions like iodine that are concentrated at less than one ppm all the way down to one part per billion (ppb). Any ions in concentrations less than one ppb are considered trace elements.

As you can see, naturally occurring saltwater is pretty complex stuff, and some aquarists have taken that to suggest that natural seawater must be superior to seawater you make with a salt mix—synthetic seawater. While there are situations in which naturally occurring seawater is a viable alternative to saltwater made with synthetic salt mixes, we believe that the great majority of marine aquarists are best off using synthetic salt mixes. Why? Well, we honestly could write a whole book on the pros and cons of natural versus synthetic saltwater, but suffice it to say for now that when you use naturally occurring seawater, you are getting all of the major, minor, and trace ions discussed above—*and* a whole lot more. In this case, more is often *not* better. For example, most natural saltwater collected close to land will have loads of additional organic matter and, unfortunately, various pollutants. The reality is that you would have to spend just as much time (and nearly as much money) testing and preparing most natural seawater as you would mixing and aging synthetic saltwater.

Synthetic Saltwater

Many good synthetic salt mixes on the market mean that the beginning aquarist needn't be a chemist to experience success. Most of the commonly available commercial salt mixes have all of the major and minor elements listed previously. Where they may differ somewhat is in what trace elements they contain. In other words, even a commonly available, relatively inexpensive salt mix like Instant Ocean will provide a perfectly adequate starting point for nearly all marine aquaria.

As you begin to specialize within the hobby, the plot thickens a bit. For example, if you intend to have a full-blown reef tank full of SPS corals, you might decide to either start using a more expensive salt mix with more of the trace ions your corals require to thrive, or you might choose to stick with a less expensive salt mix and add trace ions through commercially available supplements. Ask around, as aquarists have major opinions about salt mixes (they are opinionated about most everything, actually), and then go with a brand that has the major and minor ions listed earlier.

To mix your saltwater, follow the instructions on the package, but here are a few tips about buying salt mixes and preparing saltwater for your aquarium:

- Make sure your synthetic salt mix contains seawater levels (or higher) of magnesium.
- Allow your saltwater to age before adding it to your aquarium. While aging, keep it warm and circulating.
- Consider testing the pH, temperature, and salinity before adding the new water to your tank.

Important Water Parameters

While the synthetic saltwater you added to your aquarium should be of excellent quality and relatively stable when first introduced, it will rapidly change over time based on many factors. This is why it is essential to monitor the quality of your water and make adjustments when necessary. In this section, we discuss the major parameters you will want to monitor, and we tell you the acceptable ranges for each.

Ammonia

When aquarists refer to ammonia, you need to know whether they are talking about total ammonia, NH_3, or NH_{4+}. NH_3 is what we are concerned with here. NH_3, sometimes called free ammonia, is highly toxic to your livestock. NH_{4+} is ammonium, a less toxic form of ammonia. When you have NH_3 in your system, you also have NH_{4+}. The ratio of NH_3 to NH_{4+} is dependent mostly upon pH and to a lesser extent temperature. When you measure for total ammonia (sometimes called TAN for total ammonia nitrogen), you measure for NH_3 and NH_{4+}, but generally aquarists are most interested in the NH_3 levels only.

NH_3 is nitrogenous waste and is a natural by-product of your livestock's metabolism. Most NH_3 is a result of your fishes' metabolic activity and, as we say in Chapter 2, is excreted from your fishes' gills. NH_3 is also produced in the aquarium when organic materials decompose (e.g., a dead fish or uneaten food).

NH_3 is toxic on contact with fish, and it causes burning of the gills that results in the production of excessive mucus. This mucus reduces a fish's ability to use dissolved oxygen in the water, essentially suffocating that fish.

In a healthy, fully cycled marine aquarium, there should be no detectable ammonia present. Nitrifying bacteria in a healthy, mature system feed on ammonia and turn it to less toxic nitrite. In fact, after a tank has cycled, most marine aquarists stop testing for any form of ammonia unless they encounter a problem.

Common causes of NH_3 include the following:

- Not enough nitrifying bacteria

- Uneaten food or decomposing organic matter

- High bioload or too many fishes added too quickly

- Untreated tap water (not using RO/DI)

Signs of NH_3 poisoning include the following:

- "Gasping" fishes and clamped fins

- Fishes lying on the bottom of the tank and breathing heavily

- Unexplained disease outbreaks

Nitrite (NO$_2$-)

As mentioned in the above discussion, ammonia is converted to nitrite in the mature saltwater aquarium by nitrifying bacteria (called *Nitrosomonas* bacteria). Nitrite (NO$_2$-), like free ammonia (NH$_3$), is toxic to your fish and other livestock and should be undetectable (0 ppm) in a properly cycled tank. NO$_2$- levels can increase for the same reasons that ammonia levels increase (see above). After the tank has cycled and stabilized, many marine aquarists stop testing regularly for NO$_2$-.

Nitrate (NO$_3$-)

Nitrate (NO$_3$-) is a water parameter for which many marine aquarists (especially reef aquarists) regularly monitor in a mature, healthy system. Some aquarists do choose not to test for NO$_3$- in a healthy, cycled system because the signs of elevated NO$_3$- levels are relatively easy to spot (e.g., algae). Nonetheless, the beginning aquarist will want to regularly monitor NO$_3$ levels throughout the cycling process, and, unlike ammonia and nitrite, he or she will want to regularly test for NO$_3$- until becoming attuned to any fluctuations in the system.

NO$_3$- is converted from NO$_2$- by anaerobic nitrifying bacteria (a different kind of bacteria than the *Nitrosomonas* bacteria mentioned above). NO$_3$- is the end product of the nitrogen cycle and is far less toxic than the previous two by-products—NH$_3$ and NO$_2$-. Unlike NH$_3$ and NO$_2$-, effective biological filtration does not remove nitrate from the water. As a result, it is up to the aquarist to monitor and remove nitrates from the system.

Pearls of Wisdom

It is not uncommon to suspect you have high nitrate levels based on algal growth but find that the levels are actually quite low based on testing. Actually, what is really going on in this scenario is that the algae are consuming the NO$_3$- before you can test for it. For this reason, some experienced aquarists consider NO$_3$- testing unnecessary.

Even at relatively low levels, NO$_3$- can be toxic to certain invertebrates. This is why reef aquarists are particularly interested in knowing the NO$_3$- level of their aquarium. While not as immediately toxic to your fishes as NH_3 or NO_2., elevated nitrate levels will cause stress for your fishes and can lead to disease and other problems.

Unlike ammonia and nitrite, it is not uncommon to always have low levels of nitrate in your system. It is, nonetheless, essential to keep these levels below 20 ppm in fish-only systems and below 15 ppm in invertebrate and reef tanks. Many reef aquarists aim for much lower levels.

Many things can cause elevated levels of NO_3, but some of the most common are ...

♦ Untreated tap water (not using RO/DI).

♦ Not enough (or not large enough) regular water changes.

♦ Any of the previously listed causes of increased ammonia.

While it's true that experienced marine aquarists may know they have a nitrate problem simply by visually monitoring algae growth in their system, we think it is best for beginning marine aquarists to regularly monitor for nitrate levels in their aquarium until they get a good handle on water parameters and how the water chemistry changes over time.

Hydrogen Power—pH

pH is a measure of the relative alkalinity, or acidity, of a solution, with a pH of 7.0 considered neutral. Levels above 7.0 are said to be alkaline, and readings below 7.0 are said to be acidic. A pH of 8.2 to 8.4 is ideal in the marine aquarium, as this most closely resembles natural seawater.

pH is the weight of hydrogen, or *pondus Hydrogenii*. It is potential hydrogen, or *pouvoir hydrogen* (French for "hydrogen power"). Simply stated, pH tells you how many hydrogen ions are in a solution. The more hydrogen ions that are in a solution, the more acidic that solution is. Remember how we said in Chapter 1 that ocean acidification is a bad thing? It logically follows that more hydrogen ions in your aquarium water will make your water more acidic, and that will be bad for your livestock.

It's useful to think of pH as a fraction—the bigger the bottom number gets, the smaller the total fraction. A higher pH indicates that the ratio of hydroxide (OH_-) to protons (H_+, hydrogen ions) is higher.

The best part about pH is that it is really easy to measure. We discuss ways to monitor pH in Chapter 13, where we also suggest that it is the one parameter (in addition to temperature) that you absolutely should monitor regularly (if not continuously).

The pH of the ocean is usually somewhere between 7.5 and 8.5, depending on many factors such as depth and, increasingly, ocean acidification. In general, it can be said that the average pH of the ocean is around 8.2 or 8.3. Most saltwater aquarists keep their tanks' pH between 7.8 and 8.4, although if you have a reef tank, you will probably shoot to keep your aquarium's pH somewhere between 8.2 and 8.5. The most important factor is stability, and you should aim to not have pH fluctuations greater than 0.2 in any given 24-hour cycle.

pH that is either too low or too high is dangerous to your livestock. Likewise, wildly fluctuating pH can easily throw a fish into *osmotic shock*. pH can also be an indicator of other serious issues in the aquarium, and the changes to pH in your tank over time indicate a lot about the general health of your system. For example, if you have an undetected dead animal in your tank, your pH will drop. If your alkalinity levels have fallen too low, you will measure a decreased pH level in your tank. In the vast majority of cases, if a water parameter is out of whack in your tank, it will drive your pH down, so monitoring pH over time can be very useful in terms of looking at general health trends in your aquarium.

def•i•ni•tion

> **Osmotic shock** refers to a sudden change in the parameters between the water inside a fish's body and the water outside its body. Moving a fish from one body of water to another can cause osmotic shock if the fish is not acclimated properly. Basically what happens is that a fish will either pump too much water into its body or out of its body in an attempt to self-regulate, resulting in dehydration and death or hemorrhaging and death.

Alkalinity

Alkalinity, like ammonia, may be defined in several different ways, but it always has something to do with how much acid it takes to drop the pH to a predetermined level. The marine aquarist is most interested in total alkalinity (sometimes referred to as TA), which is a measurement of the amount of acid required to drop the pH to the *carbonic acid endpoint*. Total alkalinity tests generally require the aquarist to drop the pH of a water sample to somewhere between 4.0 and 5.0.

def•i•ni•tion

Carbonic acid is what you get when you add hydrogens to carbonate ions. Lower pH means more H+ ions, so they are more likely to pair up with carbonate and form carbonic acid. The **carbonic acid endpoint** is that point where carbonate and bicarbonate can be converted to carbonic acid. Saltwater's endpoint is around a pH of 4.2. This endpoint is sometimes referred to as the carbonic acid equivalence point, and it is usually this to which we are referring when we talk about our tank's alkalinity.

A high alkalinity is necessary in a saltwater tank as a buffer capable of maintaining high pH. Stated differently, alkalinity is the acid-neutralizing capacity of your water. Saltwater is a basic solution with a pH around 8.2 or 8.3, and when the pH in the ocean changes for whatever reason, the high alkalinity present is usually capable of bringing the pH back to 8.2 or 8.3. Your aquarium is a much smaller system than the ocean and does not have the same buffering capacity over time. That is why you, as the aquarist, need to monitor your system's alkalinity and intervene when necessary. You must ensure that your aquarium can resist (or neutralize) acids produced in the system.

How does high alkalinity maintain high pH? In essence, water with high alkalinity has plenty of negative ions in the form of carbonates and bicarbonates. These negatively charged ions counteract the positively charged hydrogen ions in the water and maintain a high pH. Your alkalinity will drop over time, because some of your livestock require calcium to grow and thrive. These animals (corals, snails, calcareous algae, etc.) pull calcium carbonate from the water and, in turn, reduce your water's buffering capacity.

Without maintaining sufficient levels of calcium carbonate in the water, your calcium-hungry animals will not thrive. In addition, your pH will fall as your water loses its alkaline buffering capacity. Assuming you agree with us that these are both undesirable outcomes, you must also agree that we must find a way to measure calcium carbonate. Luckily for us, there is a relationship between carbonate and alkalinity. In fact, carbonate hardness is alkalinity.

Carbonate (and bicarbonate) is essentially the same as total alkalinity in almost all marine aquarium situations. The icing on the cake is that total alkalinity is quite easy to measure (carbonate is not). Alkalinity is measured either as dKH (degrees of carbonate hardness) or meq/L (milliequivalents per liter). Since the alkalinity of natural seawater is about 8 dKH, you should aim to keep your aquarium water at about the same level. With a high dKH, your buffering capacity should be able to compensate for any event that could rapidly drop your pH.

We recommend that all marine aquarists regularly test for alkalinity. Some reef aquarists use alkalinity as the primary test for aquarium health in their system, relying on the assumption that a high alkalinity will keep most everything else in check.

Calcium

Calcium, as was suggested in the previous section on alkalinity, is closely related to carbonate hardness. You need to keep your calcium levels high in the marine aquarium. This is less difficult in a fish-only system and more difficult in a reef system, but the bottom line is that all marine aquarists need to have a method for increasing and maintaining healthy calcium levels in their aquaria. Calcium is generally measured in ppm, and natural seawater has a calcium content of around 410 ppm. In the aquarium, you should shoot to keep your calcium stable somewhere between 400 and 500 milligrams per liter (mg/L).

Magnesium

Magnesium, like calcium, is a major ion in seawater, yet marine aquarists rarely talk about it. The reason we don't spend a lot of time talking about magnesium is because magnesium is plentiful in natural seawater. It is also generally plentiful in synthetic salt mixes, and partial water changes are generally capable of maintaining more than adequate levels of magnesium regardless of what is in your tank. Many marine aquarists never give magnesium a thought because it never causes them problems.

Magnesium is a critical component for maintaining appropriate calcium and alkalinity. If you are having trouble maintaining calcium and alkalinity, you might want to test for magnesium. Magnesium also plays an essential role in photosynthesis (chlorophyll requires magnesium), and as such, magnesium is necessary for photosynthetic corals and algae. When magnesium levels fall below 800 mg/L (natural seawater has magnesium levels upwards of 1,350 mg/L), pH will start to drop, and the proper combination of calcium concentration and alkalinity will be disrupted. This can be catastrophic for your corals and calcareous algae. The leading cause of depleted magnesium levels is the use of Kalkwasser or a salt mix that contains less magnesium than naturally occurring saltwater.

Strontium

Strontium is part of the chemical triad formed by calcium, magnesium, and strontium. We call it a chemical triad because these three ions are very close to one another in their chemical properties; they belong to the same chemical family, the alkaline earths, and some reef aquarists dose all three regularly. In reality, strontium's benefit to coral is little more than anecdotal. While it's clear that calcifying organisms deposit strontium in their skeletons, there is a great deal of debate about whether this is intentional or incidental. Some aquarists claim that strontium supplements have aided coral growth tremendously, while other aquarists claim that strontium can be toxic at doses above naturally occurring levels. Our advice? If you want to dose strontium, read up on it first and then dose in small amounts making sure to keep levels at 8 mg/L or less (this is the level in natural seawater). Using a strontium supplement absolutely necessitates the frequent monitoring of pH, calcium, and alkalinity.

Trace Elements

In addition to the parameters and ions mentioned previously, there are a variety of trace elements for which the marine aquarist can test. The majority of these tests are truly unnecessary for the vast majority of us. Remember that 99.9 percent of the ions in saltwater are major and minor ions.

156 Part 3: Putting It All Together

Phosphate

Inorganic orthophosphate is a very basic form of phosphorus that exists in natural seawater but at very low levels (as low as 0.005 ppm in the ecosystems we are most often replicating). When we talk about phosphate in the marine aquarium, we are usually talking about testing for inorganic orthophosphate as opposed to total phosphorus. Many marine aquarists do not test for phosphates on a regular basis for two main reasons:

♦ The presence of algae is an indicator of high phosphate levels.

♦ The presence of lots of algae can consume the phosphate so it does not register on the test even though the levels are quite high.

We suggest you have a phosphate test kit on hand, especially as a beginning aquarist, but you probably won't need to regularly test for this parameter. There are some very good, albeit somewhat expensive, phosphate test kits that make testing for this parameter very easy and quick. The Hanna Instruments Low Range Phosphate Photometer, for example, measures phosphate content in seawater in the 0.00 to 2.50 mg/L (ppm) range. Accurately measuring low-range phosphate levels (below 0.03, for example) is beyond most test kits' capability, yet may be essential in keeping some of the more difficult corals.

The Least You Need to Know

♦ The vast majority of marine aquarium hobbyists should use salt mixes to make synthetic saltwater for their aquaria.

♦ Understanding the most important water quality parameters is essential to success.

♦ While you will only want to test NH_3 and NO_{2-} while cycling your tank, you will want to regularly monitor NO_3, pH, alkalinity, calcium, and phosphate once the tank is up and running.

Chapter 12

Aquascaping

In This Chapter

- ◆ Adding substrate
- ◆ Adding live rock
- ◆ Filling the aquarium with synthetic seawater

Once the system is fully plumbed, you will need to start aquascaping. Aquascaping is like landscaping underwater, and, like landscaping, some people love it and others don't. Regardless of your artistic ability, by following some simple guidelines, you will be able to create a system that is easy to maintain, provides for the health of your animals, and is (of course) visually stunning.

How you aquascape can have a major impact on the overall success of your system. Will you use live rock? Will you have a substrate-covered bottom (such as sand) or a bare bottom? If you have a substrate-covered bottom, will you use live sand, crushed coral, or a synthetic substrate? Will it be a deep sand bed or a shallow sand bed? This chapter covers what you need to know to make these choices and create an aesthetically pleasing and healthy environment for your soon-to-be-added animals.

Add Water

We called the last chapter "Just Add Water—Water Quality," but now you actually get to do it. Once the tank is fully plumbed and you have mixed up enough saltwater (using RO/DI water, of course), you are ready to fill the tank. For a small tank, this can be a pretty simple process, but for a large tank, it can take over a day to completely fill the tank (mostly because of the limits of your RO/DI system). Why not mix the saltwater in the tank and let it age and stabilize there? Perhaps you can, especially if there is nothing else in the tank and you can observe that the salt is completely mixed (dissolved) before proceeding to the next step.

Warning

Many aquarists like to give their tank a test run with freshwater (non-RO/DI) first to see if everything is working and there are no leaks. It stinks to spend the time to make enough RO/DI water, mix the salt and fill the tank only to have to drain it again. Whether you do this or not is entirely up to you.

We, however, prefer to mix the saltwater in a separate container and add our substrate first, but you needn't do it this way. By mixing your salt in a separate container without substrate present, the salt has a chance to totally dissolve before you add anything that may interfere with the salt's solubility. Because this is the way we do it, we're going to talk about substrate (or lack thereof) before filling the aquarium with synthetic seawater.

Substrates

Beginning from the bottom and working up, one of the first choices you will need to make concerns your substrate. The substrate is the material that covers the bottom of the tank, and the first choice you need to make is if you intend to have a substrate at all. If you choose not to have a substrate, you will have what is generally called a bare-bottom tank (or BB).

Bare-Bottom Tanks

Bare-bottom tanks have no substrate. As such, they are a cinch to clean (simply by vacuuming up the detritus). The deeper your substrate, the more organisms (and more diversity of organisms) can live in it. Some aquarists like to have these organisms living in their tank because of the biological functions they perform (we are talking about nitrifying bacteria and more here), while other aquarists worry that a substrate only becomes a reservoir for potentially toxic elements, which can build up over time. In short, the bare-bottom crowd believes that the risks and necessary maintenance associated with a substrate are too great, even though many also feel that a bare-bottom tank is less aesthetically pleasing.

There isn't a whole lot more to say about bare-bottom tanks in terms of aquascaping. With a bare-bottom tank, the rock that might other-wise sit on top of the substrate simply sits on the bottom of the tank or on rock lifts (greatly decreasing the risk of in-tank rock slides caused by animals that move sand). In a bare-bottom tank, you don't have to worry about powerheads or returns blowing sand about the tank, and you can therefore set up your flow patterns for maximum detritus clearing in every area of the tank. Finally, with a bare-bottom tank, you never have to debate whether or not your sand bed needs to be changed, cleaned, or renourished. If you do decide to go bare bottom, make sure you realize you are limiting the types of animals you can keep in your tank (jawfishes, wrasses, and certain gobies immediately come to mind).

Tanks with Substrate

There are many reasons to not have a bare-bottom tank. For example, you may choose not to have a bare-bottom tank because you don't like the look of a bare bottom, because you want to keep substrate-dwelling animals, or because you believe a substrate bottom can provide benefi-cial biological filtration for your tank. If you decide to use a substrate, you need to first decide what you are going to use as your substrate. Many different substrates are available in a plethora of grain sizes, from sugar fine to entire seashells. We prefer using a form of calcium car-bonate called aragonite for the substrate in most saltwater aquaria, and we generally prefer small grain size over large.

We like the finer-grained substrates because they provide excellent burrowing habitat for certain species, and because they have more surface area on which nitrifying bacteria can grow. You will remember from our previous discussions regarding biological filtration in Chapter 6 that it is of great benefit to have nitrifying bacteria colonize parts of your system. Using fine-grain sand in a sand bed of 7.5 centimeters (3 inches) or deeper can add a tremendous amount of biological filtration to your system.

While all sand will become "alive" over time (as it is colonized by bacteria), you can purchase sand that is alive right out of the bag. Certain commercially available "live sand" substrates like the CaribSea Arag-Alive substrates contain nitrifying bacteria that can "seed" the tank by adding live organisms to the substrate. Whether you buy live sand or not, small grain size provides lots of habitat for nitrifying bacteria to grow. CaribSea calculates that their special-grade reef sand (1–2 mm grain size) has approximately 129,032 square centimeters (20,000 square inches) of surface area per cubic inch. That's a lot of surface area for nitrifying bacteria to colonize.

Pearls of Wisdom

Live sand contains countless heterotrophic (can't make its own food), autotrophic (can make its own food), and chemolithotrophic (can make their own food but don't need sunlight to do it) bacteria. In addition, it provides numerous major, minor, and trace ions like calcium, strontium, magnesium, carbonate, potassium, molybdenum, barium, boron, selenium, and beryllium. Avoid live sands that contain anything but trace levels of phosphates. Also, avoid buying any substrate that contains silica. It's best to avoid beach-collected substrate for the same reason it's best to avoid natural seawater, which may contain harmful organics and other impurities.

The "arag" in CaribSea's Arag-Alive product is a reference to the fact that the substrate is aragonite. Aragonite is a carbonate mineral, which is an excellent choice for all saltwater tanks (remember our discussion of buffering capacity and carbonate in Chapter 11?). Aragonite is created by mollusk shells and coral, and it is the most dissolvable form of calcium carbonate available as a substrate for the marine aquarist. It is, in our opinion, highly superior to calcite-based substrates. Aragonite dissolves at a pH over 8.0 (where many marine aquarists like to keep their tank), while calcite-based substrates need a much lower pH to become dissolvable.

Regardless of what substrate and what grain size you choose, the next choice you need to make is how deep you want your sand bed to be. Generally speaking, you can choose to have either a deep sand bed (DSB) or a shallow sand bed (SSB). These terms are somewhat arbitrary, but for our purposes, we'll consider a sand bed deeper than 8 centimeters (3 inches) to be a DSB, while anything less will be called an SSB. A DSB is generally chosen because of its filtration capacity, although this is a topic of heated debate amongst aquarists. An SSB is often employed primarily for aesthetic reasons. Before deciding between a DSB and SSB, be sure to consider the habitat your animals will need. Go back to the stocking list you developed in Chapter 3 and see if there are any animals on your list that have substrate requirements. You will find that certain species of fishes, corals, and invertebrates need a DSB to thrive (or in some cases, to even survive). The reason a DSB is a sand bed deeper than 8 centimeters (3 inches) is because at that depth, the bottom layer of the sand bed becomes excellent habitat for anaerobic bacteria that can carry out effective *denitirification*. In a large tank, it is not uncommon to employ 13 to 18 centimeters (5 to 7 inches) of substrate, turning the entire sand bed into a massive biological filter colonized by aerobic and anaerobic bacteria.

def•i•ni•tion

Denitrification is the process of converting nitrate into nitrogen-containing compounds. This is an essential component of the nitrogen cycle and maintaining a healthy aquarium.

Pearls of Wisdom

When discussing substrate, you will hear some aquarists speak of their plenum. They are referring to a water-filled space directly beneath their substrate (usually a deep sand bed) designed to aid biological filtration. While the use of a plenum has been shown to be very beneficial in huge systems (like public aquaria huge) with very deep sand beds, the benefit to the average marine hobbyist is, in our opinion, negligible. If you want to experiment with a plenum, feel free, but know that you don't need a plenum to experience success with a deep sand bed.

In general, DSBs are quite forgiving for the beginning aquarist, but this does not mean you should be lax about your regular aquarium maintenance. Tanks with DSBs usually have few nitrate and phosphate problems, even in the absence of good husbandry practices. If you miss a water change or consistently overfeed, for example, a tank with a DSB will often compensate for your delinquency. Over time, however, the cumulative effects of poor husbandry will cause the DSB to become a liability to the tank, and this is why some people are such proponents of bare-bottom tanks. They say that any DSB will eventually max out its filtration capacity and will start releasing toxins back into the aquarium water. How long will it take for a DSB to max out on its filtration capacity? It depends on the system, but it will certainly take at least several years, and there are many aquarists who believe a DSB can be indefinitely sustained.

A deep sand bed provides a home for anaerobic nitrifying bacteria as well as animals such as the blue spot jawfish (Opistognathus rosenblatti), *nassarius snail (*Nassarius spp.) *and Tonga fighting conch (*Strombus gibberulus*).*

(Courtesy Karen Talbot.)

With good husbandry practices, excellent aragonite substrate, and appropriate sand-sifting animals, you should expect your DSB to have a life span of more than a few years. Part of the reason is that the substrate will dissolve over time (perhaps as much as half in two years if you are using fine grain), and you will replace it with new substrate. In addition, sand-sifting animals will keep the surface layer of a DSB stirred so small amounts of waste are constantly being picked up by your current and eventually driven into your mechanical filtration. A DSB is not for everyone, but, in our opinion, with good husbandry practices and good materials, there is no need to believe that a DSB is a ticking time bomb in your tank.

Substrate Grain Sizes and Recommended Usages

Grain Size (mm)	Common Name	Recommended Usage
0.2–1.0	Sugar-fine grade	DSBs designed for denitrification. Good for sand-sifting detritivores.
1.0–2.0	Medium grade	Deeper DSBs for denitrification. Marginal for sand-sifting detritivores.
2.0–4.0	Coarse grade	Poor choice for a DSB fish-only system.
4.0 +	Very coarse grade	SSB or 12 mm or less fish-only system

Adding Substrate to the Aquarium

Even if the instructions say you do not need to rinse the substrate, we recommend that you thoroughly rinse all substrate before adding it to the aquarium. This can be easily accomplished by poking many holes in the bottom of the plastic bag in which the substrate is packaged and placing the bag inside a 5-gallon (or larger) bucket. Cut a hole in the top of the bag and stick a hose in the hole. Allow it to run for a good 10 minutes (while the excess water overflows the top of the bucket) before lifting the bag out of the bucket and allowing it to drain. Shake the bag vigorously and repeat. Finally, empty any water out of the bucket and pour the sand into the bucket. Fill the bucket half full with water (so the top of the sand is covered) and stir it aggressively. Allow the sand to settle, and then skim off any floating material and discard. You are now ready to add the sand to your aquarium.

If you are using live sand, you need to treat it in a slightly different fashion. Live sand must be rinsed with saltwater instead of tap water, and you probably won't want to produce that much waste saltwater. Live sand can be effectively rinsed by pouring it into a bucket, filling the bucket with saltwater to several inches above the level of the sand. Stir the sand in the bucket and siphon off the debris that accumulates on the surface. Discard the water, and add the sand to your tank.

Once your sand has been rinsed, drain off the water (you don't want to add non-RO/DI water to your aquarium) and gently pour the substrate into the aquarium, and spread it out evenly. Before adding the substrate, especially in a tank with a deep sand bed, consider adding rock lifts or a PVC frame (we discuss this below) so that your live rock is resting on the lifts or frame at the top of the substrate. This will help both in terms of effective filtration and avoiding potential rock slides.

After the substrate (and any lifts or PVC frames) has been installed, fill the aquarium halfway with warm, aged synthetic saltwater, and allow it to settle. When adding the water, you may choose to place a plastic container on the sand and pour the water into the container, so it does not disturb the substrate. You are now ready to start adding your live rock if you already have it and have finished curing it. If you do not have your live rock yet, be sure to place one or more small powerheads in the aquarium and a heater to keep the water oxygenated and between 24 and 28°C (75–82°F).

Live Rock

Few advances in the marine aquarium hobby have been as important as the now almost-ubiquitous use of live rock in marine aquaria. Unfortunately, the name "live rock" is a poor choice and tends to confuse beginning marine aquarists. How can rock be alive, you might ask? Well, the rock itself is not actually alive (although at one time it probably was the skeleton of a living coral). Instead, when we say live rock, we mean it is loaded with life. What kind of life, you ask? You'll be amazed.

We cannot emphasize enough the benefits of using live rock to the overall health of the marine aquarium. For starters, good-quality live rock comes to you full of live micro- and macrofauna essential for biological filtration. This is why we say our favorite way to cycle a new marine aquarium is to mix up seawater and then add good-quality live rock—but more on this in Chapter 13. In addition to all of this beneficial fauna, a virtual kaleidoscope of life will emerge from good-quality live rock over a period of days, weeks, months, and even years. Calcareous algae, brittle stars, *Asterina* stars, snails, feather dusters, and much more may come "free of charge" as so-called "hitchhikers" on live rock.

While the vast majority of hitchhikers are beneficial (or at least pose no immediate threat to your system), there are a few hitchhikers you don't want in your system. Live rock is generally collected from reef rubble zones in the ocean. Reef rubble zones are made up of porous rock and dead coral skeletons that have broken off the reef face as a result of storm activity or other natural processes. Live rock is also aquacultured in some places, but it is generally considered unnecessary to aquaculture live rock given that it is a highly renewable resource when collected properly. In terms of understanding live rock, however, it is worth thinking about what it means to aquaculture live rock.

Aquaculturing live rock can be as easy as placing any porous rock into the ocean and allowing it to be colonized by life before "harvesting" it. If you apply this concept to your aquarium, you will realize that any rock put into a healthy, mature aquarium will become live rock in time. This is the reason that some people use less expensive base rock "seeded" with a few quality pieces of live rock when starting a new aquarium. In time, it all will become live rock.

To return to aquascaping, live rock is added to the aquarium at around the same time that the substrate is added. We say "at around the same time" because some aquarists choose to add it first, since it is generally best if your live rock is sitting directly on the bottom of the aquarium. This greatly reduces the potential for rock slides caused by burrowing animals, but it also makes the base of the live rock, which is now buried in the substrate, a trap for detritus and other organic waste. To avoid this, some aquarists build rock racks or rock lifts so that the live rock is placed on top of the substrate but is not supported by the substrate.

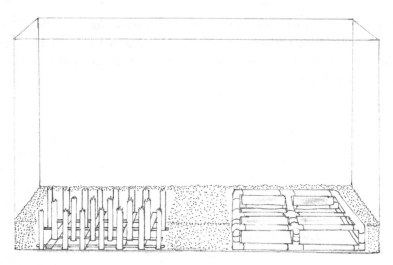

Rock lifts and rock rack used to support the weight of the live rock at the level of the substrate.

(Courtesy Karen Talbot.)

No matter how you add the live rock to the tank, you will want to add it in such a way that water can freely flow around and through it (see Chapter 10 for recommendations on creating water flow). You will also want to arrange the live rock in such a way that it provides the appropriate habitat for the species you intend to keep. For example, nocturnal fishes will prefer a large cave in which to retreat during the day, and low-light, nonphotosynthetic organisms such as deep-water gorgonians will want a shady area of the tank to thrive. Many larger fishes (e.g., angelfishes and triggerfishes) will want plenty of swimming space and several rocky crevices in which to retreat.

How Much Live Rock?

The general rule of thumb is to add at least 1 pound of live rock per gallon of system water. This rule is highly variable, however, based on a number of factors. The most important factor is the weight of the rock compared to its size. Dense rock (i.e., heavy rock) is not as good as porous rock (i.e., light rock). It will not surprise you to know that extremely porous, light live rock fetches a premium price, but you generally can get away with less of it. A compromise is to buy some high-quality live rock and then purchase a bunch of lower-quality "base rock." Use the base rock (which will become live rock over time) as the base of your aquascaping, and then use the live rock as the external facade on your artificial reef.

Care of Live Rock

While live rock is not alive, it is full of life, and as such, you need to treat your live rock as if it were alive. Make sense? What we mean when we talk about taking care of live rock is placing it in an environment with stable water conditions conducive to the survival of the flora and fauna growing on your rock. Plan to keep live rock in heavily oxygenated, properly aged synthetic seawater kept between 21 and 28°C (70–82°F). This is why it is a practical solution to set up your aquarium, fill it with synthetic saltwater, turn on the circulation systems and heater(s), and then add your live rock directly.

Adding live rock to your system is going to cause your system to cycle in 99.9 percent of all situations. This is why you cannot add live rock to an existing system unless it is cured live rock. Cured live rock is live rock that has already experienced significant die-off of flora and fauna that did not survive the traumatic shipping process and acclimation to the holding tank at the dealer's facility. Many retailers will offer you "cured" live rock (usually for a significantly higher price). In theory, this rock has already experienced any die-off, and has been given a chance to "cure" in the retailer's holding facility where most of the dead and decaying life has been cleaned from the rock. Be forewarned, even cured live rock will probably need to be cured again when you introduce it to your aquarium. Why? Because an additional die-off will happen during transport between the local fish store or online retailer and your house. No doubt this second cycle will be far smaller than the first cycle when the rock was initially cured by the dealer, but depending upon how the rock was handled during transport to your house, you should expect to experience another curing cycle.

We prefer to cure live rock directly in our new aquarium because the nutrient levels produced by the die-off and subsequent decomposition of organic matter initiates the nitrogen cycle (described in Chapter 13) and promotes excellent growth of life on the rock as it cycles. The downsides to curing your live rock in your aquarium have to do with maintenance and odor. During the curing process, you will need to do many partial and full water changes. In addition, you will need to physically remove dead organisms from the rock, and change your mechanical filtration media frequently. Because curing live rock often produces an odor ranging from a pleasant low-tide smell to a house-clearing stench, some aquarist choose to cure their live rock in rubber or plastic tubs or trash cans in the garage. This is perfectly acceptable so long as you place both a heater and a powerhead in the curing container. You will still need to physically remove dead organisms and do frequent partial and full water changes, and you will also be well served to vacuum accumulated detritus from the bottom of the container.

Regardless of how you cure your live rock, once it is cured, we like to lay it out on the floor and look closely at each piece of rock to determine how it can be most effectively utilized in the aquarium. During this process, keep the rock covered with newspaper soaked in seawater, and work as quickly as you can to prevent any additional die-off. The methods for aquascaping with live rock are numerous and really only bounded by your imagination. Here are a few tips to keep in mind:

- Make sure your live rock structure is stable. In-tank rock slides can injure and kill sessile invertebrates. In a worst-case scenario, they can actually break the tank.

- If you are stacking live rock, make sure that each piece is securely resting on the piece beneath it.

- Live rock can be affixed or attached to other pieces of live rock or the tank itself with epoxy, plastic ties, or polyurethane foam.

- Attaching live rock to a frame of some sort (e.g., PVC pipe) can be quite effective.

- Avoid live rock structures that prevent free flow of water in and around the rock.

Other Alternatives to Live Rock

In our way of thinking, there really are few alternatives to live rock in a marine aquarium. While it used to be very popular to use bleached, dead coral skeletons in a marine tank, these are highly inferior to live rock in terms of aesthetics, habitat considerations, and filtration capacity. Using "dead rock" (often sold as base rock) is totally acceptable, but realize that it will take a significant amount of time for it to become live rock. Many aquarists mix base rock and live rock in order to save some money up front, and this technique works fine, so long as you do not increase your bioload beyond what your biological filtration can handle.

The Least You Need to Know

- You can have either a bare-bottom tank, a tank with a deep sand bed, or a tank with a shallow sand bed.

- Tanks with deep sand beds of aragonite provide both additional buffering capacity and biological filtration.

- Live rock is the best form of primary biological filtration in a marine aquarium, and should be a part of almost every saltwater system.

- Plan to use at least 1 pound per gallon of live rock.

Chapter 13

Hurry Up and Wait– Aiming for Consistency

In This Chapter

- ◆ Understanding the nitrogen cycle
- ◆ How to test for the major water parameters
- ◆ The importance of consistency

So you can't wait to get fish in the tank, but now is when patience, as the cliché goes, is a very real virtue. This chapter explains day by day how to properly cycle your tank and monitor the cycling process so you know when it is safe to add fishes. We then look at test kits for the major parameters you will want to monitor, and we make some recommendations regarding which kits are best.

Cycling the System—the Nitrogen Cycle

Using "cycle" as a verb is no longer just for Lance Armstrong. Cycling for the marine aquarist is the process of making your tank's water safe (not poisonous) for your livestock. Making your tank safe for livestock means initiating and observing a complete nitrogen cycle where ammonia is created and then converted to nitrite and then nitrate.

While you already know a lot about ammonia, nitrite, and nitrate (the water parameters most essential to you when cycling your tank), we'll go into a bit more depth here and walk you through the day-by-day process of cycling a new tank. The actual length of time a given tank requires to fully cycle depends on many factors (e.g., quality and quantity of live rock, size of tank, etc.). You will only know how quickly your tank is cycling (and when the cycle is complete) by monitoring your tank's water parameters.

The following scenario assumes you are cycling your tank with live rock. There are other ways to cycle your tank, such as initiating the cycle by putting a whole (dead) table shrimp in the aquarium and allowing it to decompose, or using a commercially available nitrifying bacteria product such as SuperBac, BioSpira or Microbe Lift. Our favorite way to cycle the tank is to cycle it the way described here, but it is not the only way (although *please* do not use live fish—even damsels—to cycle your tank).

Day 1

You have finally finished plumbing your new saltwater system and checked it for leaks and any equipment issues. Everything appears to be a go for starting the cycle.

Perhaps you already started making RO/DI water and mixing it with a salt mix in anticipation of this moment, but if you didn't, it's time to start. Start by purchasing a 32-gallon plastic trash can with a lid. This should cost you no more than going to the movies and buying a box of popcorn (depending on where you live!), but it will be worth its weight in gold as you progress into this hobby.

Rinse the trash can thoroughly and then direct the outlet from the RO/DI system to this trash can, and start filling it. Depending on the size of your tank and the efficiency of your RO/DI filter, it may take hours or days to fill the 32-gallon trash can (this is why you may have wanted to do this in advance of the day you are ready to start filling your new aquarium).

Once the trash can is filling, go ahead and add the appropriate amount of salt mix (following the directions on the container). When there is enough water, add a heater and powerhead to the water in the trash can. Set the heater at about 25.5–26.5°C (78–80°F), and occasionally stir the water as the trash can fills to ensure that all the salt mix is dissolved.

Eco Tips

Realize that you will make around four times as much wastewater as RO/DI water, and as such, we prefer to not have our RO/DI wastewater go down the drain. Instead, we collect the wastewater (which is actually better than our standard tap water) and use it to water the gardens.

While you are making your synthetic salt mix, you can head online (or over to the LFS) and buy your substrate (we discuss various substrate options in Chapter 12). For this tank, say you are using fine-grain aragonite sand (not live sand—if you use live sand, you must treat it like it is alive). Rinse the sand as described in Chapter 12.

Pour your sand carefully into the bottom of your tank (which was thoroughly rinsed with freshwater when you tested the system). If you are using an acrylic tank, be especially careful not to scratch the tank with the sand. Keep in mind that if you are planning a deep sand bed, you may want to have already installed rock lifts, a PVC frame, or the base rocks so that they will remain stable even when animals burrow, sift, or tunnel in the sand (many aquarists also believe this helps with filtration and circulation). Smooth out the substrate and add just enough synthetic seawater (assuming the salt is completely dissolved before you add it) to fully cover the sand bed.

Good first day! Keep making the RO/DI water overnight, but know that it will not overflow while you are sleeping. If your RO/DI water is already made and you have mixed your salt, allow it to sit in the trash can with the heater and powerhead running. Giving it a good stir from time to time will not hurt.

Day 2

Fill up the rest of your tank with the garden hose and add fish ... just kidding. Depending on the size of your tank and the efficiency of your RO/DI system, you may be ready to fill your tank halfway today, or you may have to wait a couple days. Let's say your tank is small enough that you have enough premixed synthetic saltwater on hand to fill your tank halfway. First siphon off any floating debris from the tank, and then go ahead and fill the aquarium halfway with saltwater. Depending on how your tank is plumbed, there probably will not be enough water in the tank to run your filtration system yet. That's fine. Simply add a heater and powerhead to the half-full tank, and let things settle.

Day 3

You wake up early and are eager to test your water parameters. Enjoy this moment—the novelty of conducting water tests will soon wear off. At this point, you want to test for pH, temperature, and salinity.

If all your parameters are in order, then it's time to add live rock. Assuming you have a local fish store that sells quality live rock, you head on over with a bunch of coolers and newspaper, and start picking through their holding containers full of beautiful "cured" live rock. You buy about 1 pound of live rock per gallon of tank water, place it in the coolers, cover it with wet newspaper, and get it home ASAP. When you get home, you transfer the live rock to your half-full tank so that all of it is covered with water. This is not aquascaping time! You are simply using your tank as a holding facility in which you will cure your live rock.

"Cure my live rock?" you gasp. "But didn't you say I bought cured live rock?" Indeed we did, but you probably had some additional die-off during transportation from the store to your house, and you will probably have some more die-off as a result of acclimation to your system. This is okay, and you needn't worry. In fact, this is good, because you want your tank to cycle, and it can only do so if there is decomposition leading to the necessary ammonia spike.

Once all the rock is in the tank, fill the remainder of the tank with premixed saltwater and turn on the return pump, CLS, or other water-movement system, as well as the protein skimmer. Do not turn on your lights. Make sure you have a mechanical filter in place such as a filter sock or a sponge filter to catch all of the detritus. Your rock is now curing (sometimes referred to as "cooking"), and the nitrogen cycle will soon begin. Do a baseline water test now for ammonia, and start making up a new batch of saltwater—many a water change is in your future.

Day 4

You wake up and test the water. At this point, you are most interested in ammonia, as you are hoping to see an ammonia spike indicating that your tank is starting to cycle. You observe your rock closely and physically remove whatever dead matter you see. Keep in mind that the more flow, the better in terms of knocking off detritus, blowing it into suspension, and, ultimately, moving it to your filter where you can remove it. Clean your filter daily during this stage of the curing/cycling process. Continue to keep the lights off on the tank at this point, as the high nutrient levels produced will create massive algae blooms.

Days 5–15

During this time, you are going to test your water daily and record the results. Perform a 50 percent water change around day six or seven (three or four days after you added the rock to the tank). Take this opportunity to inspect the rock and remove any obviously dead organisms (a toothbrush can be useful). You will most likely see your ammonia peak in the beginning of the second week of having the rock in your tank. You will know that the ammonia spike has happened because the ammonia level will start to fall. Again, keep the lights off to prevent massive algae blooms.

Day 16–26

Continue to test the water daily, and you will see the ammonia levels drop and the nitrite levels rise. The nitrite is probably going to rise to concentrations more than twice that of the highest ammonia readings. Once the ammonia has dropped off to zero, you can stop testing for ammonia (unless you run into a problem down the road). If your ammonia levels won't drop, consider doing a 75 percent water change. As the tank continues to cycle, you may consider doing a 20 percent water change every four or five days. Continue to clean your filter media daily, and keep the lights off.

Day 26–36

Once the nitrite has peaked (probably around the third week after adding the live rock), you want to start testing for both nitrite and nitrate. Somewhere around the first week of the second month after placing the live rock in your tank, you will see nitrite levels drop to close to zero. This is a very good sign. When this happens, test once more for ammonia and nitrites—ammonia should be at zero and nitrites should be either undetectable or very, very low (using a low nitrite test kit like the one discussed later in this chapter), and your nitrates should be under 20 ppm. Throughout this period you have continued to keep the lights off, done 20 percent water changes every week, and cleaned the filter media daily.

Day 37

This is a banner day—although day 37 will be day 27 or day 47 depending on each situation, but the important thing is that on a certain day, your ammonia and nitrite levels will be zero, and your nitrate level will be below 20 ppm. Your tank is now cycled and should remain relatively stable.

Starting today, you will run your lights (although you are going to slowly build up to a full lighting cycle, as described in Chapter 9). In addition, you will begin testing daily for new parameters like alkalinity, phosphate, and calcium.

It is now time to add your clean-up crew (discussed in Chapter 14) and maybe a few hardy, herbivorous fishes. These animals will produce the waste needed to feed the bacteria now living in your system.

What Just Happened? Nitrification–Denitrification

Repeat after us: ammonia is converted to nitrite, which is converted to nitrate. That is the nitrogen cycle, and it converts toxic ammonia into relatively harmless nitrates and nitrogen gas. This happens because ammonia is metabolized by tiny bacteria that, in the process, turn the ammonia to nitrite. Different bacteria then feed on the nitrite and convert it to nitrate.

The nitrogen cycle is what allows us to keep life in an aquarium over a long period of time, but in order for it to happen, we need to have the bacteria present. To have the bacteria present, we need to provide it with food, and, because it feeds on toxic ammonia, we must add ammonia—even though it's toxic—to our new aquaria.

A new tank, filled with newly mixed synthetic saltwater, may look pretty, but, in reality, it is not an appropriate home for any waste-producing animal. Think back to Mark's glass box theory in Chapter 1. When he added a fish to the glass box, the fish immediately began producing waste in the form of ammonia from its gills. This observation has led some old-school aquarists to add hardy fish to their new aquarium as a means of jump-starting the nitrogen cycle. We do *not* advocate this technique, because, in a sterile environment with no nitrifying bacteria present, the ammonia quickly reaches toxic levels, and while a hardy fish such as a damsel *may* survive, it is nonetheless being subjected to a very unpleasant experience.

Test Kits for Cycling and Continued Monitoring

We have mentioned the importance of testing your water parameters many times, but we have not actually told you how to do that. As you probably surmised, you use a test kit, of which many varieties are available. It's important to understand that a saltwater test kit is different from a freshwater test kit, and we recommend you buy individual tests for each parameter rather than buying a prepacked saltwater or reef test kit.

Generally speaking, test kits come in the form of dry powder reagent test kits, tablet reagent test kits, and liquid reagent test kits. You will notice here that the common denominator is "reagent." A reagent is something that is consumed as a chemical reaction takes place. Reagents are used as indicators when testing. You remember our discussion of alkalinity in Chapter 11? We explained there that alkalinity is measured by seeing how much acid it takes to drop the pH of a water sample to somewhere between 4 and 5. The reason we know when the pH has reached the desired level for the test is because the reagent makes the sample change color, alerting us to the fact that a chemical reaction has occurred.

Liquid reagent test kits are the most common test kits used by marine aquarists, but all liquid reagent test kits are *not* the same. Studies conducted for the purpose of researching this book confirmed a long-standing belief amongst marine aquarists: spend the money to get good tests and then stick with that brand. We like Salifert test kits (and they are not paying us to say that) because they are reliable, relatively user-friendly (bold color changes and easy-to-read color-comparison charts), and measure very small changes in water parameters.

Whichever brand you use, remember that the purpose of a test kit is not to get a one-time reading of a parameter. Instead, test kits should be used to chart a parameter over time. There are no 100 percent accurate hobbyist test kits out there for sale at your local fish store, and very few aquarists test their water under true lab conditions. Sure, you can spend a ton of money on "more accurate" test kits or "lab-grade" test kits, but why? The entire goal of testing is to paint a picture of the chemistry of your tank and to map the trends that the chemistry follows. For this, you do not need 100 percent accurate test kits. You just need ones that are easy to use and give fairly accurate results, which can be compared over time.

By no means are we telling you not to buy the very best test kits you can find; we are just saying you don't need to spend the money on something like a digital titration kit. Having said this, you will notice that the Salifert test kits are more expensive than the reef test kits sold at the big-box pet stores. As we said before, our recommendation to you is to buy the individual tests you need for your system. Here's what we recommend for the beginning aquarist:

Fish-Only System	Reef Systems
Ammonia	All the kits for fish-only,
Nitrite	and calcium. Consider a low-
Nitrate	range phosphate test kit if
pH	you plan to keep difficult
Phosphate	corals.
Alk/Carbonate Hardness	

You may want to also consider the following test kits: iodine, strontium, silicate, boron, and magnesium.

Testing for Ammonia

As explained earlier in this chapter, somewhere during the first week or two, you are going to see ammonia levels in your tank spike. If you had livestock in your tank, this would be bad, as you would essentially be poisoning them, but because there are no animals yet, this is a good development. During this time, you are testing for ammonia daily and somewhere early in the second week—maybe around day 11—you are going to see the ammonia peak and then begin to fall. This indicates that the nitrifying bacteria colonies are growing and consuming the ammonia.

Most ammonia test kits are easy to use. Generally they measure the total ammonia nitrogen (TAN), which includes both NH_3 and NH_{4+}. This test takes about five minutes, and should measure ammonia down to 0.5 ppm.

Testing for Nitrites

At this point, you will start testing for both ammonia and nitrite. As your ammonia falls, you should see your nitrite levels skyrocket. If you were to graph these levels, you would see that the nitrite levels will be about twice as much as the ammonia levels. This high concentration of nitrite is not as toxic as the ammonia, but it is still quite toxic to livestock, so still no fish. Somewhere around the third week, the nitrite levels should peak and start to fall. By this point, your ammonia levels should be at zero.

We said earlier that your nitrite levels should drop to zero and stay at zero. Generally speaking this is true, but the reality is a little more complicated. Without getting into too many details, nitrite is converted to nitrate and the nitrate is transformed anaerobically into nontoxic nitrogen gas through the process of denitrification. During denitrification, the nitrate is briefly converted back to nitrite before becoming nitrogen gas. As such, very low levels of nitrite will actually be present even in a properly cycled aquarium.

Most nitrite test kits will show that there are no nitrites in the tank, but this is often a result of the fact that the nitrite test kit in question is giving an inaccurate reading due to something called "amine interference." It's not important what that is, but it is important to understand that when the process of denitrification is interrupted, your nitrite may reach high levels undetected by many nitrite test kits. As a result, we recommend a test kit that does not suffer from amine interference (e.g., Salifert's nitrite test kit). Make sure that whatever nitrite test kit you use, it can test for very low levels of nitrite.

Testing for Nitrates

As your nitrite levels fall, you will begin to see nitrate levels rise. Somewhere about a month into the cycle, you should see no ammonia, very low levels of nitrites, and only low levels of nitrate. High levels of nitrates often create algae blooms that can interfere with coral growth, so the aquarist—especially in the reef tank—wants to maintain nitrates at a very low level (lower than 1 mg/L, an equivalent of 1 ppm for a reef tank).

A nitrate test kit often converts nitrate to nitrite to give you a result, and it follows that this process will suffer from the same amine interference from which nitrite test kits suffer. This amine interference will result in reading much lower levels of nitrate than are actually present in the sample. As such, make sure you use a nitrate test kit that does not suffer from amine interference (again, Salifert's nitrate test kit is a good choice). Your nitrate test kit should be able to detect levels as low as 0.05 mg/L as nitrate-nitrogen or 0.2 mg/L as nitrate ion.

Alkalinity

We know that typical seawater is a basic solution with a pH around 8.2 or 8.3. When the pH in the ocean changes for whatever reason, it is generally capable of readjusting back to a pH of 8.2 or 8.3. Your aquarium, a much smaller system than the ocean, does not have the ability to perpetually compensate for fluctuations in pH because it does not have the same buffering capacity as the ocean.

Carbonate and bicarbonate, in addition to promoting the growth of corals and calcareous algae, are important to keeping your pH in the target range. Because the alkalinity and carbonate hardness can be easily converted back and forth, a single KH/Alk test can measure both. It is important that this parameter not fluctuate more than 0.14 meq/L or 0.4 dKH, and this requires a test kit capable of measuring changes as small as 0.14 meq/L. Again, the Salifert test is superior to most other test kits because it measures changes as small as 0.1 meq/L or 0.3 dKH, and it does so with a sharp color change, which makes reading the test easier.

Alkalinity in the ocean is about 2.7 meq/L (7.5 dKH), and your aquarium should not fall below this number. It is best, in fact, to keep your alkalinity higher than natural seawater.

Testing for Phosphate

Phosphate is a natural component in seawater, but only at very low levels. In the aquarium, elevated phosphate levels can lead to nuisance algae blooms, stunted coral growth, and a lack of calcareous algae.

A basic phosphate test kit will work in most situations, especially for the beginning aquarist. If you want to see rapid calcareous algae growth and are intent on keeping some of the more difficult corals, you will want to ensure your phosphate levels are lower than that for

> **Pearls of Wisdom**
>
> One scientific study shows that a phosphate concentration higher than 0.05 mg/L decreases he growth of calcareous algae by 90 percent.

which most phosphate test kits can test. Low-range phosphate photometers are becoming more popular with marine aquarists. The Hanna Instruments phosphate photometer, for example, can measure phosphate content in seawater in the 0.00 to 2.50 mg/L (ppm) range.

Testing for Calcium

As already discussed, calcium is very important in the marine aquarium, especially in the reef aquarium. In the ocean, calcium levels are usually measured between 400 and 450 mg/L calcium, and we want the same levels (or higher) in our aquaria. Again, consistency is critical, which is why we shoot for calcium levels to not fluctuate more than 15 mg/L. As such, your calcium test kit should be able to monitor changes of 15 mg/L and less (good test kits measure fluctuations as small as 10 mg/L).

Other Tests

We have covered the major test kits for a fish-only and a reef aquarium. You can (and may choose to) test for additional parameters such as iodine, strontium, silicate, boron, magnesium, etc. To test for these, use a brand that you like based on the previous recommendations, and follow the instructions on the test kits. Remember that the most important thing is consistency over time. This means that unless you have a compelling reason to switch brands, use the same brand and chart your results over time.

There are a few parameters that many aquarists like to monitor continually through the use of a testing probe and an electronic monitor or controller, such as the ones we discussed in Chapter 7. These parameters can be tested using liquid reagent test kits such as those already described, but accurate and relatively inexpensive probes are available for pH and temperature, and we recommend their use.

Testing for pH

There are essentially three zones on the pH scale that allow us to generally define a sample of water as either acidic, nonacidic (which we call base or alkaline), or neutral (in between acidic and alkaline). If you test distilled freshwater or "pure water" at 25°C (77°F), you would find that it has a pH of 7.0, which is considered neutral. Water is said to be acidic if it is lower than this, and it is said to be alkaline—like seawater—if it is higher.

Most pH test kits do a reasonable job of accurately telling you the pH of your aquarium. pH is such an important parameter to measure over time, however, that we prefer to use a pH probe to monitor and log our pH levels continuously. A pH probe, attached to a controller with a data-logging feature (such as the Neptune AquaController discussed in Chapter 7), is an excellent way to monitor the health of your system over time. The probe simply goes in the sump, and the data log can be read on the controller or on your PC. The only maintenance required is to calibrate (and periodically recalibrate) the probe. Most pH probes are used in conjunction with a temperature probe because temperature and pH are so closely linked. We recommend you use a temperature and a pH probe attached to a data-logging controller for optimal monitoring of these two critical parameters.

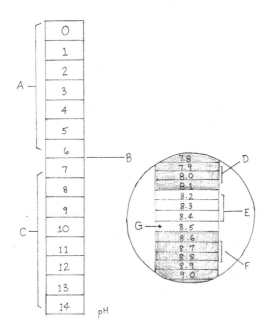

The pH scale. A = Alkaline, B = Neutral, C = Basic, D = Okay for fish-only system, E = Seawater, F = too basic—only go here to treat parasite infestation, G = higher than most ocean water but okay for reef tanks.

The Most Important Parameter to Monitor?—Testing for pH

Ret's a fly fisherman (which, in case you're wondering, isn't really all that ironic), and he has participated in a fly fishing competition in Wyoming called the One Fly. In this competition, anglers are only allowed to use (you guessed it) one fly. It's an incredibly difficult choice to make, as generally an angler will employ many flies over the course of a day as conditions change. But the competition rules are strict—you can only pick one fly.

What if you could only pick one water parameter to monitor in your saltwater aquarium? Which one would you choose? We're going to go out on a limb here and say pH. Of course, we would never only monitor one parameter, but in theory, if we had to, we'd pick pH (assuming, of course, that there is a thermostat in place to keep the temperature stable).

Robert Fenner, the author of *The Conscientious Marine Aquarist* (a book you should own!), refers to pH as "a window into water quality," and we agree. Monitoring changes to your pH over time is a good indicator of what is going on with other parameters in your aquarium. For example, pH is closely tied to alkalinity, ammonia, nitrites, nitrates, and carbon dioxide.

If alkalinity is the water's ability to maintain a high pH, we can surmise that if you monitor pH, and your pH is consistently high (alkaline), then your alkalinity is also high. On the other hand, if your pH begins to fall over time, then your alkalinity levels may be the culprit. Observing a descending pH trend therefore prompts the aquarist to test for alkalinity.

Changes in ammonia, nitrites, and nitrates will also have an effect on the pH of your aquarium. An increase in any of the parameters associated with the nitrogen cycle will cause a descending pH trend. As a result, if you observe a downward trend in pH over several days and testing for alkalinity shows that alkalinity is not to blame, then consider testing for nitrates, then nitrites, and finally ammonia.

Although we have not explicitly discussed it, we are quite concerned about CO_2 in our marine aquaria, and, like the parameters previously discussed, a change in CO_2 will affect your pH levels. CO_2 is a critical component in many of the important chemical reactions that occur in a saltwater tank. It is a normal by-product of respiration, but it can also be caused by a decomposing animal in your system. Excessive amounts of CO_2 in your aquarium will have a detrimental effect on your livestock, and so you need to know if the CO_2 levels are getting too high.

Like the other parameters discussed, excessive CO_2 will lower your pH over time and key you in to the fact that something is not right. If you observe a descending pH over time, and your alkalinity, nitrates, nitrites, and ammonia levels are all okay, you may want to consider excessive CO_2 as the culprit.

We are not suggesting that you address each small fluctuation in pH as a problem requiring additional testing and corrective measures (if you did this, you would have time for little else). What we are suggesting is that you look out for (and address) sudden large changes in pH or slow trends over the course of several days or weeks. Monitoring pH is by no means a silver bullet, but it is an excellent parameter to monitor over time in order to stay on top of your system's overall health.

A Matter of Life and Death—Consistency

When it comes to managing water parameters in the aquarium, it is usually about more than comfort. Let your ammonia climb too high? Livestock will die. Let your pH fall too low? Livestock will die. When it comes to monitoring and controlling the water parameters in your saltwater aquarium, it is often truly a matter of life and death.

Okay, now that we have scared you, we want to reassure you about what we said in the introduction—maintaining water quality in your marine aquarium is relatively easy. At the most basic level, you are analogous to the thermostat in the above example. Using a test kit or sensor probe, you regularly test the water parameters. Then, based on the results of your tests, you control the parameters by fixing a problem with your husbandry, adjusting a piece of equipment, adding a supplement, or in some other way manipulating the system so that your test results consistently fall within the target range.

Keeping your parameters consistent and within the target range is essential to the health of your livestock. Notice that we said consistent and within the target range. It is our opinion that, within reason, consistency is the most important factor when it comes to water parameters.

Will the larger temperature fluctuation kill the fish? No, not in and of itself, but keep in mind that the animal's natural environment—the ocean—is a remarkably stable one. While small variations do occur in some areas of the ocean over a 24-hour period, it would be unheard of for the Auriga butterflyfish's habitat to fluctuate 6 degrees every day. Even if it did, the fish could easily swim to a different location with a different temperature. Prolonged exposure to wildly fluctuating temperatures—even within a particular species' acceptable range—can and will cause stress that can contribute to disease and ultimately death.

The Least You Need to Know

- Take the time to properly cycle your tank—everything else you do in the hobby depends on it.
- Be sure to test the major water parameters.
- Use the same brand test kit for the sake of consistency.
- Respond to water quality changes over time; record everything.

Part 4

Adding Livestock

Some would say that this is the part of the book they've been waiting for—adding animals to your aquarium. We'll show you how to select a clean-up crew of invertebrates to take care of tank maintenance, and then how to gradually select, acclimate, and add fishes, corals, and other invertebrates to your new system. If you have not done so already, this would be a good time to use the CD-ROM included with the book to better understand the hierarchy of fishes (discussed in Chapter 15), noncoral invertebrates (discussed in Chapter 16), and corals (discussed in Chapter 17).

14

The First Bold Explorers—the Clean-Up Crew

In This Chapter

- Selecting a clean-up crew
- Choosing the best snails
- Sea cucumbers and crabs
- Selecting herbivorous fishes

Chances are, you will want to add a "clean-up crew" first—usually a collection of snails, hermit crabs, and other critters—to start cleaning up the algae and detritus produced during the cycling process. Some aquarists also add hardy or herbivorous fishes like damsels or tangs early on, especially since the waste produced by these animals will help feed the growing populations of beneficial bacteria. This chapter will help you decide which animals you will add to your system first and how to acclimate them to their new home.

The Clean-Up Crew

After your tank has cycled and ammonia and nitrite levels are undetectable, you can consider adding your first tank inhabitants. Frequently referred to as the "clean-up crew" or CUC, this industrious gang of organisms serves many purposes, but first and foremost, their role in the reef tank is janitorial.

With the cycling of your tank (and possibly also the curing of your live rock), you have provided extraordinarily high nutrient levels to your aquarium—much higher than you will ever intentionally do again (unless you have to cycle a new tank). All of those nutrients have fed various algae that may now appear to be overtaking the tank (especially once you get your lights up to speed). Adding a well-researched and carefully chosen clean-up crew will be your first step in bringing your tank back under control and stabilizing its parameters.

In this section, we will discuss three separate groups of clean-up crews—algae clean-up crews, detritus clean-up crews, and sand-stirring clean-up crews. In reality, you will want a clean-up crew to deal with all of your janitorial tasks, and we have therefore included a so-called "ultimate" clean-up crew. Keep in mind that each system is unique, and what works for one system may not work for another. The table we provide here should be a good starting point, but, as always, do your research and choose what is right for your specific situation. Keep in mind, too, that the numbers provided are based on a mature tank with an average bioload. Remember, the primary purpose of the clean-up crew is to do the following:

- Clean up nonliving particulate organic matter (a.k.a. detritus) resulting principally from die-off during the shipping and acclimatization of live rock.

- Take care of algae blooms commonly associated with a newly cycled tank.

- Keep nuisance algae and detritus in check as the tank continues to mature.

Algae Clean-Up Crew

The size of an algae clean-up crew will vary greatly based, primarily, on the size of the tank. There are other variables to consider, but the following table provides a rough guideline based on how many of each species should be added to various tank sizes.

	25 Gal	50 Gal	75 Gal	100 Gal	150 Gal	200 Gal
Asterea Snails	5	9	16	22	30	38
Nerite Snails	10	16	22	28	35	42
Margarita Snails	10	16	22	28	35	42
Turbo Snails	0	3	6	9	14	18
Onyx Nassarius Snails	10	20	30	40	60	80
Red Leg Reef Hermit Crabs	10	16	22	28	35	42
Zebra Hermit Crabs	10	16	22	28	35	42
Emerald Crabs	1	2	3	4	5	6

Detritus Clean-Up Crew

The size of a detritus clean-up crew will vary greatly based, primarily, on the size of the tank and what else is in the tank. If your algae is under control, but you are still worried about your parameters, a detritus clean-up crew may be what you need to eat the detritus that is caught amongst the rocks and in dead spots in the aquarium. The small hermit crabs from the genus *Calcinus* are particularly good at controlling detritus in tanks with lots of live rock. Make sure to only include species that need a sand bed (e.g., Nassarius snails) in tanks with a sand bed. There are other variables to consider, but the following table provides a rough guideline based on how many of each species should be added based on tank size.

	25 Gal	50 Gal	75 Gal	100 Gal	150 Gal	200 Gal
Tonga Fighting Conch	1	2	3	4	5	6
Bumble Bee Snails	5	8	14	18	26	32
Cerith Snails	10	16	22	28	35	42
Nassarius Snails	0	3	6	9	14	18
Atlantic Sand Cucumbers	0	1	1	2	3	4
Blue Leg Reef Hermit Crabs	10	16	22	28	35	42
Scarlet Reef Hermit Crabs	5	8	14	18	26	32
Sally Lightfoot Crabs	0	1	1	2	3	4

Sand-Stirring Clean-Up Crew

Like the other two clean-up crews, the size of a sand-stirring clean-up crew will vary greatly based, primarily, on the size of the tank and what else is in the tank. Obviously, a sand-stirring clean-up crew is only appropriate for tanks with sand beds. There are other variables to consider, but the following table provides a rough guideline based on how many of each species should be added to various tank sizes.

	25 Gal	50 Gal	75 Gal	100 Gal	150 Gal	200 Gal
Sand-Sifting Starfish	0	1	2	3	5	7
Tiger Tail Cucumber	0	1	1	2	3	4
Tonga Nassarius Snails	6	10	15	20	30	40
Onyx Nassarius Snails	10	20	30	40	55	70

Ultimate Clean-Up Crew

This is the ultimate clean-up crew, and, while it will vary greatly based on the size of the tank, it is, in our opinion, the clean-up crew you should plan for your tank. While not inexpensive, this combination of animals should effectively deal with algae, detritus, and the stirring of sand beds. The following table provides a rough guideline based on how many of each species should be added to various tank sizes.

	25 Gal	50 Gal	75 Gal	100 Gal	150 Gal	200 Gal
Lettuce Slugs	1	2	3	4	5	6
Lawnmower Blenny	0	1	1	1	1	2
Serpent Starfish	0	1	1	2	3	4
Sand-Sifting Starfish	0	1	2	3	4	5
Asterea Snails	5	9	16	22	28	35
Nerite Snails	7	12	17	24	30	38
Margarita Snails	7	12	17	24	30	38
Turbo Snails	0	3	6	9	14	21
Onyx Nassarius Snails	7	14	21	28	40	55
Nassarius Snails	7	12	17	24	30	38
Cerith Snails	7	12	17	24	30	38
Tonga Fighting Conch	1	2	3	4	5	6
Red Leg Reef Hermit Crabs	7	12	17	24	30	38
Blue Leg Reef Hermit Crabs	7	12	17	24	30	38
Scarlet Reef Hermit Crabs	3	6	10	14	21	28
Sally Lightfoot Crabs	0	1	2	2	3	4
Emerald Crabs	1	2	3	4	5	6
Atlantic Sand Cucumbers	0	1	1	2	3	4

Snail Specifics

As you can see from the preceding tables, snails often define the
workforce when it comes to cleaning-up. In addition to the guidelines
offered in the tables, there are some additional points to be made about
certain snails.

The following four snail species—asterea, trochus, cerith, and nerite
snails—should, in our opinion, be added to every newly cycled saltwater system to control nuisance algae. In addition, turbo snails are
commonly available and utilized as part of a clean-up crew; however,
their large size (and penchant for knocking over rockwork) make some
aquarists leery of introducing them into their systems.

Asterea Snails

Asterea snails (e.g., *Astraea tectum*), also sometimes called astrea snails,
are particularly useful herbivores for clearing algae (both green and
brown) from the walls of the tank. They will also clean the substrate
and live rock and will not grow in excess of about 2.5 centimeters (1
inch). Despite their excellent algae-eating ability, slow-moving asterea
snails have one major downside—they are unable to right themselves
if they flip over. In the wild this is not a problem, for they are coastal
snails that only need wait until the next wave flips them over. In the
aquarium, you may have to perform this task for them.

We generally recommended adding only a few asterea snails to start—
perhaps one snail for every 6 or 7 gallons of water.

Trochus Snails

Trochus snails (*Trochus* spp.), like asterea snails, are fantastic algae eaters and are adept at controlling a wide range of algae in the saltwater
aquarium. Like asterea snails, trochus snails generally remain small
(although some get quite large like the so-called zebra trochus, or
turbo, snail). Be sure to check on the specific adult sizes of individual
species. Trochus snails, unlike asterea snails, are able to self-rescue
upon flipping upside down.

Some aquarists include as many as one trochus snail for every gallon of water in the tank. It is, however, a better idea to begin with perhaps one trochus snail for every 3 gallons of water in a newly cycled tank. Our advice? Do your research and know what you're getting. Mark once had a "pet" zebra trochus. It was a pet because it was the size of a good-size rodent.

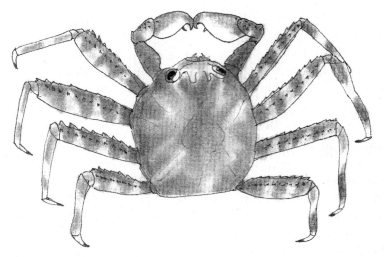

Sally lightfoot crab.

(Courtesy Karen Talbot.)

Cerith Snails

Cerith snails (*Cerithium* sp.) will aggressively target nuisance algae in the newly cycled tank. In addition, they are extremely useful for agitating the sand bed. As such, this relatively small snail (rarely larger than 2.5 centimeters/1 inch) is an excellent candidate for any tank with a sand bed.

One cerith snail for every 5 gallons of water is a reasonable number to add to the newly cycled tank.

Nerite Snails

Nerite snails (*Nerita* sp.) are yet another small snail (2.5 centimeters/1 inch) adept at eating film algae from the aquarium sides. These snails will come completely out of the water from time to time, and as such, they are sometimes referred to as "suicide snails" (suicidal when they climb over the edge of the tank and down the glass on the outside of the tank—make sure your tank has a sizable lip or even an egg-crate cover). In addition to their effectiveness in combating nuisance algae on the tank walls, they also do an excellent job tending marine plants (including macroalgae) and are well suited for the refugium. In addition to their janitorial duties, if you are interested in studying the small species of organisms in your tank, these guys will knock your socks off. Many marine aquarists populate their tanks with one nerite snail for every gallon of water.

Other Snails

In addition to the four species of snails we discuss here, there are many other snails and organisms that should be considered as part of a comprehensive clean-up crew, especially as the tank matures. Four additional snails that bear mention are turbo snails, margarita snails, nassarius snails, and bumble bee snails. We believe these snails need comment either because they are misunderstood or require specific conditions. All are commonly touted as excellent clean-up crew candidates, and we would agree so long as you know what they need to thrive.

Turbo snails (*Turbo* sp.) are undoubtedly some of the most effective snails at controlling filamentous algae. They are also, however, some of the most destructive snails commonly seen in the hobby. A turbo snail's wake of destruction is almost always unintentional, but its large size (not to mention the speed at which it moves) means that anything not firmly anchored will most likely be toppled. In addition, turbo snails are so effective at eating algae, that it is not uncommon for them to starve in a mature tank where there is not enough food. This puts the aquarist in the ironic position of needing to supplement the clean-up crew's diet. Having said this, turbo snails can be kept in the home aquarium with success so long as the aquarist only adds a few of them and makes sure everything is firmly anchored. Owing to their size, a dead turbo snail can really cause a problem in a small tank. Turbo snails are awesome in fish-only systems with predators such as puffers and triggers because they are about the only clean-up crew member that can survive in such a tank.

Margarita snails *(Margarites pupillus)* are another snail species commonly included in a clean-up crew package, but one that usually should not be added to a tropical marine system because they are a temperate species. Actually, we have to qualify that statement slightly. While margarita snails are excellent hair algae eaters, and they will survive for some length of time in tropical reef tanks, knowingly adding a temperate species to a tropical environment is (and should be) frowned upon. So why are they so commonly sold as part of clean-up crew packages such as the one Mark's company sells? The reason is that some margarita snails are collected from farther south and do fine in a tropical marine aquarium. How do you know from where your margarita snails come? A quick trick Mark uses is to look and see if their shells are encrusted with coralline algae. The pink type of coralline algae marine aquarists love so well is a tropical species, so if the margarita snails you are purchasing have pink coralline algae, you know they have most likely been collected near the Tropics (not from the tide pools of Laguna Beach).

Nassarius snails *(Nassarius* sp.) are fantastic additions to an effective clean-up crew with one major caveat—the tank into which they are introduced must have a sand bed. Nassarius snails bury themselves in the sand bed and emerge to feed, making them ideal and continuous agitators of the substrate (a critical function for a tank with a sand bed). In addition to agitation of the sand bed, nassarius snails will feed on detritus, carrion, and organic waste that other snails are likely to ignore.

Consider adding one nassarius snail for every 2 to 3 gallons of system water in a standard-size tank (or one for every 5 gallons of water in a tall tank given the reduction in substrate surface area).

Onyx nassarius snails are very good at keeping sand beds completely clean of algae as well as other organics. Sometimes they are too good, and they may occasionally strip a sand bed of enough nutrients that there will be none left to support copepod or amphipod populations. If you keep dragonets, such as green mandarins, that rely on healthy populations of copepods and amphipods, you may want to reconsider the addition of onyx nassarius snails, although Mark points out that their onyx nassarius snail–holding tank is loaded with healthy populations of copepods and amphipods. In addition to eating everything other nassarius snails will eat, onyx nassarius will eat hair algae and red algae, and will keep a sand bed spotless.

Finally, bumble bee snails (*Engina mendicaria* and *Pusiostoma mendicaria*), while alluring due to their attractive coloration, may not be the best choice for the tropical marine aquarium with a deep sand bed, but they are fantastic snails. Bumble bee snails are carnivores and may prey on beneficial fauna in the sand bed. There is also some anecdotal evidence that they will feed on zooanthids and polyps, but this is not generally a problem. For tanks with a deep sand bed, we prefer nassarius snails rather than bumble bee snails, but for all other tanks, we tend to like bumble bee snails.

Cucs and Crabs

Some people are afraid of the dark. Other people fear spiders. Many marine aquarists fear sea cucumbers and crabs. Is there a good reason for fearing sea cucumbers and crabs? Sure, in the same way that dark provides an opportunity for a mugger to mug me, and some spiders can kill me. Thankfully, it is rare to get mugged or bitten by a poisonous spider, and likewise, it is rare to have an aquarium catastrophe with the crabs and cucumbers recommended earlier in this chapter. This is not to say that cucumbers have not wiped out entire tanks. It's also not to say that all crabs are not opportunistic. We are simply saying that the cucumbers (tiger tail and Atlantic sand) and the crabs (red leg reef hermit, blue leg reef hermit, scarlet reef hermit, Sally Lightfoot, and emerald mentioned here) are not likely to cause problems.

First Fishes—Blennies and Tangs, Oh My!

Hardy herbivorous fishes should be amongst the first fishes added to a system, with one major caveat: don't introduce an herbivorous fish just because you have algae. This is the first major test of your willpower. Stick to your stocking list you developed in Chapter 3. A lot of good, hard work went into making that list, and you don't want to change course in midstream just because you want to address a "problem."

Actually, we'd suggest that the algae growth you may be seeing in your tank is not a problem at all. Your tank is progressing nicely and the clean-up crew, along with stabilizing parameters and regular maintenance (read: water changes), will bring the algae under control. You have to be patient.

If, however, you already had a peaceful herbivorous fish such as a Chevron tang *(Ctenochaetus hawaiiensis)* on your stocking list, then by all means, go ahead and add that fish now. Lawnmower blennies *(Salarias fasciatus)*, as their name suggests, are also great at mowing down fields of filamentous hair algae (although the adult of this species can become belligerent and may preclude the addition of many other blennies down the road). Keep in mind that the lawnmower blenny, like most herbivorous fishes, may require supplemental feeding when the hair algae is gone.

Pearls of Wisdom

Ctenochaetus tangs, frequently called bristle-tooth tangs, will spend their day picking at rockwork in search for hair algae to eat. They are one of the best-equipped fish for assisting your clean-up crew in hair algae removal. These largely peaceful fish can get bullied, so only add them if you plan to not add bullies down the road.

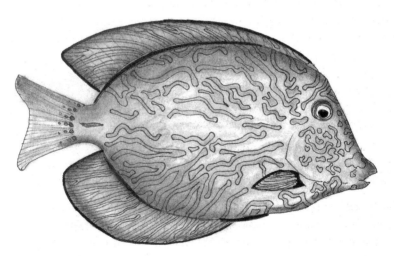

Chevron tang.

(Courtesy Karen Talbot.)

Amazing Animals Working Magic

The clean-up crew provides some of the first large animals (at least larger than most of the life that will emerge from your live rock) in your system. Don't waste the opportunity to enjoy seeing these fascinating organisms work their magic. No, they are not flashy angel-fishes or puppylike puffers, but they are incredibly interesting and highly adapted life forms that will amaze you if given the chance.

Be sure to read up on how to acclimate invertebrates and fishes before purchasing any species. You can find all the acclimation procedures in later chapters, and you can learn a tremendous amount more about most of the species mentioned in this chapter on the CD-ROM.

The Least You Need to Know

- ◆ Choose a well-balanced clean-up crew made up of a variety of different organisms.

- ◆ Resist the urge to add an animal simply to address a temporary problem—stick to your stocking list.

- ◆ Don't forget to observe the fascinating behavior of your clean-up crew members.

Chapter 15

Selecting, Purchasing, and Acclimating Fishes

In This Chapter

- ◆ Reviewing your stocking list
- ◆ Selecting individual fish
- ◆ Transporting fishes
- ◆ Acclimating fishes

So you've taken the time to set your system up right and allow it to fully cycle. Now you are *finally* ready to add the fishes (although you may have added a few last chapter). Back in Chapter 3 (and using the enclosed CD-ROM), you created your stocking list. This chapter discusses how to select, purchase, transport, and acclimate your individual specimens. It also covers the order in which you should add your new specimens and how much time you should leave between each new addition. The chapter does not include species-specific information, because all of that is on the CD-ROM.

Stocking List Revisited

It is absolutely amazing how much you have learned about your aquarium and marine species in general since getting into this hobby. Pat yourself on the back—you've come a long way since those first tentative steps into the marine aquarium world. And now you are finally ready to begin stocking your tank with fishes.

We are going to start by discussing fishes, because some of you may be planning a fish-only aquarium. If you are planning an invertebrate or reef aquarium, we suggest that, with the exception of one or more herbivorous fishes such as the ones mentioned in Chapter 14, you begin with corals instead of fishes. Why? Corals are significantly less in terms of bioload, and, if your system is stable, you can slowly build up your coral population before adding fishes. This will give your aquarium a chance to build up better biological filtration capacity and larger populations of copepods and amphipods before adding fishes that may benefit tremendously from their presence.

Regardless of the order you choose, these next three chapters will go over the finer points of purchasing, transporting, and acclimating the animals on your stocking list. Before acquiring any animals, this would be a great time to return to your stocking list with all of your new-found knowledge and make any adjustments.

Selection and Purchasing

So you know the fishes you want. You've used the CD-ROM to re-search compatibility issues, and have a stocking list that is right for you.

But what if you're a little tentative on your fish identification? And what if you're not really sure exactly what to look for or exactly what questions to ask? Or what if you don't have a good local fish store that sells marine fishes (or, heaven forbid, no local fish store at all)? Online shopping may be for you.

Whether you buy from the local fish store or online, the desired outcome is the same. You want to purchase a healthy fish that is going to thrive in your aquarium. Shopping at the local fish store and online both have their pros and cons. We've been to more than one local fish store where fish were mismarked, obviously inappropriate fishes were being foisted on beginning aquarists, and tanks from which fishes were being sold possessed fishes with obvious parasitic infections. Likewise, we have purchased from online retailers who have sent us individuals that look nothing like the pictures we saw online, and are malnourished and diseased specimens.

Color and General Health

When selecting a fish, it is important to know something about the general anatomy of fish in general. That way, you can assess, at least partially, the health of the animal before you buy it. If you are shopping online, you will not usually see a picture of the actual fish you are going to receive. This actually isn't really a bad thing, as the online retailers' business is dependent upon sending you a healthy fish. If the online retailer is always sending out poor specimens, they won't stay in business very long. Also, online retailers tend to have better guarantees.

Regardless of where you shop, if you're going to take responsibility for the care of a living animal, you should know something about that animal. One of the first things you will notice about a fish is the overall shape and its fins. The shape of the fish gives you a major clue as to how that fish lives. In general, fishes have (from front to back) pectoral fins, pelvic fins, a dorsal fin, an anal fin, and a caudal fin. It is important to inspect these fins when selecting a new fish. It is also important to frequently check the fins on your fishes. Many signs of trouble from illness to aggression will be evident by observing fin damage. Generally speaking, fins should be intact and not clamped to the body.

Most fishes possess a swim bladder. Why? Because they need to be able to hold their position in the water column without constantly readjusting and expending valuable energy. The swim bladder—a gas-filled organ—allows them to do this. The swim bladder is very similar to the scuba diver's buoyancy compensator (BC). We mention the swim bladder here because it is important to make sure the swim bladder was not damaged during collection. If a fish cannot maintain its position in the water column, it may well have a swim bladder injury, and you should not choose that fish. Look out for swim bladder trauma on fishes collected at depth.

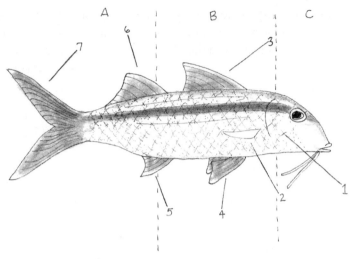

Fish fins: A = "caudal region" B = "trunk" C = "head" 1 = "gill cover 2 = "pectoral fin" 3 = "spinous dorsal fin" 4 = "pelvic fin" 5 = "anal fin" 6 = "soft dorsal fin" 7 = "caudal fin"

The fish's gills are essential to the animal's survival. These organs are highly developed breathing apparatus, and it is important to make sure that the gills are healthy before purchasing a fish. Signs of gill damage or injury include redness or excessive mucus. The fish's respirations, evidenced by the movement of the gills, should be slow and steady—no gasping.

A fish's color is critical to its success in the wild, and you should make sure the fish's color is natural and vibrant. Fishes with pale coloration may be stressed or even diseased.

Most fish species have scales, and these scales should be intact with no visible ulcers or wounds. Avoid a fish with any unnatural spots on its scales.

Behavior

Because most saltwater fishes are wild-caught, the fish you are contemplating for purchase has, most likely, been through a grueling ordeal involving capture, acclimation to a holding facility, a long airplane trip, more acclimation, and more transportation. Having said that, most fishes are remarkably resilient, and within a few days, they should be acting normally. Normal, of course, is a relative term, but because you planned your stocking list so carefully, and because you referenced the CD-ROM for each species you are purchasing, you know what to expect. It is always best to purchase fishes that are acting normally in the retailer's tank. What is one of the best ways to determine normal behavior? Ask the salesperson to feed the fish for you.

If you are purchasing your fish online, you will not have the opportunity to see the fish's behavior before you purchase. One thing you can do is make a down payment on the fish and ask the online retailer to hold the fish in their system until it is eating a captive diet and behaving normally. Not all online retailers will do this, but you can feel confident that the ones that do are as interested in the health of your fish as you are.

Transporting Fish

You want to do your absolute best to reduce stress during transportation. If you are ordering online, then it's up to the retailer to package your fishes appropriately, but you should be sure to discuss their shipping procedures with them. The industry standard is to ship fishes in doubled individual plastic bags inside a larger plastic bag inside a Styrofoam container. Heat packs or cooling packs are added depending upon the time of the year. As of this writing, Federal Express (FedEx) certifies anyone shipping live animals; United Parcel Service (UPS) does not. Does this mean FedEx is always your best bet? No. But you at least know that the retailer had to be trained and approved to ship live animals with FedEx. Also, FedEx provides round-the-clock customer service for live animals. UPS does not.

If you are transporting the fishes yourself (e.g., from the local fish store to your home), you will rely on the salesperson at the local fish store to appropriately bag your fishes. Some local fish stores will provide a Styrofoam cooler for you to transport your fish home. If they don't, consider bringing your own cooler. The cooler will help to insulate the fishes from temperature changes.

Regardless of how your fishes make it to your house, there will be some major changes to the water chemistry in the bag during transport. As you learned in the early chapters of this book, the fish excretes waste in the form of ammonia upon being bagged. In short, the water in the bag is becoming more and more toxic as time goes by. Your goal? Get the fish to your house as quickly as possible, and take the time to acclimate it using the drip acclimation procedure detailed next. As you may have guessed from what we have already said, a fish can do fine in an adequately sized bag with sufficient oxygen for up to 24 hours, but the sooner the better.

Acclimating

One of the most important aspects of a healthy aquarium is proper acclimation of new arrivals. The theory behind acclimation could (and does) fill a book, but we have outlined the procedure for you here in order tell you what you need to know to successfully acclimate your fishes to your aquarium.

The water in which your fishes are bagged for transport is going to be different than the water in your aquarium. Over the time between bagging and reaching your aquarium, the water will undergo slow chemical changes. For fishes used to living in a vast and stable ocean, these differences can be quite a shock and, sometimes, deadly if not slowly allowed to adjust.

Temperature, pH, and Salinity

The three important parameters to which you need to pay most attention during acclimatization are temperature, pH, and salinity (or specific gravity). The best equalizer for disparities in these parameters is time. Spreading out changes in temperature, pH, and salinity over time allows your new fishes to gently adjust to the conditions in your aquarium.

We highly recommend using a quarantine tank to reduce the possibility of introducing disease and parasites into your established aquarium and to ensure feeding success and overall good health of new fishes before introducing them into your display tank.

The Tools

You will need the following tools to successfully acclimate your new fishes:

Drip line

Stress guard

Acclimatization bucket (or other dedicated aquarium container)

Fully aerated and mixed saltwater

Scissors or knife

Plastic spaghetti strainer or strawberry baskets

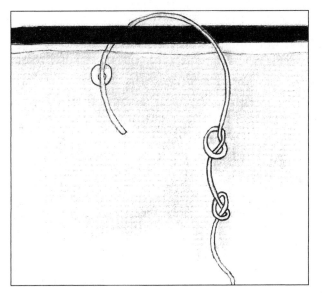

Drip line.

(Courtesy Karen Talbot.)

The Procedure

We recommend drip acclimating all new arrivals. The drip method is considered the best for sensitive animals and is used by every importer and wholesaler when receiving shipments of livestock from overseas.

Because most retailers have separate holding systems with different water parameters for fishes, corals, and invertebrates, you will need to separate your fishes out from any other animals during acclimatization. Always acclimate your fishes first, then move on to the other groups of animals (discussed in Chapters 16, 17, and 18).

Do not float the shipping bags in your aquarium, as you may have been instructed in the past, unless you know that the difference between the water in the bag and the water in your tank is within a few degrees of one another. It is not uncommon for the water to be as much as 10, 15, or even 20 degrees different, and floating the shipping bags will change the temperature of the water inside the shipping bag too quickly.

Use a dedicated 3- to 5-gallon bucket for acclimatization. A new bucket works just fine as long as you rinse prior to use. Label it as an aquarium bucket and never use any cleaners in it. Alternatively, you can use the Styrofoam box in which your animals were transported (some local fish stores will give you a Styrofoam box when you purchase animals, and most online retailers will ship your fishes in a Styrofoam box).

Open the bags with scissors or a knife and gently pour the fishes from each bag into the acclimation bucket along with all shipping water. You may need to prop up one side of the bucket in the beginning to allow water to fully submerge the fishes. The level of the water inside the bucket after all bags are emptied should not be more than halfway up the bucket. If it is, split the acclimation up between multiple containers. Add Stress Guard to each acclimation container. Make sure to cover the acclimation container so that fishes do not jump out and to reduce light and stress.

Prepare your drip line by submerging one end of the drip line under the aquarium water (you can secure it with a suction cup). Tie a loose knot somewhere in the middle of the drip line—this will control the amount of flow by tightening or loosening.

Begin a siphon by sucking gently on the end of the tubing, and place that end into the acclimation container. Start by having the knot tighter and then loosen it to achieve the desired flow rate of two to four drops per second. You want the water volume in the container to double in 45 to 60 minutes. Remember, it is better to fill slowly than to fill too fast.

Keep an eye on the progress of the acclimation so that the container does not overflow onto the floor. It is helpful to make a mark on the inside of the acclimation container to indicate where the water level should be after the shipping water volume has doubled. You may adjust the flow so that the water will double within the 45- to 60-minute time frame.

Once water volume doubles, discard half of the total water volume from the container and then repeat. After you have doubled the water volume twice, you are almost ready to add your new fishes to your quarantine aquarium. Empty half the water in the acclimation bucket, undo the knot in the drip line, and let the water flow freely until you have doubled the water volume one last time. This last step will equalize the temperature of the acclimation bucket and your quarantine aquarium.

Adding the Fishes to Your Aquarium

While it is acceptable to net many fishes, we prefer capturing them in a cup or small container and then submerging the entire cup under water and allowing the fish to swim out. The reason for this is that some fishes (tangs and butterflyfishes, for example) can easily become entangled and injured in a net. Unfortunately, these wounds often lead to infection and death. Second, we prefer to move our animals in this fashion so as not to expose them to air any more than is absolutely necessary. Many people use a net, and generally there is not a problem, but we believe using a cup to move fishes represents better husbandry practice.

Regardless of how you move your fishes from the acclimatization bucket to the aquarium, only move one at a time. Never dump the acclimatization water into your aquarium. You will release a small amount of heavily diluted shipping water into your system using the cup method of moving fish, but it should not cause any adverse effects if you have drip acclimated as explained previously.

Once you have added your new fishes, it is best to leave the aquarium lights off for several hours. It is also best to avoid feeding for the first 24 hours.

Some Final Thoughts

As we discussed in Chapter 3, you do not want to add all of your fishes at once. When you created your stocking list, you also established a stocking order based on aggressiveness. Just to remind you here, you generally want to add the most aggressive fish last.

Allow time between your additions. How much time? Well, there are two key considerations. First, adding new fishes increases bioload, and your system needs time to adjust. In short, your system will experience a minicycle after each new addition. Depending upon how many fishes you introduce at one time, the minicycle may or may not be detectable, but it's best to test the water parameters associated with the nitrogen cycle (e.g., ammonia, nitrites, and nitrates) a week after new additions. If these numbers have all returned to normal levels, then you are probably safe to add your next addition.

Some fishes need to be introduced at the same time. This is particularly the case with harematic fishes (one male with several females or one female with several males) and shoaling fishes.

The Least You Need to Know

- Take your time when selecting a fish to purchase.
- If you're buying from a local fish store, observe the fish's health, and ask to see it eat before purchasing.
- If in doubt, put down a down payment on the fish, and ask the store owner to keep it for a few days in his or her holding system (you can make the same request with online retailers).
- Drip acclimate all fishes.
- Generally speaking, add your most aggressive fishes last.
- Don't add too many new fishes at once, but do be sure to add shoaling or harematic fishes together.

Chapter 16

Selecting, Purchasing, and Acclimating Invertebrates

In This Chapter

- ◆ Invertebrates to know
- ◆ Selecting invertebrates
- ◆ Acclimating invertebrates

This chapter, like the last one on fishes, discusses how to select, purchase, transport, and acclimate your individual invertebrate specimens. While corals are indeed invertebrates, we will not discuss them here. Instead, we will deal with corals exclusively in the next chapter.

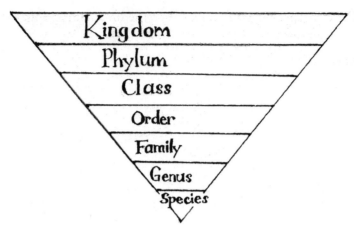

To review, here is the taxonomy pyramid that organizes life into manageable categories.

(Courtesy Karen Talbot.)

Most Reef Animals Without a Backbone

When it comes to invertebrates for your marine aquarium, here we are speaking of reef animals that are neither fishes nor corals. Of course, this makes sense when discussing fishes since fishes have vertebrae, but corals are invertebrates, too, aren't they? Indeed they are; yet, in the hobby, corals (and coral-like animals we call corals) are generally put in their own category as opposed to being a subcategory of invertebrates. In short, the term *invertebrate* is a horrid term, as it groups the vast majority of life on earth (include the seas) by what that life is not. It is also, in our opinion, hopelessly anthropomorphic that we have chosen to put such value on animals that, like us, have vertebrae, yet are significantly outnumbered.

Alas, we're not out to change the taxonomical world here, and, as we discuss corals by themselves in Chapter 17, this chapter will deal exclusively with those marine animals that are not fishes and not corals (although we will deal with some of the cnidarians here, such as sea anemones from the order Actiniaria and tube anemones from the order Ceriantharia).

Alphabetically speaking, we might divide the invertebrates into the following categories:

Anemones	Scallops
Clams	Sea slugs/nudibranchs
Crabs	Shrimp
Cucumbers	Snails
Feather dusters/worms	Sponges
Lobsters	Starfishes
Octopuses	Urchins

This of course leaves out the barnacles, chitons, comb jellies, copepods, corallimorphs, cowries, cuttlefishes, forams, hydrocorals, hydroids, isopods, jellyfishes, squids, and tunicates (and probably a few others), but it's a good starting point (especially since many retailers organize their animals as such).

However, because we want to give you good information unmarred by errors associated with using common names exclusively, we've chosen to clean up this list a bit. We have chosen to break invertebrates into the following categories:

♦ Hexacorallia inverts—anemones and tube anemones

♦ Sponges

♦ Spiny-skinned invertebrates—Echinodermata

♦ Mollusks

♦ Crustaceans (crabs, shrimps, lobsters, and such)

♦ Ornamental worms—feather dusters

Anemones and Tube Anemones

Both groups of anemones are actually from the subclass Hexacorallia, and as such, we could have dealt with them along with the other hexacorals in Chapter 17 (e.g., zoanthids, mushroom corals, and stony corals, but we didn't. Anemones are a good place to start our discussion of marine invertebrates because they are exclusively marine animals and represent, in a way, the foundation of the whole animal kingdom, which emerged from the sea.

Anemones are from the order Actiniaria, and tube anemones are from the order Ceriantharia. The latter have no pedal disc and, very generally speaking, are somewhat easier to keep. The true anemones, however, are, for many aquarists, an animal they have dreamed of keeping. Several can be successfully kept if they are added to a mature, stable aquarium (at least six months old) and provided with appropriate lighting. Supplemental feeding is highly recommended if not obligatory.

The novice aquarist may consider anemones belonging to the following genera: *Condylactis* (condy, Caribbean or pink-tipped anemone), *Bartholomea* (curleycue anemone), *Macrodactyla* (long tentacle anemone), and *Entacmaea* (bubble tip anemone). The most common tube anemones seen in the hobby are from the genera *Arachnanthus*, *Cerianthus*, and *Pachycerianthus*.

Sponges

The phylum Porifera, or what we call sponges, is a large grouping with at least 5,000 known species. Sponges are beautiful and interesting animals, and make good additions to most invertebrate and reef tanks, where they provide filtering functions and are useful bioassay organisms. While there are species to avoid, these unique filter feeders can make excellent display specimens and should not be overlooked.

Porifera translates roughly as "bearing openings," and they possess no organs whatsoever. These are very simple multicellular animals—far simpler than the corals (cnidarians) with which they are sometimes grouped. Most sponges are sessile animals that attach themselves to the substrate. Sponges are polymorphic, and they vary greatly based on environmental factors such as depth and water flow even within the same genus. This makes identification somewhat difficult at times, but we'll touch on a few of the species you might try (and a couple you want to avoid).

Chances are that some sponges will be imported into your system as hitchhikers on live rock. Remember Anna from Chapter 1? She actually did some of the first important work on sponge reproduction. For the modern aquarist, the genus *Agelus* (sometimes sold as elephant ear sponges) is a good starter sponge, as are species from the genera *Cinachyra* and *Callyspongia*. Red sponges from the genus *Latrunculia* are also great choices. Blue sponges from the genus *Haliclona* are relatively common and quite stunning, but a little more difficult to keep. Sponges from the genus *Acanthella* are out-of-this-world beautiful, but very difficult for the beginning aquarist. Likewise, the so-called tree sponges from the genus *Ptilocaulis* are dramatic in appearance but difficult in terms of care.

Be wary of the infamously temperamental (and toxic) genus *Tedania*, and, if you intend to keep stony corals, avoid boring sponges that will bore into stony corals (e.g., *Siphonodictyon* and *Cliona*).

Regardless of which sponge you intend to keep, be sure to never remove it from the water. Doing so will cause air to be trapped in the atria, which can be fatal to the specimen. Most sponges require supplemental feedings of microplankton.

The Spiny-Skinned Invertebrates– Echinodermata

The phylum Echinodermata includes the sea urchins, sea stars, brittle stars, basket stars, and sea cucumbers, all of which are frequently seen in the marine aquarium hobby. While there are obviously many differences between these animals, they all share some common traits. All have tube feet and an internal *calcareous skeleton*, and are radially symmetrical (they are actually pentamous, meaning that they can readily be divided into five mirror images). We can divide the echinoderms into roughly five classes (with more than 6,000 known species):

- Starfishes (class Asteroidea)
- Brittle and basket stars (class Ophiuroidea)
- Sea lillies and feather stars (class Crinoidea)
- Sea urchins and sand dollars (class Echinoidea)
- Sea cucumbers (class Holothuroidea)

def•i•ni•tion

> A **calcareous skeleton** is a skeleton composed primarily of calcium carbonate. Calcareous skeletons are hard and provide either support or protection (or both) for the organism.

Starfishes, Brittle Stars, and Basket Stars

We will deal with the first two classes together for obvious reasons. The starfishes, brittle stars, and basket stars are truly amazing animals with hundreds of tube feet on each arm that help the animal both move, and collect and manipulate food. Small brittle stars may come with your live rock as hitchhikers. They are outstanding (some would even say essential) inhabitants of a tank with live rock as they tirelessly clean detritus from all the nooks and crannies you can't reach. If you didn't get any freebies with your live rock, consider purchasing some. One or more per 10 gallons is a good starting point.

While a large starfish draped over a piece of live rock may look peaceful, consider their feeding method before naming them something cute. Starfish are adept at attacking shelled creatures such as bivalves; they literally slide their stomach inside the shell, release a digestive enzyme, and then consume the entire animal leaving an intact shell behind. Wow! Thinking twice about getting a starfish now?

Given the right environment, a starfish can be a wonderful addition to a marine aquarium. Here are a few tips. Some retailers will divide starfishes into reef-safe and non-reef-safe. Usually this refers to the predatory nature of a given animal and the voraciousness of its appetite. You will commonly see industrious sand-sifting starfish from the genus *Archaster*, colorful orange and red starfish from the genus *Fromia*, and bold blue starfish from the genus *Linckia* (although many so-called *Linckia* starfishes are not *Linckia* starfishes—get a positive ID before purchasing).

When selecting a starfish, ask if the dealer will flip it over for you. A healthy specimen should be able to right itself. Avoid starfishes with any obvious blemishes or wounds. Also avoid the following sea stars unless you know exactly what you are in for:

◆ The green brittle star from the genus *Ophiarachna* is a well-known predatory fish eater.

- Basket stars are very difficult to keep alive.

- Knobbed starfishes from the genera *Protoreastor, Pentaster,* and *Pentaceastor* (e.g., chocolate chip starfishes) will eat clams, oysters, and coral.

Sea Urchins—Class Echinoidea

Sea urchins from the class Echinoidea are, as you probably know, covered with spines (*echinoidea* actually translates from the Greek as something akin to "like a hedgehog"). Many urchins—there are about 800 known species—have spines that can deliver a painful (and venomous) wound. Do your homework before purchasing, but do consider purchasing one or more—even in a reef aquarium. Sea urchins are hard to beat for their algae-grazing ability, although they are nondiscriminate algae grazers (in other words, they will eat red and purple coralline algae just as readily as green algae). In terms of our favorite species, we like the long-spined sea urchins from the genus *Diadema,* but we have included several other genera on the CD-ROM.

Sea Cucumbers—Class Holothuroidea

Finally rounding out phylum Echinodermata (we will not deal with sea lilies, feather stars, or sand dollars, as they are not common in the hobby) we have the sea cucumbers from the class Holothuroidea. Sea cucumbers have gotten a pretty bad rap in the hobby, and while they definitely have their risks (especially certain species), there are sea cucumbers that make excellent (and useful) aquarium species. The best sea cucumbers for the home aquarium are truly vacuum cleaner–like animals—they take sandy substrate in through their mouth; purge it of all detritus, algae, etc.; and deposit it out the back end as clean sand. Wow!

The reason sea cucumbers have a bad rep is they have been known to turn themselves inside out (essentially), releasing a toxin reported to take out entire tanks. The toxin is called holothurin, and if bothered by hermits, fishes, or any other animal in the aquarium, it has the ability to eject its viscera as a survival mechanism. *Wow!*

While there are sea cucumbers we would never put in our aquaria, we are big fans of a couple of species that do not pose any great risk. In particular, we like the tigertail sea cucumber *(Halathuria hilla)*, as well as some of the species from the genus *Holothuria*. These species will keep the top layer of your sand bed detritus- and algae-free (they need a sand bed—no bare-bottom tanks for these guys). Despite what the nay-sayers say, in an established and well-balanced aquarium, an originally healthy sea cucumber specimen such as the ones mentioned here will offer years of hassle-free service.

Soft-Bodied Inverts Mollusca

The phylum Mollusca is a massive group of invertebrates second only to arthropods. The name is a Greek derivative of the word for "soft-bodied," and all mollusks do indeed have a soft body (known as a mantle), although they also have a calcareous shell. Some are filter feeders, others are active predators, and yet others are parasites—you name it, there is probably a mollusk that feeds that way. To make it a little easier, we can break this very large group down into four groups frequently seen in the hobby:

Snails (Gastropoda)

Sea slugs (subclass Opisthobranchia)

Clams and scallops (Pelecypoda, formerly Bivalvia)

Octopuses (Cephalopoda)

Snails—Gastropods

Snails make up the biggest group of mollusks, with more than 35,000 known species on land and sea (and in freshwater, too). All snails make a calcareous shell which is uniquely twisted so that the animal can pull its soft body back into it when threatened. We cover some specifics on snails in Chapter 14 when discussing clean-up crews. All of these and more are also included on the CD-ROM. Beware of murexes (family Muricidae), coralliophilids (family Coralliophilidae), thiads (family Thiadidae), olives (family Olividae), auger shells (family Terebridae), and turrid shells (family Turridae).

Sea Slugs–Subclass Opisthobranchia

The sea slugs, like snails, are gastropods but from the subclass Opisthobranchia. Without a shell (or with a shell that is greatly reduced compared to their snail brethren), sea slugs need another form of defense. This alternative defensive mechanism is what has earned sea slugs their bad rep in marine aquarium circles—chemical toxicity. In reality, there are many sea slugs appropriate for the marine aquarium, and we'll look at three groups here: sap-sucking slugs (order Sacoglossa), headshield slugs (order Cephalaspidea), and nudibranchs (order Nudibranchia).

The most popular of the so-called sap-sucking slugs is probably the lettuce slugs that go by the scientific name of either *Tridachia crispate* or *Elysia crispate*. Sometimes sold as a nudibranch, this animal is not one. Often noted as an algae eater, lettuce slugs are frequently added to the home aquarium to control nuisance hair algae. The lettuce slug doesn't eat hair algae; however, they eat bryopsis (a noxious weed that can take over a large aquarium in a very short time, choking out corals). Few fish or invertebrates will eat the lettuce slug.

The headshield slugs of the order Cephalaspidea are frequently seen in the aquarium hobby, especially as flatworm hunters. In particular, the velvet nudibranch *(Chelidonura varians)* is a nocturnal and often cryptic nudibranch that spends its time cleaning up problematic flatworms. Unfortunately, this animal will die when flatworms are no longer in the aquarium, as it will not likely eat anything else and will slowly starve.

True nudibranchs are considered expert-only animals, but their striking appearance and interesting behavior does make them something to aim for as a hobbyist. Of all the nudibranchs out there, the polycerid dorids may be the best suited for captivity. Again, we suggest the beginning marine aquarist steer clear, but if you do find the nudibranchs simply irresistible, then look to ones from the genera *Nembrotha*, *Roboastra*, or *Tambja*.

Clams and Scallops–Pelecypoda, Formerly Bivalvia

Some mollusks are called bivalves for their hinged shell (actually they have two opposing shells connected by a hinge). Most famously in the aquarium hobby, the bivalves include giant clams from the family

Tridacnidae, but we are also talking about other less glamorous clams, a few "sexy" scallops, oysters, and mussels here. Most of these animals are filter feeders and, as such, provide some benefit to the aquarium as a whole. A few, like the giant clams, contain zooxanthellae (like photosynthetic corals), and they are therefore in need of appropriate lighting. If you decide to have a go at keeping clams from the family Tridacnidae, be sure to read up first. These can be highly rewarding aquarium animals, but they do have some special requirements, and some are much harder to keep than others.

Mollusks generally are sessile, attaching themselves to live rock or burying themselves partially in the substrate. A few, such as the flame scallop *(Lima scabra)*, do move about the aquarium, propelling themselves with blasts of water. These latter animals are actually not really scallops, and they are also not really good aquarium specimens given their somewhat delicate nature.

Octupuses—Cephalopoda

In addition to octopuses, we also have squids and cuttlefishes in the group of head-footed mollusks. Octopuses are the only ones seen with any frequency in the hobby, and we'd suggest the beginning aquarist steer clear. While they are amazing, intelligent animals, they are difficult to keep in anything but a species-specific tank, and even then they are difficult to keep. If you decide to go this route, do yourself a favor and spend some time with other marine aquarium species first.

The Jointed-Leg Inverts—Anthropoda

Anthropoda are the largest phylum of animals. Period. We are most interested in the subphylum Crustacea, of which there are nearly one million individual species. With so many species, what commonalities can there possibly be? Actually there are several, and they are readily identifiable by even the beginning marine aquarist. First, crustaceans have a segmented body (this is called *metamerism*) with a pair of appendages accompanying each section. Next, they all have a chitinous skeleton (chitin is a naturally occurring polymer) which is external. There are other commonalities, but those may be better left to the scientists for our present purposes. We are, of course, talking about, amongst others, shrimp, lobsters, and crabs. Copepods and krill are also included in this group.

Shrimp

There are several families of shrimp frequently seen in the aquarium hobby, and by all means, we would encourage you to keep some in your aquarium. There are a few things you need to know about some of these shrimp, as the wrong shrimp can cause a world of hurt to you (not to mention its tankmates). Likewise, adding the wrong shrimp to the wrong tank will be little more than offering popcorn shrimp to your fishes. While there are many more families, we will briefly mention the pistol shrimp of the family Alpheidae, the cleaner shrimp of the family Hippolytidae, the dancing shrimp of the family Rhynchocinetidae, the anemone shrimp of the family Palaemonidae, and the harlequin shrimp of the family Gnathophyllidae.

Pistol shrimp get their name from their ability to make a snapping sound audible to you if you keep one or more in your aquarium. These shrimp are prized by some aquarists for the mutualistic relationship many have with fishes such as gobies.

The cleaner shrimp from the family Hippolytidae sprang into the limelight along with that pesky animated clown Nemo. Despite the resulting somewhat clichéd inclusion of cleaner shrimp in marine aquaria, you should not pass up on keeping one or more of these very beneficial anthropods. You needn't travel far outside the genus *Lysmata* when looking for a cleaner shrimp. Try the hardy *L. amboinensis* (white-striped cleaner shrimp) for fish cleaning power, and *L. wurdemanni* (peppermint shrimp) for aiptasia (a common pest anemone) control. Both can be kept in groups, which is more than can be said for many shrimp. Also in this family is the genus *Thor* with the intriguing sexy shrimp *(T. amboinensis)*, which live in association with anemones and various corals (e.g., genus *Euphyllia*).

Dancing shrimp from the family Rhynchocinetidae are potentially problematic with some corals, but given their nocturnal behavior, you probably won't see them at it directly. They are named because they, well, dance. Generally small, these shrimp are sometimes sold as pep-permint shrimp, which they are not if by peppermint shrimp we mean aiptasia-eating *Lysmata wurdemanni.* Don't be fooled if you like your zoas and mushrooms, which species from the genus *Rhynchocinetes* are known to consume.

In a small (nano) aquarium, you may want to really look into the anemone shrimp of the family Palaemonidae. These are small shrimp that live in close association with other invertebrates (especially anemones and sea cucumbers). Try members of the genus *Periclimenes* such as *P. brevicarpalis* (clown anemone shrimp), which will readily host with anemones. They are great in large tanks, too, but their small size and ability to change color make them hard to spot in a big tank.

Harlequin shrimp of the family Gnathophyllidae are decidedly cool-looking anthropods. Be warned, these shrimp eat sea stars.

Lobsters

When matched with larger tankmates, lobsters make very interesting additions to the reef or fish-only aquarium. Omnivores, lobsters are capable of eating most anything they can catch. Some of the smaller ornamental lobsters may be kept in a large reef tank if the hobbyist is prepared for a nocturnal loss or two. If you really must have a lobster, consider one from the genera *Panulirus* or *Enoplometopus.* The latter remain smaller, up to 13 centimeters (5 inches), and are considered reef-safe by some aquarists.

Crabs

We discuss some crabs such as hermit crabs in Chapter 14 when talking about clean-up crews, and here we'll touch on a few more.

Porcelain crabs (sometimes called anemone crabs) from the family Porcellanidae are filter-feeding crabs that live in the tentacles of anemones. Porcelain crabs from the genus *Neopetrolisthes* are your best bet, such as *N. maculosus,* which has a white body with red spots and readily accepts an anemone host in captivity. These crabs pose little danger to other animals in your system (though they are easily preyed upon if not kept with an appropriate host).

Arrow crabs (sometimes sold as spider crabs) from the family Latreillidae are commonly available and often touted for their ability to control bristle worms and fire worms. Arrow crabs are often at the mercy of larger fishes, and smaller fishes are often at the mercy of arrow crabs. If you have a bristle worm problem, by all means try an arrow crab such as *Stenorhynchus seticornis*. Most arrow crabs will likely not bother your corals, but big arrow crabs may well eat neon gobies (*Gobiosoma oceanops*) and other small to medium-size fishes.

The mithrax crab (also called the emerald crab or *Mithrax sculptus*) is somewhat legendary for taking down algae and being reef-safe. When talking crabs, reef-safe is a very relative term, as all crabs are opportunistic omnivores. Having said that, this crab is about the reef-safest, and it will consume hair algae and any other algae. Some people have used this crab to go after bubble algae, but be warned that the crab does not have the ability to swallow the bubble whole. Instead, it pops the bubble, which releases the spores.

Like the mithrax crab, the Sally Lightfoot crab *(Percnon gibbesi)* is often purchased for algae control. It is somewhat more likely to go after small fish than other so-called reef-safe crabs, especially if it is underfed. Offering it finely chopped marine flesh and occasionally some type of dried marine algae like spirulina or nori will go a long way toward keeping your small fishes around.

Finally, we want to mention one crab that is somewhat of an oddity, but may be just the species for which you are looking for a nano tank or biotope-specific reef tank. We are thinking of the pom pom crab *(Lybia tessellata)*, which carries one Bunodeopsis anemone in each claw and uses these to catch food out of the water column. While too small to be seen much in a large aquarium, in a properly aquascaped nano tank, this crab will be a joy to watch. This is one crab that is truly reef-safe.

Feather Dusters

These marine segmented, tube-bearing worms of the phylum Annelida (meaning "little ring" in Latin) are generally hardy sessile invertebrates that either attach themselves to a rock or anchor themselves in the substrate. While they do have certain requirements such as good water quality and supplemental feedings, feather dusters can add an intriguing, colorful display for the marine aquarium. We will discuss ones from the genera *Bispira, Protula, Sabellastarte,* and *Spirobranchus.* Don't plan on keeping feather dusters in the same aquarium as butterflyfishes. Also use caution with many crabs, some wrasses, and a few hawkfishes.

Dwarf Feather Dusters from the Genus *Bispira*

Feather duster species from the genus *Bispira* are the most commonly available feather dusters in the hobby, and for good reason. They are generally hardy and many reproduce easily in the aquarium. These are commonly sold as dwarf feather dusters and grow to about 10 centimeters (4 inches) in length. They are frequently available in flashy green and yellow or pink and white. The variegated feather duster *(Bispira variegata)* and the social feather duster or cluster duster *(Bispira brunnea)* are both from the family Sabellidae, although the latter appears to not be nearly as hardy as most feather dusters. *Bispira viola*, on the other hand, is very common and very hardy. *Bispira variegate* grows somewhat larger than *Bispira viola* and prefers dwelling in the substrate (as opposed to *Bispira viola*'s preference for rockwork). The variegated feather duster is an excellent choice for the beginning aquarist.

Giant Feather Dusters from the Genus *Sabellastarte*

The genus *Sabellastarte* is home to species commonly called giant feather dusters. These feather dusters will grow to 18 centimeters (7 inches) and can be quite hardy with proper husbandry. Most all feather dusters appreciate (or need) supplemental feedings with a marine invertebrate food for filter feeders.

Christmas Tree Worms from the Genus *Spirobranchus*

Species from the genus *Spirobranchus* most frequently live in stony corals or fire corals. Sometimes referred to as porites worms, as this is the most common host coral, they do not require a living host coral to survive. The appearance of a host coral covered with these worms resembles multicolored Christmas trees and is a sight to behold earning the host "rock" the title "jewel rock" or Christmas tree rock. This worm is not a beginner species, as it requires target feeding and conditions necessary to support the host coral (high-intensity lights, high calcium and alkalinity, and low nutrients).

Coco Worms from the Genus *Protula*

The so-called coco worm (or hard-tube coco worm *Protula bispiralis*) is a real beauty (and relatively expensive as far as feather dusters go). This is not a beginner feather duster, as it is pretty finicky about water quality (especially high alkalinity and calcium).

Transporting Invertebrates

Transporting invertebrates varies by the type of invertebrate and the person packing the invertebrate. Overall, be sure that invertebrates with spines (e.g., urchins) are packaged with some protection for the bag and that delicate invertebrates are packaged with some protection for the invertebrate. Most snails and hermit crabs will be transported with very little water (usually they are shipped with newspaper or moist paper towels in their shipping bags).

Special Acclimating Considerations for Inverts

It is advisable to follow the drip acclimation guidelines detailed in Chapter 15 for most marine invertebrates, being very careful to match specific gravity and pH. Don't acclimate your invertebrates in the same water in which fish were shipped.

While you can acclimate most all of the individuals from each group together in the same bucket, those invertebrates that can possibly release toxins into the acclimation water (e.g., sea cucumbers and sea slugs) should be acclimated in separate containers to avoid poisoning other animals in the event of a loss due to shipping trauma or stress.

Some animals must never be exposed to air at any point during acclimation or transport to your aquarium. This includes sponges, some gorgonians, and smooth-skinned starfish like those of the genera *Linkia* and *Fromia*. Simply remove these animals from the acclimation container using a specimen container or clean, sterile Tupperware and release them into your aquarium by submerging the entire container under the water and inverting it. A small amount of shipping water will be introduced into your aquarium, but this is fine.

The Least You Need to Know

- ◆ As always, do your homework before acquiring an invertebrate.
- ◆ Take the time to acclimate invertebrates properly—most are quite sensitive.
- ◆ Drip acclimate all invertebrates discussed in this chapter.

Chapter 17

Selecting, Purchasing, and Acclimating Coral

In This Chapter

- ◆ What is coral?
- ◆ Families of coral
- ◆ Selecting coral
- ◆ Acclimating coral
- ◆ "Starter coral" suggestions for the beginning aquarist

The Greek word *cnidos* means "stinging needle." Members of the phylum Cnidaria are all stinging-celled animals, and all of them sport nematocysts (or stinging cells). Soft or hard, reef building or non–reef building, large polyp or small polyp, sea fans, zoanthids, mushrooms—they are all (well, almost all) Cnidaria. In this chapter, as in the other species chapters, we will rely on scientific names rather than common names since common names (such as brain coral) are often applied inconsistently and can lead to confusion.

Phylum Cnidaria

The phylum Cnidaria is consists of more than 11,000 species in four major classes. Three of the classes are made up of the various jellyfishes (Scyphozoa, Cubozoa, and Hydrozoa), and the corals and anemones (Anthozoa) make up the fourth class. While cnidarians come in many forms, they have some general common characteristics beyond their nematocysts. For example, all cnidarians possess a gastrovascular cavity with a polyp or opening that serves as both mouth and anus. Cnidarians are part of the subkingdom Radiata, which means they are radially symmetrical (in other words, you could cut them in half and have two halves that look the same). In this chapter, we are interested in cnidarians from the class Anthozoa.

In the class Anthozoa, there are roughly 6,000 known species of so-called corals and anemones, and the vast majority are sessile animals which are stuck to the substrates where they live. We can divide this class into three subclasses: Octocorallia (with eight tentacles, including the soft corals and gorgonians), Hexacorallia (with six or multiples or six tentacles, including mushroom corals, anemones, and, most famously, stony corals), and Ceriantipatharia (including tube anemones, which we discuss in Chapter 16).

The Main Players

We will not attempt to comprehensively discuss all cnidarians in this chapter (although we do list many species of coral on the enclosed CD-ROM). Instead, we will touch on some of the most common corals in the aquarium hobby, including soft corals and gorgonians (Octocorallia) and mushroom and stony corals (Hexacorallia).

Soft Corals and Gorgonians—Subclass Octocorallia

Corals from the subclass Octocorallia include the blue corals (order Helioporacea) and the soft corals (order Alcyonacea), mat corals (order Zoanthidea), and sea fans and sea whips (order Gorgonacea). It is very hard to make generalizations, but if we were pressed, we might tell you that soft corals—sometimes called "leather corals"—are relatively easy to keep, fast growing, and quite attractive. Soft corals also tend to be adept, however, at a certain brand of chemical warfare (they actually release toxins into the water) that leads some experts to warn against mixing soft corals in a tank with stony corals. The reality is that it depends on your specific situation, but do be aware that soft corals may well cause stony corals in the same aquarium to cease growing and even recede.

If you are interested in soft corals, you may want to take a look at the order Alcyonacea where you will find the genera *Clavularia* and *Pachyclavularia*—both relatively hardy encrusting soft corals that form attractive mats that readily spread. There is also the genus *Tubipora* (often sold as pipe organ coral) in the order Stolonifera, which is an attractive octocoral with interesting calcite tubes that are not typically found in this genus (most octocorals lack any calcium skeleton).

The leather corals of the family Alcyoniidae are readily available and very popular, and most are quite appropriate for the beginning aquarist. Look for species from the genus *Alcyonium* to be usually sold as encrusting leather coral, finger leather coral, or colt coral. The growth patterns of leather corals are quite varied and may present with finger-like appendages, lobes, or even globular shapes. You will find these leather corals in a range of colors. In particular, look for *A. digitatum* and *A. fulvum* as good choices. Leather corals from the genera *Cladiella*, *Lobophytum*, and *Sarcophyton* are also commonly available, hardy leather corals. You will often see species from the first two genera sold as the generic "finger coral" (*Lobophytum* species are also sometimes sold as devil's hand, lobed, or cabbage leather corals), and species from the latter genus are sold as toadstool corals.

Soft corals from the genus *Sinularia* are also quite attractive and very hardy. This is a very common genus of soft corals in the aquarium hobby often sold as cabbage coral, flower coral, knobby coral, or flexible leather coral. Species from this genus are well represented in the wild on shallow reefs, indicating their ability to withstand stronger water current than many other soft corals. *S. dura* and *S. flexibilis* are good choices for the beginning aquarist—they are very common, relatively inexpensive, tolerant of a wide range of conditions, and they grow quite large. If you plan to keep stony corals in the same tank as *Sinularia*, consider steering clear of *S. flexibilis*, which is perhaps the most toxic of the *Sinularia* corals. In fact, we suggest not keeping species from the genus *Sinularia* in the same tank as stony corals unless that aquarium is very large or your chemical filtration is very robust.

While somewhat more delicate, soft corals from the family Nephtheidae are quite attractive and can grow to be very large. These are frequently sold as cauliflower coral or tree coral, with species from the genera *Capnella* and *Dendronephthya* being two of the most common (although the latter is more particular and best left to the advanced aquarist). The pulse corals making up the family Xeniidae (e.g., pulsing *Xenia*) are both widely available and alluring given their common namesake pulsing action, but they are definitely not the hardiest of the soft corals. If you want to attempt any of these, consider ones from the genus *Xenia* (frequently sold as pulsing xenia or simply pulse coral).

The magnificent gorgonians include the sea whips, sea fans, sea plumes, and sea fingers, as well as the so-called tree gorgonians. There is a fair bit of disagreement regarding their ease of care, and as such, we are not going to enthusiastically recommend any of them to the beginning aquarist. Having said that, these are amazing animals that can be successfully kept with a little research and consistent husbandry. We have included several commonly available species on the CD-ROM, but suffice it to say for now that photosynthetic gorgonians such as species from the genus *Briareum* (often sold as dead man's fingers or corky sea fingers) are far easier to keep than species from the *aposymbiotic* genus *Diodogorgia* (red and yellow tree gorgonians). Gorgonians from the genus *Muricea* (the spiny sea fans or spiny sea whips) are commonly available and quite hardy, and we can recommend sea rod species from the genera *Plexaura*, *Plexaurella*, and *Pseudoplexaura*. Sea fans from the family Gorgoniidae are notoriously difficult to keep, but if you want to try members of this family, we'd suggest species from the genus *Pseudopterogorgia* (sea feathers, frilly gorgonians).

def•i•ni•tion

Aposymbiotic corals are corals that do not host mutalistic algae (called *zooxanthellate*). These corals are generally considered easier to keep because they do not have the same intense lighting needs as corals that do host zooxanthellate. Sometimes aposymbiotic corals are called *azooxanthellate* corals.

Zoanthidea and Mushroom Corals

Zoanthidea—button polyps, sea mats, or colonial anemones—are hardy, colorful, and very common in the aquarium trade. Polyps and sea mats from the order Zoanthidea are cnidarians with no skeletons that are amongst the easiest coral species to keep. While zoanthids look like anemones and are often called colonial anemones, they are not sea anemones from the order Actinaria or coral anemones from the order Corallimorpharia. While we identify several genera and individual species of zoanthids on the CD-ROM, we need not say more here about zoanthids than that these (along with the corallimorpharians or mushroom corals) are amongst the best of the cnidarian animals for beginning aquarists. So long as you give them sufficient light and water flow, most zoanthids will flourish in even the most inexperienced marine aquarist's tank.

The corallimorpharians (commonly known as mushroom corals, mushroom anemones, and disc anemones) are as hardy as zoanthids and, as such, are excellent cnidarian choices for the beginning marine aquarist. They are also interesting and attractive. Sometimes referred to as false corals, corallimorpharians have roughly the same structure as "real" stony corals, except they lack the sweeper tentacles. Within the order Corallimorpharia, the two species from the genus *Ricordea*—*R. florida* and *R. yuma*—are somewhat less hardy corallimorpharians, but still adapt well to aquarium life. Species from the genera *Actinodiscus* and *Rhodactis* (the hairy mushrooms) are common, quite hardy (especially the latter), and good choices. In captivity, clownfishes are known to host in species from the genus *Rhodactis*. In general, corallimorpharians prefer lower light and less flow. Species from the genus *Discosoma* are often quite large (and capable of capturing small fishes), but are also generally more tolerant of brighter lighting.

The True or Stony Corals—Order Scleractinia

Stony corals are the true corals, and, in fact, they are the only group of cnidarians that, taxonomically speaking, are actually coral. They are called stony corals because they build a "stony" or hard skeleton on top of which the "soft" living tissue resides. This group of cnidarians is somewhat arbitrarily divided up in the hobby as either large polyp stony corals (LPS) or small polyp stony corals (SPS). Generally speaking (very generally), the LPS corals have larger polyps and are easier to keep, while the SPS corals have smaller polyps and are far more difficult to keep.

As Eric Borneman points out in his indispensible book *Aquarium Corals*, it is far better for the hobbyist to approach the true or stony corals of the order Scleractinia by focusing on taxonomic families first. Within the families, it is then useful to discuss traits that are directly tied to the species' care, such as symbiotic corals and aposymbiotic corals. Trying to systematically list all of the families of stony corals here would be futile—it would require a book of its own. We have, however, included many of the stony corals commonly available in the hobby on the CD-ROM.

On the CD-ROM, we organize scleractinian (stony) species by family instead of by the LPS/SPS distinction frequently used in the hobby. We include the brain corals as scleractinian species (because they are), although most retailers designate them as a separate category. The brain corals can be found in the families Mussidae, Faviidae, and Trachyphylliidae.

Below is a chart of stony corals organized by family:

Family	Genera			
	LPS	**SPS**	**Brain**	**Unknown**
Astrocoeniidae		*Madracis*		
Pocilloporidae		*Pocillopora, Seriatopora, Stylaphora*		
Acroporidae		*Acropora, Astreopora, Montipora*		
Poritidae	*Alveopora, Goniopora*	*Porites*		
Siderastreidae				*Siderasterea*
Agariciidae		*Pavona, Pachyseris*		
Fungiidae		*Cycloseris, Fungia, Heliofungia, Polyphyllia*		
Oculinidae		*Galaxea*		
Pectiniidae	*Echinophyllia, Mycedium, Oxypora*	*Pectinia*		
Meandrinidae		*Hydnophora*		

| Family | Genera | | | |
	LPS	SPS	Brain	Unknown
Mussidae	*Cynarina, Scolymia*		*Acanthastrea, Lobophyllia, Micromussa, Symphyllia*	
Merulinidae		*Merulina*		
Faviidae	*Caulastrea, Echinopora*		*Cyphastrea, Cyphastrea, Diploastrea, Favia, Favites, Goniastrea, Montastrea*	
Trachyphylliidae			*Trachyphyllia*	
Caryophylliidae	*Catalaphyllia, Euphyllia, Nemanzophyllia, Physogyra, Plerogyra*			
Dendrophylliidae	*Duncanopsammia, Turbinaria*			
Rhizangiidae				Uncommon in Hobby
Flabellidae				Uncommon in Hobby

Purchasing Coral

Purchasing coral, like purchasing fishes, should never be done on impulse unless you absolutely know what the coral is, how it behaves, and what requirements it has. Do not necessarily trust what the shopkeeper tells you or what is written on the tank. I'm not trying to suggest they would intentionally dupe you, but the reality is that many corals are frequently misidentified or simply thrown into one of the "hobby categories." People who keep and know corals are a subset of all aquarists, so don't expect every successful marine aquarist to necessarily know what he or she is talking about when it comes to coral husbandry.

Once you know what a specimen is and how it behaves and what it requires, then you need to take the time to assess the individual specimen before purchasing. If you are purchasing online, you are trusting selection to (hopefully) an experienced aquarist at the company from which you are buying, but you should still carefully assess the coral once it reaches you (after it has been placed in the quarantine tank). If you notice tissue recession, discolored or torn tissue, or excessive slime/jelly when assessing a coral at the local fish store or once you have unpackaged an online purchase, speak with the shop owner or salesperson directly (on the phone if it was an online purchase).

Notice that we did not put polyp size or expansion on the above list of signs for which to look. The reason is that many corals will be stressed from travel and less than ideal conditions in the dealer's tank. If otherwise healthy, these corals will expand (some up to five times the size they were!) once presented with excellent conditions in your aquarium

Starter Corals—Some Specific Suggestions for the Novice

Beginning aquarists (or even more experienced aquarists new to coral) may want to start with some of the so-called "starter coral" species. In particular, we are talking about corals from the subclass Octocorallia, including those from the order Alcyonacea and suborders Alcyoniina (soft corals) and Stolonifera (mat corals).

Within the suborder Alcyoniina, the beginner might look at any of the genera within the family Alcyoniidae—the so-called leather corals. These include the popular and commonly available genera of *Alcyonium* (finger leather coral), *Cladiella* (colt coral), *Lobophytum* (lobed, devil's hand, or cabbage leather coral), and *Sarcophyton* (toadstool and mushroom leather coral). You may want to avoid soft corals from the genus *Sinularia* if you intend to keep stony coral in the same aquarium. Species such as *S. flexibilis* are extremely toxic and quite capable of waging effective chemical warfare against stony corals.

Within the suborder Stolonifera, there are several hardy species from the genera *Clavularia* (glove or clove polyps, fern polyps, palm tree polyps), *Pachyclavularia* (star polyps, green star polyps, daisy polyps), and, to a lesser extent, *Tubipora* (pipe-organ coral).

From there, you will probably want to branch out into the zoanthids (button polyps, colonial anemones) and mushroom corals (or corallimorpharians). Just about all of the commonly available zoanthids are hardy, and we'd recommend mushrooms from the genera *Discosoma* or *Rhodactis* (elephant ear, metallic or hairy mushroom).

For the beginner looking to move into the stony corals (the scleractinians), we'd recommend researching (in alphabetical order) the following organisms:

> *Anacropora* (briar coral)
>
> *Caulastrea* (candy cane, trumpet)
>
> *Cynarina* (tooth coral, modern coral)
>
> *Diploastrea* (moon brain)
>
> *Euphyllia* (frogspawn, grape)
>
> *Favia* (pineapple brain)
>
> *Favites* (closed brain)
>
> *Fungia* (plate coral)
>
> *Lobophyllia* (carpet brain)
>
> *Montipora* (velvet coral)
>
> *Platygyra* spp. (maze brain)
>
> *Plerogyra* (bubble coral)
>
> *Siderastrea* (starlet coral)
>
> *Trachyphyllia* (open brain coral)

Acclimating Coral

We do not recommend drip acclimating coral, as corals use water in a different fashion than fishes. For coral, we suggest temperature acclimation by floating the bag for 20 minutes. Then cut open the top of the bag and transfer the specimen into your quarantine tank (we do recommend quarantining all new coral for 10 days to two weeks).

Your corals have been through a very stressful experience en route to you, and perhaps the most important item is to not cause them any additional stress. How you do this is to get them into "good" water with strong flow quickly. In the process, handle the specimen as little as possible, and do your best to keep it underwater at all times (use collection cups). Avoid touching the soft fleshy part of the coral, which can cause trauma and lead to bacterial infection. Like always, keep as much shipping water as you can out of your system (although if you move the coral with a collection cup to the tank, a small amount of shipping water will enter your system—this is often preferable to exposing the animal to air.

Whether or not you want to dip your corals as part of the quarantine procedure is up to you. If, however, you choose not to quarantine your corals, then seriously consider dipping them for 20 minutes in a commercial coral dip solution such as Seachem's Reef Dip. If you quarantine (and we suggest you do), consider using appropriate medications (e.g., Interceptor, Flatworm Exit, etc.) to ensure your specimen is clear of all parasites.

Regardless of whether or not you use a quarantine tank, make sure to acclimate your coral to your lighting. In the quarantine tank, this means leaving the lights off at first and then increasing the photoperiod for two hours each day. In your display aquarium, either start all corals on the bottom and gradually move them up to their final position, or place them in their final position and use multiple layers of plastic screening to shade them. Remove layers gradually until your coral is exposed to your regular aquarium lighting.

When you have sited your coral in its final position, you will want to make sure that other animals (or even currents) will not knock it over. We suggest using a two-part epoxy designed for aquarium use or simple cyanoacrylate gel (superglue). You can also rely on wedging the base of the coral between rocks, so long as you don't damage the coral in the process.

The Least You Need to Know

- Coral is a living animal.
- Try not to rely on broad generalizations such as the somewhat arbitrary distinction of LPS versus SPS.
- Start with "starter corals" and move up to more difficult species.
- Quarantine all new coral specimens, or at least use a commercially available coral dip.

Part 5

Caring for the System

Providing and maintaining optimal conditions for your animals are the key to success in this hobby. In this part of the book, we'll show you how to feed and maintain your system. We'll also look at some common parasites, infections, and diseases, as well as address some of the latest trends in treatment. While algae is a part of the marine environment, nuisance algae can become a real headache for you, so we'll discuss how to identify the various algae growing in your tank and how to limit the growth of nuisance algae and cultivate "good" algae. Finally, we'll offer a few tips on dealing with so-called "problem fishes" and on adding (or replacing) animals as your tank matures.

Chapter 18

Feeding and Maintaining Healthy Livestock

In This Chapter

- ◆ Feeding basics
- ◆ Types of eaters and types of food
- ◆ How to feed
- ◆ Observing your animals
- ◆ Maintaining your system

This chapter discusses feeding your livestock based on the dietary information contained on the CD-ROM. It also helps you establish a maintenance routine that will keep your livestock healthy and happy for many years.

The Basics of Feeding

A well-balanced diet is an essential part of a marine animal's health. This goes for fishes, corals, and other invertebrates. Feeding is not as simple as giving the proverbial pinch of food or feeding only enough that your fish consume all visible food in three minutes. No, to be successful in this hobby, you must approach food as part science and part art. It is quite likely that more marine aquarium animals die of starvation or diseases and illnesses brought on by malnutrition than any other cause. Let us repeat that—improperly feeding livestock is the number-one cause of death in the marine aquarium hobby. Advances in what we feed and how we feed is, to us, one of the most exciting frontiers in the hobby and is an area the hobbyist will definitely want to read up on.

The Three Main Categories

It is absolutely essential to research the dietary needs of any species you are considering for purchase. Generally speaking, you will see marine animals listed as carnivores, herbivores, or omnivores.

Carnivores

Carnivores, not surprisingly, eat flesh. They need plenty of protein in their diets. Proteins are made up of amino acids, and these amino acids are critical to carnivorous fishes and invertebrates, including corals. Amino acids are also important to herbivores, but we'll touch on that in a minute.

Carnivorous marine animals appreciate live food or fresh meaty seafood. The most common foods in the category include the following:

Brine shrimp (*Artemia* spp.)

Table seafood

Glass shrimp (also called ghost or grass shrimp)

Pods (e.g., (copepods and amphipods)

Feeder fish (saltwater baitfish, live shrimp, or mollies raised in saltwater)

Tubificid worms (a.k.a. black worms and red worms)

Prepared carnivore foods (flake, pellet, freeze-dried, and frozen foods)

In addition to prepared carnivore food, we like to feed meaty seafood to our carnivorous marine animals. Many of these foods are available at your local fish store or online. If you live near the ocean, you may want to buy baitfish used by saltwater fishermen. It is easy to hatch and feed your own brine shrimp with either a simple improvised or manufactured brine shrimp hatchery (again, available at your local fish store or online). Both copepods and amphipods are available as commercial food products sold by many retailers. Feeder fish should only be used as a very special treat for certain predators, and we always prefer marine fish as opposed to freshwater goldfish. If you do feed meaty bits of table seafood (e.g., shrimp, scallops, mussels, etc.), you might consider briefly steaming it before feeding. This will limit the chance of introducing parasites to your aquarium.

Herbivores

Marine herbivores are generally not strict vegetarians. Most herbivorous marine animals rely on at least a certain amount of meaty seafood in order to get enough protein. This meaty seafood usually comes in the form of small crustaceans consumed "accidentally" when feeding on herbivorous food. Nonetheless, herbivorous foods should be made available to herbivorous marine animals. The most commonly available herbivorous foods include the following:

Macroalgae growing in the aquarium

Macroalgae cultivated and harvested from a refugium

Prepared seaweed (e.g., nori)

Prepared herbivore foods (flake, pellet, freeze-dried, and frozen foods)

In addition to prepared herbivore foods, macroalgae grown in and harvested from the refugium is our favorite food source for herbivorous fishes. Nori or other macroalgae food dried in sheets is also a favorite choice of ours. These can be offered to fishes on a feeding clip attached by a suction cup to the inside wall of the aquarium, or you can first soak these foods, wrap them around pieces of rock, and place them on the bottom of the tank or on the rockwork. We prefer to steer clear of terrestrial vegetables for our marine livestock, but many aquarists do offer their herbivorous livestock lettuce, spinach, kale, and other leafy greens.

Omnivores

Most of the marine aquarium animals we keep are omnivores. In fact, it could be said that all marine fishes are omnivores, as they all feed on planktonic animals during at least some stage of their development. There are many prepared foods for omnivorous marine animals, or you can combine foods from the above lists to make sure your omnivores are getting a well-balanced diet.

Prepared Foods

We previously alluded to prepared foods, and there is a virtual cornucopia of prepared foods for marine animals readily available to the hobbyist. Some are quite good, although many are more about marketing than nutrition. Basically, prepared foods come in the form of flakes and pellets, sheet food, freeze-dried food, and frozen food.

Flakes and Pellets

Anyone who has kept freshwater fish is familiar with flake food. Flake foods are the most commonly fed foods in the marine aquarium world as well, because they contain a balanced assortment of carnivorous and herbivorous food in an easy-to-store and easy-to-feed product. If you want to feed flake food to your marine animals, make sure it is a flake food specially prepared for marine animals. Using a freshwater flake food will usually result in malnutrition over an extended period of time.

Pellets also contain a balanced diet, but they are designed to either sink or float. Sinking pellets are good for animals that are bottom dwellers or not aggressive enough to join the feeding frenzy at the surface.

With both flakes and pellets, read the ingredients. You will want to see a combination of fishmeal, *Spirulina*, tubifex worms, algae, and other yummy treats. By looking at the color of the flakes, you can make an educated guess about the proportion of certain ingredients (green flakes are full of vegetable matter, red flakes are full of protein, and multicolored flakes are mixed). We do not recommend flake or pellet food alone for marine animals, but we do advocate the use of flake food as part of a balanced diet.

Sheet Food

Sheet food comes in sheets and may be prepared for marine animals or for humans. The most common sheet food used by marine aquarists is nori, which is often sold in the oriental foods section of your local market. Nori is kelp, and it is what is used in making sushi. It happens to be an excellent food source for marine animals in the aquarium as long as it has no additives or preservatives. Various manufacturers also make sheet food especially for marine aquarium fishes.

Freeze-Dried Food

Freeze-dried food has had its moisture sucked out of it, yet most of its nutritional value remains. We prefer freeze-dried foods over frozen foods (although the latter are generally cheaper), and we really like freeze-dried krill and tubifex worms. Freeze-dried bloodworms are popular and readily available, but they are not our favorite. Probably the best freeze-dried food currently available is freeze-dried copepods. A product called Cyclop-eeze should probably be in every marine aquarist's home.

> **Pearls of Wisdom**
>
> Bloodworms, a popular freeze-dried food, are not really worms. They are actually the larvae of a freshwater insect from the genus *Chironomus*. We prefer to feed foods of marine origin like freeze-dried copepods or krill to our marine livestock.

Frozen Food

Frozen foods are widely available, and they are generally quite nutritious. You can purchase a variety of preparations ranging from frozen foods designed for specific species of marine animals to frozen foods representing a specific food source. Keep in mind that freezing does have a negative effect on the nutritional value of the food, and, for this reason, we recommend soaking all frozen foods in a vitamin supplement like Selcon, which provides not only vitamins but also fatty acids.

How to Feed

While you may have left instructions for the housesitter feeding your freshwater tank that said something like "Feed a pinch of flake food twice a day," chances are your instructions for your marine aquarium feeding will be slightly more involved. Depending on your livestock, you will have a regimen of feeding that suits each animal's dietary needs. In general, it is best to feed a very small amount of food several times a day. It is also a good idea, in our opinion, to vary what you feed. A well-balanced flake food in the morning, a small sheet of nori midday, and freeze-dried or frozen food in the evening might be one example. You may choose to replace the freeze-dried or frozen food with small pieces of meaty table seafood several times a week or live food such as newly hatched brine shrimp (*Artemia* spp.).

As we said, what you feed and when you feed will vary greatly depending on what livestock you keep. We once again emphasize the importance of researching your species' dietary needs. Some fishes, for example, must have a constant source of live food, while other fishes must be fed many times a day. Don't acquire a fish unless you know you can properly care for it.

Some marine animals will need special attention at feeding time. Corals and other sessile invertebrates, for example, cannot move to the food, and so you must often move the food to them. While many corals host algae, which in turn provide the majority of their food, almost all corals benefit from targeted feedings of either a specially formulated, invertebrate food or small pieces of meaty seafood. Plan to deliver this food with either a feeding stick or a turkey baster. On the CD-ROM, we give specific dietary instructions for all listed invertebrates.

In conclusion, overfeeding is generally more of a problem than under-feeding, but underfeeding can also lead to serious problems. In addition, feeding the right amount of the wrong kind of food will lead to definite problems. There are all sorts of rules of thumb for how much to feed, but no single piece of advice outweighs the value of knowing your species' needs. That's why we have included the CD-ROM with this book, but even the information contained on the CD-ROM is only a starting point. Remember, more marine animals die as a result of improper feeding and malnutrition than any other cause.

Warning

Overfeeding is not only bad for your animals from a nutritional standpoint, but uneaten food is also a leading contributor to poor water quality. Having said that, some voracious eaters (e.g., lionfishes and eels) just need to eat a lot and are particularly messy eaters. With these animals, plan to provide a beefed-up filtration system.

Observation Is Power

We like to use feeding time as observation time.. When your animals feed, they are usually active, and this gives you the perfect opportunity to look for any abnormalities in physiology or behavior in your nonsessile invertebrates.

First and foremost, your nonsessile animals should react to food in the tank, and so your first question might be: are all my nonsessile animals eating? Then inspect each for any obvious signs of skin parasites. Do fish have any missing scales or lesions? Are the fins clear or opaque? Are they bulging or frayed at the tips? Are the eyes clear? You will get to know your animals over time, and the most important question might be: is anything different from yesterday?

If you see anything unusual, investigate further. In Chapter 19, we discuss many of the common diseases and parasites you may see, but don't always assume the worst. Sometimes a fish such as a Banggai cardinalfish is not eating because it's carrying young in its mouth (these fishes are mouthbrooders). Likewise, your shrimp may simply be molting or your anemone may be dividing. We strongly suggest you keep a written daily log of your observations. Some of the software available for aquarium controllers allows you to keep a log and all of the aquarium data in one electronic place. However you choose to keep track, just make sure you have a system that will work for you over the length of your aquarium's life.

Dosing

In addition to feeding your marine animals, you may well want to dose certain supplements into your water column to assist with various water parameters or add supplemental nutrition or trace elements to help certain animals grow and thrive.

Unfortunately, dosing is often a slippery slope. In other words, you start dosing to correct one issue and then you find you have to start dosing for another issue caused by dosing for the first issue. Phew! Generally we suggest that the beginning marine aquarist address issues in his or her tank with better husbandry rather than supplements. Having said that, there are a few supplements that we heartily encourage you use. When used as a daily supplement, vitamin C enhances the immune system of marine animals. It helps facilitate the metabolism of fatty acids, and it stimulates the healing of tissue secondary to disease or coral propagation. The dosage amount depends on the product, but the most readily available vitamin C supplement, Marine C by Kent Marine (ascorbic acid in aquaculture grade form of 2-sulfate dipotassium dehydrate), can be used daily at a concentration of 1 milliliter per 50 gallons. Marine C is acidic, but it is also buffered. Nonetheless, we recommend regularly checking for pH and alkalinity while using vitamin C.

Chores

In addition to feeding, observing, and possibly dosing on a daily basis, you should include the following chores in your maintenance regimen.

Daily

Visually observe all components of the aquarium and plumbing for leaks, excessive salt creep, and general functioning. Make sure all hoses are secured (preferably with hose clamps), and clear all strainers and other filters of debris that may decrease their effectiveness.

Check and record your water parameters (we discuss water parameters in Chapter 11) depending upon your system and your experience. Dose any additional supplements or additives after you have recorded the current levels.

Empty your protein skimmer's collection cup, clean out your filter sock, and rinse any filter sponges if you have them. You do not want these last two items to become part of your system's biological filtration.

Top off the water level with freshwater (or better, use an automatic top-off system).

Push salt creep back into the tank (but make sure to not let it settle on sessile invertebrates). We like to simply wipe salt creep into the over-flow or sump itself.

Clean the front glass from the outside using a magnetic algae pad (if you have an acrylic tank, be sure to use one designed for use on acrylic). This keeps your hands out of the tank.

Weekly

At a minimum, perform a 10 percent water change weekly. Some aquarists choose to do more frequent, smaller water changes, while others prefer less frequent, larger water changes. As a general rule, be sure you are changing at least 20 percent of the water twice a month.

Before performing the water change, use a turkey baster or a small handheld powerhead to blow detritus from the rockwork. The better your flow patterns are, the less detritus will accumulate from week to week. Once you have lifted the detritus into suspension, perform your water change. Allow the tank to clear completely and then clean your filter sock.

Clean the side and back walls of the aquarium, and anything you were unable to clean off the front panel using your magnetic algae pad.

Depending on what type of substrate you have, consider vacuuming the substrate.

Vacuum the sump.

Check any chemical media you are using, such as activated charcoal or a phosphate remover. Clean and/or replace the media when appropriate.

Clean lights and aquarium top (if one is present).

Monthly

Clean the protein skimmer inside and out.

Change filter media that needs changing.

Check all pumps and perform maintenance if necessary.

Check all wavemakers and powerheads and perform maintenance if needed.

Yearly

Replace bulbs (actually Mark suggests every nine months).

Take apart and service your pumps.

The Least You Need to Know

- ◆ Improper feeding is a leading cause of mortality.
- ◆ Different marine species have different dietary needs.
- ◆ Most species are omnivores requiring a varied diet.
- ◆ Don't forget to target feed sessile invertebrates.
- ◆ Don't overfeed. Don't underfeed.
- ◆ Observe your fish closely daily, and stick religiously to a daily, weekly, monthly, and yearly maintenance regimen.

Chapter 19

Diseases and Care

In This Chapter

- Setting up a hospital tank
- How to dip
- Identifying infestations, infections, and diseases
- Treatment protocols
- What's in your medicine cabinet?

Even the best aquarists will eventually have to deal with parasites and diseases. This chapter discusses the major ailments from which your animals can suffer and the standard treatments and treatment protocols to nurse a sick animal back to health.

The Hospital Tank

To treat most diseases, infections, and infestations, you will want a separate hospital tank, and a small 10- or 20-gallon tank will suffice for most fishes. The reason you will want to treat a fish in a separate hospital tank is because some of the treatments we will recommend in this chapter would wipe out the corals and other invertebrates in your display tank. Moving the sick fish to a hospital tank also gives you the opportunity to observe that fish closely and keep it separated from other (hopefully) healthy fishes.

The hospital tank is a simple affair, requiring little more than an external power filter, a heater, and possibly a substrate reactor. We like to add a piece of PVC pipe to give the sick fish some cover, and in the case of fishes that need a sandy substrate (e.g., wrasses), we add a sterile Tupperware container filled with substrate for them. Keep in mind that after treatment, everything in the tank will need to be sterilized.

Dips

Throughout this chapter we will frequently refer to "dips" and "baths." We quite literally are talking about dipping your fish in a solution to attempt to treat a particular affliction. While the solution will vary depending upon the issue at hand, the mechanics of dipping are pretty much the same.

We like to use water in the dip that is the same pH and temperature of the water of the tank to which the fish is destined. Use a container like a bucket that is big enough for the intended fish. Add the dip mix to this bucket (methylene blue and freshwater is our go-to dip, but there are others we discuss later in this chapter). If this is not a freshwater dip, you can use system water for starters. If it is a freshwater dip, you will have to bring the pH of the freshwater up before using the dip.

Once the dip is ready, capture your fish in a net or collection cup, and put it in the dip. It's that easy. Be sure to observe your fish for the duration of the dip (if it's a long dip, add an airstone or powerhead for oxygenation). If the fish's behavior becomes frantic, remove it from the dip.

Signs of Sickness

Because you observe your fish daily and keep meticulous notes regarding their appearance and behavior, it is easy to identify when something is awry. Here are some of the most common signs that you have a sick animal:

◆ Rapid or labored breathing—Just as in people, this is a bad sign if it is prolonged. There could be unseen damage as the result of parasites or poisoning to the fish's gills, and this can readily result in death by suffocation.

- ◆ Spots—This is bad. Nothing good comes of spots appearing on your fishes' skin, gills, eyes, or fins.

- ◆ Flashing—This is not lewd behavior, rather it is an attempt by a fish to rub or scratch parasites off its skin by rubbing against objects in the aquarium.

- ◆ Lethargy—Fishes should be active much of the time (and certainly during feeding time). If your fish appears to be lethargic, this is usually a sign of trouble.

- ◆ Anorexia—Has your fish stopped eating? This is rarely a good sign.

Protozoans

Protozoa are single-celled organisms that are usually microscopic and include amoebas, ciliates, flagellates, sporozoans, and the like. Why do you care? You care because *Cryptocaryon irritans* is a ciliated protozoan (a cilia is simply a hairlike locomotion and food-capturing mechanism). Still don't care? Well you should, because *Cryptocaryon irritans* is one of the most lethal and common diseases marine aquarists face. You may have heard it referred to as ich, but that is most decidedly a misnomer, as ich is a freshwater disease. Some marine aquarists call it marine ich or saltwater ich, which, while slightly better, is still not all that good. White-spot disease is certainly more descriptive, and cryptocaryonosis is most accurate.

Pearls of Wisdom

No matter what someone tells you, marine fishes do not suffer from ich ... ever. They suffer from a disease known as cryptocaryonosis, which is caused by the *Cryptocaryon irritans* parasite. Ich is a freshwater disease caused by a ciliated parasite called *Ichthyopthirius multifilis*. Cryptocaryonosis is also called marine ich, saltwater ich, and white-spot disease. The proper name, however, is cryptocaryonosis, or, if you must, "crypto."

Cryptocaryonosis, sometimes simply called "crypto," is a disease caused by the parasite *Cryptocaryon irritans*. Regardless of what you call it, it's a killer. Crypto attacks the infected fish by boring into its skin and gills. The parasite is then covered with mucus produced by the fish as part of the fish's natural defense mechanism. It is this mucus buildup that the aquarist is referring to when he or she says, "My fish has white-spot disease." You may also see the spots on the eyes of the fish or on the fins or tail. In addition, the parasites bore into the gill structure, causing respiratory difficulty for the fish.

What the aquarist is observing in this stage of a crypto outbreak is the trophont phase (feeding phase) of the parasite's life cycle. After this phase, the parasite moves into the dividing or reproductive stage (called the tomont stage) and falls off the host. In a period of time ranging from three days to one month, the parasite reaches the third and final stage of its life cycle—the swarming (or tomite) stage, where the divided cysts open, and the parasites seek new hosts for the next trophont phase. Sounds like something straight out of science fiction, eh?

Combating crypto is actually quite easy if you catch it early, but avoiding it altogether is even easier. To do the latter, simply quarantine all new fishes before introducing them to your aquarium. Also, running a UV sterilizer on the system will kill any parasites during the swarming stage that make it into the sterilizer.

If you do experience a crypto outbreak, the best course of action is to remove the infected fish or fishes to a bare-bottom hospital tank where they can be treated. Catching crypto early is essential—even before the white spots appear, you will notice some of the symptoms as well as a velvety sheen on the fish's body. Treatment usually involves some or all of the following procedures:

Dipping in freshwater dosed with methylene blue plus formalin

Lowering specific gravity (hyposalinity = 1.010–1.013), but never in your display tank

Continuous exposure for at least 28 days to 0.15 to 0.20 ppm copper, although copper in and of itself can have long-term negative effects

Antibiotic feeding (preventative against secondary infection)

Pearls of Wisdom

Some research has suggested that chloroquine phosphate (sold as Aralen) may be a less stressful treatment than copper for fish suffering from crypto. The recommended dosage is 10 milligrams per liter (40 milligrams per gallon) in combination with hyposalinity. Chloroquine phosphate is, like copper, toxic to some invertebrates and algae, and so it cannot be used in the reef tank. In addition to working on crypto, chloroquine phosphate has been shown to effectively treat Amyloodinium, Brooklynella, and Uronema.

If the crypto was allowed to progress in the display tank to the dividing and reproductive phase, then you may have recurring outbreaks. To take care of these, you would need to remove all potential hosts (all fishes) from your aquarium for at least a month.

There are several other protozoan infestations of which the marine aquarist should be aware. They are *Amyloodinium ocellatum* (a flagellate protozoan infestation sometimes called marine velvet disease) and two additional ciliate protozoans, *Brooklynella hostiles* (Anemonefish disease) and *Uronema marinum* (Uronema). All three of these can affect all bony fish (despite the fact that Brooklynella is often called anemonefish disease), and all can be devastating to your system if not treated quickly. All three infestations present in roughly the same way (skin damage, rapid breathing, rubbing on rocks and substrate, and extreme lethargy), are the results of very similar parasitic organisms with almost identical life cycles, and are treated with the same procedures.

The take-home point is to quarantine all new fish until you know they are free of an infestation and use preventative measures such as UV sterilization. If you do have an outbreak, you must act quickly and definitively.

Other Infestations

There are several other infestations from which your marine animals may suffer. A variety of crustaceans ranging from isopods to copepods can infest your fishes. Many of these (such as isopods) are visible to the naked eye and can be seen attached to the fish's mouth or body, where it pierces the skin of the host. If you see these crustaceans, remove them. Try forceps or freshwater dips. Copper may also be effective. If you physically remove the crustacean with forceps, swab the area afterward with either iodine or hydrogen peroxide to limit secondary infection. Some parasitic copepods are not easy to remove without harming the fish. For these situations, use a formalin (or formalin/malachite green) dip. The treatments will have to be repeated to kill the parasite in all its life stages.

Black-spot disease (sometimes called tang turbellarian disease or black ich) is caused by a parasitic flatworm from the genus *Paravortex*. An infected fish will have small black spots on its body, fins, and gills. An infested fish can be cured with freshwater dips or a formalin (or formalin/malachite green) dip. Other worms (such as monogenic trematode worms) are impossible to see and difficult to treat.

Fungal Diseases

A variety of fungal diseases afflict marine fishes. They include Exophiala disease and Ichthyophonus disease. Fungal diseases are different from parasitic diseases, because fungal diseases are caused by parasitic fungi. Unfortunately, little can be done for a fish infected with a fungal disease given the internal nature of the disease. Remove the suspected host from the aquarium. Common signs of fungal disease include damage to the skin (including erosion and ulcers), malnourishment, spinal curvature, and erratic swimming (especially in the case of Ichthyophonus disease, often called whirling disease).

Bacterial Infections

A host of bacterial infections can afflict marine animals. Some of the most common are so-called wasting disease, ulcer disease, and the aptly named fin rot. The bacteria responsible are Mycobacterium, Vibrio, Aeromonas, and Pseudomonas bacteria, and a variety of aquarium antibiotics can be used to address infections. The most common antibiotics are furanace, augmentin, and ciprofloxin (for fin rot); kanamycin, erythromycin, and streptomycin (for wasting disease); and halquinol and nitrofurazone (for ulcer disease).

Unfortunately, many bacterial infections are hard to diagnose and even harder to treat. Certainly remove a sick-looking or -acting fish from the display tank, and try some of these antibiotics in a hospital tank. Your goal should be to not spread the infection to other fishes. If the infected fish survives, that's icing on the cake.

Your Aquarium Medicine Cabinet

Going to the local fish store or the big-box pet store in search of medication for your ailing fishes is often a frustrating experience. With so many products boldly proclaiming wonder cures, it's hard to figure out what you really need. We've decided to try to make it easy for you. Procure these treatments prior to having a problem, and you will never find yourself dazed and confused in the aquarium fish medication aisle.

Formalin

This has been a go-to drug for the aquarist for many years. Formalin is a formaldehyde gas in water solution that has long been used to rid fishes of infestations such as crypto and marine velvet. It can be used quite effectively in conjunction with malachite green in baths and dips. While it is somewhat of an aquarium wonder drug, it is fairly dangerous (it's a carcinogen) and should be kept out of reach of children and used only with caution by well-informed adults.

Hydrogen Peroxide

You probably don't even have to go out and buy this, as it's most likely already in your medicine cabinet. This stuff is magic for the marine aquarist, and you should not be without it. In addition to using it as a topical disinfectant for fish wounds (on the fish and on the ones the fish imposed on you), it can be a lifesaver in the event of a power outage. Huh? Yep, that's right. Adding a 3 percent solution of hydrogen peroxide to your aquarium at a dosage of 1 teaspoon for every 50 gallons can significantly elevate oxygen levels in your aquarium for the duration of the power outage (you must repeat the dosage every six hours). An injured fish or a fish suffering from various bacterial infections can be removed to a hospital tank with a 7.5 ppm solution of 3 percent hydrogen peroxide (1 milliliter per gallon).

Malachite Green

This is admittedly some nasty stuff, so if you keep it, be careful with it. Malachite green is usually combined with formalin (discussed previously) to treat certain parasitic infestations such as Brooklynella, which is (at least anecdotally) immune to copper treatments. It can also be combined with quinine hydrochloride for an effective Brooklynella treatment.

Methylene Blue

This is great stuff, although it, too, can be quite dangerous if not used with caution. Methylene blue will turn anything it touches smurf blue, but this is not why you should have some in your aquarium medicine cabinet. The real value of methylene blue is that it can be used as a so-called "oxygen donor" for stressed and injured fishes. Used at a dosage of about two drops per gallon, it will ease stress, especially in injured fishes or fishes with gill damage. The dosage can be repeated when the blue color dissipates entirely from the water column.

> **Warning**
>
> While methylene blue can be used directly in the aquarium, it may well disrupt the nitrogen cycle and kill nitrifying bacteria eliminating all biological filtration from an established system.

Garlic

Allicin, a chemical that occurs naturally in garlic, may be a reef aquarist's best friend. *May* be. The evidence is still completely anecdotal, but it is believed by some that liquid garlic (either a commercially available brand marketed specifically for aquarium usage, or some you pick up from the health-food store) acts as an immunostimulant. But that's not the real reason reef aquarists may be thrilled. The real reason is that there is anecdotal evidence that liquid garlic may be effective at treating crypto, and (drum roll, please) it is the only known crypto treatment that can be used in the reef aquarium itself (no need to remove infested fishes to a hospital tank).

We like feeding liquid garlic to live brine shrimp and then feeding the live brine shrimp to our fishes, but there are other effective ways to deliver garlic to your fishes. You can, for instance, soak your flake, freeze-dried, or frozen food in liquid garlic before feeding. Offer daily for a month and then supplement with a weekly liquid garlic meal. As we've pointed out several times in as many sentences, this is anecdotal, but we like the odds. Be conscious of water movement and filtration (effective protein skimming and running activated carbon) while using liquid garlic.

Copper

Ah, copper. If you have not heard a lot about it up until now, prepare yourself. Copper is an oft-discussed topic in marine aquarium circles. Why is it controversial? Because 1) it's very good at killing external parasites (read very effective treatment for both crypto and Amyloodinum), and 2) it's highly toxic to marine animals. While marine invertebrates will usually be killed outright by copper treatments, marine fishes also suffer long-term side effects of having endured treatment with copper. There are certain fishes that are particularly sensitive to copper (e.g., angelfishes, blennies, dragonets, and wrasses), and great care must be used when treating these fishes with copper treatments in a hospital tank. It is best in our opinion to use copper treatments in conjunction with formalin or methylene blue. Copper treatments will also negatively impact biological filtration (not an issue generally, as you will be using it in a hospital tank) and will, over time, impair a fish's immune system. You will need to choose either copper sulfate or chelated copper (we recommend the latter) using an appropriate test kit, and you absolutely should follow the directions on the package to a T.

Antibiotics

Definitely plan to have a broad-spectrum antibiotic in your fish medicine cabinet. Both tetracycline and nitro furans are effective when attempting to combat a bacterial infection. We also like kanamycin sulfate, minocycline, and neomycin sulfate. With bacterial infections, it is often impossible to determine the actual bacteria at work, and so a fair amount of guesstimating goes into the treatment. Begin with one of the broad-spectrum antibiotics we have mentioned, and treat for several days. If after three days you observe no improvement, switch to the next broad-spectrum antibiotic. Once you find one that has a positive effect, follow the directions (usually a 7- to 10-day treatment). Be aware that these antibiotics will kill your nitrifying bacteria if massive water changes are not regularly performed throughout treatment (which is why you should use a quarantine tank!).

The Least You Need to Know

◆ Always have a hospital/quarantine tank ready to go.

◆ Use dips for treatment.

◆ Observe your livestock daily.

◆ Have the right medications on hand.

Chapter 20

Problem Fish

In This Chapter

- ◆ Causes of so-called aggression in fishes
- ◆ Fishes to avoid from the outset
- ◆ Tips, tricks, and strategies for dealing with problem fishes
- ◆ Catching problem fish

Fishes, like people, are individuals, and certain individuals tend to be more aggressive, more territorial, and more rambunctious than others (even—and sometimes especially—within the same genus or species). This chapter discusses what to do to avoid issues associated with problem fishes (and invertebrates). It also discusses what to do if you have a problem fish (or invertebrate) in your tank.

As always, we emphasize doing your homework and fully researching all species before you acquire them. In Chapter 3, we discuss how to create a stocking list to avoid undue aggression in the marine aquarium, and, as you no doubt have noticed, we include each species' disposition on the CD-ROM (e.g., peaceful, semi-aggressive, or aggressive). We also point out in Chapter 15 that virtually all marine fishes are at least capable of aggression. Having said that, there are some notable troublemakers.

Aggression or Instinct

Before listing any particular species, let's remember that fishes often act on instinct. What we may call aggressive or "mean" behavior may well be simply a genetically programmed response. When a triggerfish bites your finger (ouch!) while hand-feeding (which we suggest you do not do!), it is not being aggressive per se. It's simply feeding. Likewise, when a snowflake eel *(Echidna nebulosa)*, which we list as semi-aggressive and relatively fish-safe on the CD-ROM, bites a small fish during feeding, it probably has to do with the eel's instinctual feeding response coupled with the animal's poor eyesight.

Also keep in mind, as we have mentioned before, that the ocean (and especially the tropical reef) is a very hostile environment. For these animals to have evolved over time and succeeded, they have needed to hone an instinctual fight-or-flight mechanism. This is, in fact, frequently the philosophy Ret employs when designing and tying saltwater flies for fly fishing. The fly does not need to look exactly like a baitfish; instead, it needs to elicit an instinctual feeding response. By understanding what triggers these responses, saltwater fly fishermen can design flies that look very little like any naturally occurring animal but which are highly effective in eliciting a strike response. Keep this in mind when adding new fishes or invertebrates to your tank. Ask yourself what instinctual response the newly added animal will provoke.

> ### Pearls of Wisdom
>
> Saltwater fishes often act out of instinct. For example, saltwater fishing flies are appropriately categorized, among other things, as imitators and attractors. An imitation fly imitates the thing (perhaps a baitfish or a crab) on which the fish is feeding, whereby an attractor fly simply elicits a strike response based on color, noise, or movement stimuli. Often the aquarist provokes an instinctual response when he or she interacts with the tank.

In order to answer this question, you have to understand the territorial nature of marine animals, especially on the reef. When you place a marine animal in your aquarium, chances are it will soon establish its own territory. Many marine species establish territories large enough to provide for their needs. This usually refers to feeding, but may also be related to spawning and other behaviors. Some species will appear not to establish a territory but will instead range over the entire aquarium. This may be because your tank is smaller than the territory the fish would normally establish in the wild, or it may be because of the type of eater your fish is (grazers and planktivores will go where the food is). Even the manner in which you feed your fishes will impact their territories in the marine aquarium. Suffice it to say (one more time) that you absolutely must do your species-specific research. Having said that, some generalities are possible.

If a fish or invertebrate (including corals) has established a territory, it will likely defend that territory if another animal either enters that territory or appears to pose a threat. The result may be fighting with several possible outcomes:

> **Death**—The dominant species may kill the weaker species. In some cases, even in extraordinarily large systems, fishes of a given species absolutely cannot tolerate the presence of some other fishes. If this is the case in your aquarium, the dominant fish will hunt down the other fish and harass it to death.

> **Truce**—This is what you hope for, but don't rely on hope alone. If you carefully planned your stocking list and then designed a system and aquascaped it for the specific livestock on your stocking list, most new additions (if added in the proper order of least aggressive largest to most aggressive smallest) should establish their own territories and cohabitate just fine.

> **Continued Fighting**—This can be a real problem. If your fishes are constantly harassing each other without effectively establishing a pecking order where the alpha fish feels secure and the beta fish(es) acts appropriately submissive, then you may be in for trouble. While they may not kill each other outright, the stress of living in these conditions can lead to disease and increased susceptibility to infections and infestations. In this situation, watch to see what happens. If there is bodily damage, you probably want to remove the aggressor from the aquarium.

Some Marine Animals to Avoid

While there are few animals we would tell every aquarist to definitely avoid, there are some that are downright inappropriate for the beginner or for any aquarist who does not have a very specialized setup.

Anthias—These fishes need a mature aquarium and frequent feedings to serve their dietary needs. Not a good fish for a new aquarium or the beginning aquarist. Consider a small, reef-safe wrasse instead.

Dragonets—These fishes need a mature aquarium and frequent feedings to serve their dietary needs. Not a good fish for a new aquarium or the beginning aquarist. Be aware that the so-called red scooter blenny (*Synchiropus stellatus*) is actually a dragonet.

Family Serranidae—Groupers and basses. Many get too large, too quickly. Unless you have a huge tank, do not purchase these fishes.

Sharks—Sharks have very special requirements, including a tank that is long enough for them to build up swimming speed and turn. If you do not have an appropriate shark tank, do not purchase these fishes.

Eels—Most are simply not appropriate for anything but the largest, most secure systems. They are escape artists and many grow very large. The snowflake eel is one possible exception you might consider if you really want an eel.

Large Tangs—Large tangs can be quite aggressive and not easy to keep alive in the home aquarium, especially for the beginning aquarist.

Pipefishes—These fishes (along with seahorses, to which they are closely related) are very delicate and not appropriate for the beginning aquarist.

Rays—Rays have specialized needs that most beginning aquarists are not capable of fully providing. Don't purchase rays unless you plan to have an appropriate ray tank.

Mantis Shrimp—Unless you have an appropriate tank and plan to keep only mantis shrimp, avoid these very interesting but potentially dangerous crustaceans.

Octopuses—Notorious for short life spans in captivity, octopuses are lethal predators that cannot live successfully with the vast majority of other marine mammals in a home aquarium.

Sea Apples (*Pseudocolochirus* spp.)—This is a delicate species of sea cucumber that is toxic and can take your whole tank with it if it dies.

Some of Our Favorite Tips and Tricks

There are many things you can do to lessen the aggression in your tank. Here are a few of our favorite tips and tricks:

- ◆ Add new fishes in groups—never singly.

- ◆ Hold off on adding the most aggressive fish(es) until last.

- ◆ When you add the most aggressive fish, add a juvenile, not an adult.

- ◆ In the case of sessile invertebrates like stony corals, give them enough room to grow and consider the reach of their sweeper tentacles.

- ◆ Consider isolating an established, more aggressive fish with a sterile plastic strainer or strawberry basket when adding a less aggressive fish to the system. (This gives the less aggressive fish a chance to get established before being harassed.)

- ◆ Some fishes are naturally predators of other fishes—keep these fishes in a predatory tank or with much larger and more aggressive tankmates.

- ◆ Look at the fish's mouth size as an indicator of what other fishes can occupy the tank with them. Fishes with very large mouths (e.g., lionfishes, anglers, and stonefishes) can swallow fishes larger then themselves whole.

- ◆ While there are exceptions to every rule, certain fishes are known to be trouble in a community tank. We include groupers, snappers, some triggerfishes, and large wrasses in this group.

- ◆ Be careful about adding two (or more) fishes of the same family, genus, or species to the same aquarium unless you know they can be kept together. If you want a pair (e.g., clownfishes, jawfishes, etc.), try to buy a mated pair from your retailer.

- When it comes to coral and territoriality, keep in mind the way that corals compete on the reef. Corals with stinging tentacles need lots of space, while ones without can often be grouped closer together. Mixing too many soft corals with hard corals can be problematic even with plenty of space, because the soft corals can conduct chemical warfare.

- Always keep in mind that all fishes are individuals, so someone else's experience may not be what you experience. A fish's level of aggressiveness can have a lot to do with many factors unique to your system. Do your research, prepare for the specific livestock you want to keep, and then be an observant aquarist.

Catching Fishes

Catching a problem fish, especially from a heavily aquascaped reef tank with lots of expensive corals, can be a nightmare. What to do?

The first attempt should be "feed and net." Simply feed your tank, and then net the fish when it is distracted by the food. This is often easier said than done, and, quite frequently, you don't want to use a net on a particular fish.

There are fish traps that can be effective. Most are constructed from clear-cast acrylic with a sliding "guillotine" door at one end and a food compartment at the other. When the fish enters the trap, you drop the door. Many fishes will readily swim into the trap in pursuit of food (you may consider not feeding the day or two before you intend to trap the fish). If you are having no luck, leave the trap in the aquarium for a few days until the fishes get used to it. Also, think about placement in the tank based on the fish you are targeting.

If all else fails, you may have to dismantle the tank to remove a problem animal. This really is no fun, so do your homework when planning your stocking list. A carefully designed stocking list won't eliminate all problems, but it should reduce the need to trap a fish.

Fish traps can also be used for catching troublesome invertebrates and sick fishes.

What to Do with Fishes You No Longer Want

After you have captured that bully, and admitted to yourself that you made a mistake, you need to figure out what to do with the fish. We'd suggest you start a new tank, but the reality for most people is that one tank is more than enough, especially as a beginning marine aquarist.

Local fish stores will often buy back a fish you bought from them. They will also frequently buy a healthy fish you obtained elsewhere, if they think they can sell it. It's best to check with the store before you take the fish to them—if they don't want it (or can't take it), the fish just went through a stressful experience for nothing. Show the owner a picture of the fish along with any details regarding its history, and ask them politely if they would consider buying it. Often the local fish store will give you store credit instead of cash, which is great, as you probably are looking to purchase another fish right about now.

If they won't buy the fish (or take it on spec), ask the owner if you can post a picture and description of the fish along with your contact information in the store. Perhaps the store also has a website with a classifieds page or an electronic newsletter. If none of the above works, you may ask if there are any local reef clubs (you could, of course, also do an online search and find a local reef club yourself). Through a local reef club, you may find a potential buyer or someone who has a fish that you want as a trade for your fish.

If all of these attempts to sell or trade the problem fish fail, you may try the local newspaper or an online classified service such as Craigslist. If you still cannot sell or trade the fish, then please give it to a good home. This is a living animal that should not live indefinitely in your quarantine tank, as you attempt to recoup your costs. Sometimes local zoos and aquariums will also be interested in a livestock donation.

The Least You Need to Know

♦ Do your homework on the front end to avoid creating problems with aggression down the road.

♦ By doing your homework, you will have considered adult sizes and personalities before purchasing any animal.

- Remember that virtually all saltwater animals are territorial and have the potential to be aggressive.

- Observe your fish daily, and act accordingly if any compatibility issues arise.

- Use a fish trap to catch an animal in a heavily aquascaped reef tank.

- Always find a suitable home for any fish you remove because of compatibility issues—it's your responsibility!

Chapter 21

Adding Additional Animals

In This Chapter

- ◆ Adding new fishes
- ◆ Replacing fishes
- ◆ Replacing a member of a mated pair
- ◆ Adding corals
- ◆ Adding other non-coral invertebrates

Well, you've done it! You've learned to set up and stock a successful marine aquarium. Good job! If you reflect back on how much you've learned about the marine hobby, marine animals, and marine ecosystems, we think you'll be impressed. Take some time to observe and enjoy your new tank. You deserve it!

As you are enjoying your new tank, keep in mind that for an invertebrate or reef tank, it's going to slowly develop over the next year. Don't expect it to look like a full-blown reef all at once. Half the fun of this hobby is watching your tank grow, making small adjustments, and observing the effects they have on your livestock.

For most of you, there will come a time when you'll want to add more animals beyond your original stocking list, and we want to give you some tips about how to do that. In addition, you will probably experience some livestock loses, and so we also want to discuss a bit about replacing livestock in this chapter as well.

Adding Animals

The reason you created a stocking list way back in Chapter 3 was so that you built your tank in a manner most appropriate for the species you decided you wanted to keep. As you progress in the hobby, you are going to see other people's tanks and other species of fishes and invertebrates that you didn't even know existed. Eventually, you may decide you really want to try keeping some of those fishes like that cute little bicolor parrotfish (*Cetoscarus bicolor*) that your local fish store just got in. Or what about that majestic angelfish (*Pomacanthus navarchus*) your best buddy just got for her tank? After your initial success, it's tempting to start adding livestock somewhat willy-nilly, but remember, your tank was set up and stocked for those animals on your initial stocking list, and, as such, it might not be appropriate for some of the species you are now eyeing.

Compatibility Check

Is the fish you are considering compatible with your current setup? This is the question.

That cute little bicolor parrotfish, for example? It can get to be 90 centimeters (35 inches) long, and it is a coral-eating machine. How about the angelfish? Well that's maybe a better choice (at least size-wise), but it may not be compatible with the other angels you have in your tank already. What's our point? Even though you have experienced success, you still have to do your homework before adding anything new to your tank. Even adding a replacement individual can be a problem, but we discuss that later in this chapter.

So you still want to expand beyond your original stocking list? Well, we're not out to totally crush your dreams, and, in fact, we're here to tell you that it's appropriate (and part of the fun!) to make some additions. There are a few things, however, you absolutely must keep in mind. We've alluded to issues regarding equipment compatibility (e.g., is your existing tank really big enough for that new fish?) and livestock compatibility (e.g., will that new fish be harassed to death by the fishes you already keep?). The other big concern, of course, is bioload.

Increasing Bioload

In Chapter 3, we encouraged you to stock your tank in a conservative manner to ensure that your filtration could keep up with the waste produced by your livestock. As your aquarium matures, it will develop more biological filtration capacity, but as your livestock grow, they, too, will increase the bioload in your aquarium. So how do you know when you've maxed out your bioload or if your biological filtration capacity has increased to the point where you can safely add a new animal? Two words: water testing.

If you stocked conservatively, and your tank has been running fully stocked based on your stocking list for a few months, you may be able to safely add a new animal, if all your water parameters look good. Should you choose a large, messy predator such as a lionfish or triggerfish? Probably not (if not for compatibility issues alone), but adding a cool wrasse or a stunning dottyback to your reef tank might be fine if there are no equipment or livestock-compatibility issues. When considering bioload, do keep in mind that some of the animals you currently have may be significantly bigger in a year's time.

Adding Animals to a Mature Tank

Introducing a new animal to an established tank is a little different than adding animals to a new, largely uninhabited tank. For one, the new fish you add to a mature tank is going to be the new kid on the block, and everyone may treat that new fish like the new kid on the block at the same time. This is one reason that adding two or three new fishes at the same time may be a good idea. For example, adding both an oblique-lined dottyback (*Cypho purpurascens*) and an orchid dottyback

(Pseudochromis fridmani) to your established, 150-gallon (or larger) reef tank at the same time will mean that any potential aggressors (although these are aggressive little fishes) in the aquarium will be distracted by two new kids instead of just one. Introducing both fishes (following the proper acclimatization procedures, of course) at the same time with the lights out after the tank has been fed should prove a successful strategy for most new introductions.

Even the best-laid plans don't always pan out, though, and more aggressive measures may be required. Some people advocate rearranging the aquascaping prior to new introductions. In theory, this disrupts all of the established territories in the tank and puts everyone on a somewhat level playing field. In most cases, we don't recommend this, especially in a reef tank, where you have presumably spent a fair bit of time acclimating your sessile invertebrates to a specific tank location. If you are really concerned about a particular bully picking on your new addition, you might 1) reconsider the new addition, or 2) plan to temporarily isolate the bully while the new addition gets settled. Isolating a bully in the aquarium can be accomplished with a sterile plastic strawberry basket or a plastic colander.

Replacing Animals

Chances are that your first "next purchase" beyond your initial stocking list will be a replacement. Inevitably you will experience some losses of livestock, and when you do, you often have an opportunity to replace the animal. Even though you've already kept this animal, don't rush into a replacement purchase. In fact, never rush any livestock purchasing decision—there is no hurry. Take your time and research the animal thoroughly, even if that means researching it again for things you may not remember from your initial research. For example, that mated pair of gold-striped maroon clownfish *(Premnas biaculeatus)* you purchased? If the male dies, can you simply add another male? Well, maybe, but let's remember that clownfishes are sequential hermaphrodites. That may not have meant anything to you when you first purchased a mated pair because they came prepared. Now, however, it's very important. Why? Read on.

Replacing a Member of a Mated Pair

If you lose one member of a mated pair, you're going to need to progress very carefully. Some fishes, such as the gold-striped maroon clownfish in the preceding example, are sequential hermaphrodites. In other words, they can change sex at different times in their life cycle. Fishes that change from being male to female are said to be protandrous hermaphrodites, while those that switch from female to male are said to be protogynous hermaphrodites. Clownfishes are protandrous hermaphrodites, and it is important to take this into consideration if you plan to replace one.

Here's how it works: When you have more than one clownfish from the same species in your aquarium, the largest one will become a female and will most likely pair off with the second largest clownfish of the same species (which will remain a male). All of the other clownfish in that group will remain immature males. If the female dies, the next largest male will become a female and may mate with the next largest fish, and so on.

Placing a female in your tank with an established, dominant female may cause some serious problems. So how do you go about replacing a clownfish in a mated pair? You do it by size. Acquiring a smaller clownfish than the one remaining in your aquarium will be your best bet in terms of hopefully getting a new mated pair. This is just one example of some of the obstacles you may face when replacing an individual from a mated pair.

Some species of fishes are gonochoristic (the fish remains the same sex throughout its life cycle), but this doesn't make things easier for you. You may not be able to easily introduce another fish of the opposite sex (even if it's smaller) without causing undue aggression between the two. You can try, but watch closely, as you may need to remove the new fish if serious aggression ensues.

Another option—if you really want a mated pair—is to sell the remaining individual back to your local fish store and buy a new mated pair. Mated pairs that you purchase at the fish store or online have either been carefully paired in captivity and will most likely be fine together in your aquarium, or they are a wild-caught pair, which will almost always do well together in captivity (if provided with the appropriate conditions, of course).

272 Part 5: Caring for the System

The plot thickens with some species of fishes that are not sexually dimorphic (you can't tell who's the boy and who's the girl). With these fishes, it is often essential to buy a mated pair, although some aquarists will buy a small group for a large aquarium and watch to see if two pair off. Acquiring five fish, for example, means you have a high likelihood of getting at least one male and one female, even though they cannot be sexed by appearance alone. The problem with this approach is that you will probably need to remove the nonpaired fish, unless your system is very large. Otherwise, chances are that you will have interspecific aggression problems.

Replacing a Member of a Harem

Some marine fishes will do fine in a small shoal in a sufficiently large aquarium. Many marine fishes are haremic, meaning that they live in groups of one male and several females. In this situation, the male protects the females and reproduces with each. Keep in mind that some of these fishes are also hermaphroditic, and in some species, it is one female with several males. Again, do your species-specific research before making any purchasing decision.

It is best to introduce shoals or haremic groups together, but if you only want to replace one member of a shoal or harem, you must do so with caution. Whenever you introduce a single fish to an established aquarium (especially if there are other fishes of the same species in the tank), expect aggression and be prepared to separate the bullies if need be. As already discussed, you can do this by using a sterilized plastic strawberry basket or colander to keep the aggressor contained while the new fish establishes itself. Still, watch closely for signs of aggression over the next several days, and be prepared to remove the fish that is being harassed if the aggression does not let up.

Replacing an Individual Fish

If you experienced a loss of a fish of which you only had one individual of that species, your job is a little easier. Do keep in mind that a mature and an immature fish are quite different, behaviorally speaking. Also, the stocking order you established in Chapter 3 has now been disrupted, and you may well have trouble introducing a replacement specimen of the fish you stocked first (because of its passivity) based on the presence of the more aggressive fish you added last.

As fish mature, they generally become more territorial and aggressive. A group of fishes that mature together in a community reef tank may do alright, but adding either a new mature or immature fish to that mix can be fraught with problems. To make matters worse, like people, all fishes are (at least to a certain extent) individuals.

What to do? Again, adding two or more fishes at the same time (even if they are from different species) is probably your best bet in terms of limiting undue aggression against any one individual. If the fish you are replacing is a more peaceful fish, it is all the more important. If you are replacing a more aggressive fish, you should be all right by acquiring an immature individual. That way, the other fishes in the tank will already be established and have their territories, and the new fish will have less of a chance of having bad habits and a belligerent personality. As always, be vigilant for the first 24 to 48 hours after adding the new specimen.

Adding New Invertebrates

Adding new invertebrates is somewhat different than adding new fishes. First off, invertebrates don't have the same bioload impact that fishes have. In addition, most invertebrates are not going to pose a problem in terms of equipment compatibility issues. You will, however, experience some issues with livestock compatibility. For example, some invertebrates do form mated pairs (e.g., coral banded shrimp), and others may be incompatible with livestock you already own—for example, you can't decide to add harlequin shrimp (*Hymenocera picta*) if you already have starfish.

Adding Coral

When it comes to adding coral beyond your initial stocking list, there are some definite compatibility issues. A common mistake is to begin by keeping only leathers and softies because these are the so-called beginner corals, and then to progress to some so-called large polyp stony (LPS) corals, as they are reputedly easier than the so-called small polyp stony (SPS) corals. The problem with this approach is that once you feel confident enough in your abilities to consider SPS corals, it may well be ill-advised to add those SPS corals to a tank dominated by soft and leather corals. Why? Because those starter corals can be some of the most lethal invertebrates when it comes to chemical warfare, and many will actually sense when you add a competing coral and release a toxin that can be deadly to stony corals.

You will find, for example, that on the CD-ROM, corals are divided into hydrocorals (fire corals and lace corals from the class Hydrozoa) and anthozoans (all octocorals and hexacorals from the class Anthozoa). The anthozoans are then broken down into octocorals (the soft and leather corals) and hexacorals (which include all the stony corals, mushroom corals, and zoanthids). We want to encourage you to stock the tank you want, not the tank that some generalized, hobbyist category says you are capable of stocking. We believe there are stony corals that are just as appropriate for the careful beginner as softies and leather corals, so if you want a tank with stony corals (*Acropora, Montipora*, etc.) in a year's time, we encourage you to start with appropriate stony corals at about the six month mark.

Adding Noncoral Invertebrates

Replacing invertebrates is a reality in a marine tank. When you consider that a clean-up crew for a 135-gallon tank may include hundreds of various invertebrates, each of which plays a critical maintenance role in the tank, you come to see that replacing invertebrates such as snails and hermit crabs is just a reality. Generally speaking, beyond proper acclimation, adding these invertebrates is not as complicated as adding fishes and corals, but there are a few for which you need to look out.

Mated Invertebrate Pairs

Ret grew up in New England where lobster races on the kitchen floor before a lobster dinner created fond childhood memories ... until, of course, his mother learned that lobsters mate for life. It was never quite the same after that. We don't mean to anthropomorphize here, but it is true that there are certain marine invertebrates that do pair up, and this is something of which you need to be aware.

Coral banded shrimp (*Stenopus* spp.) are one example of a marine invertebrate that forms pairs in captivity. These are great invertebrates for a marine aquarium—they are cleaners, so they *may* pick parasites off of your fishes, they are boldly colored, and, if introduced as a mated pair, they are quite bold. Often you can buy a mated pair together, but if you can't, they actually are sexually dimorphic (you can tell the boy and girl apart). Keeping a single male will mean that, at best, you won't see him very much, but two males or two females may truly tear each other apart unless the aquarium is very large. These guys are a great example of a territorial motile invertebrate, and that's definitely something you want to know if you are adding one or more to a mature tank.

There are other invertebrates that may be inappropriate replacements for a variety of issues beyond territoriality. Also, even more so than fishes, invertebrates are often mislabeled at the local fish store. For example, you may decide you want three peppermint shrimp (*Lysmata wurdemanni)* to either deal with a nuisance anemone problem or simply because they are attractive invertebrates, especially when perched upside down on the roof of a big cave. Unfortunately, shrimp labeled peppermint shrimp are often not really peppermint shrimp—they are camelbacks (*Rhynchocinetes durbanensis*), which, unlike peppermint shrimp, will probably go after your coral polyps. Keep in mind that many invertebrates are *not* reef-safe, and an invertebrate that feasts on your coral at night can be very hard to get out of your system. Are you sick of hearing us say it? Do your homework!

Finally, there are some invertebrates that can be great additions to your system, but they can also pose huge risks. For example, a tigertail sea cucumber (*Holothuria hilla*) can be a fantastic addition capable of keeping your sand bed sparkling clean. Unfortunately, some sea cucumbers also pose a risk in that they have a very interesting defense mechanism, and in a small tank, could potentially wipe out your entire system. That's why we don't recommend them for any tank under 50 gallons. Again, do your homework.

Adding additional animals to your aquarium—or replacing ones that have perished—is both a reality and a joy in the hobby. As you can see from the examples we have shared in this chapter, adding animals is not without risk, but if you take the time to do the research, you can continue to add to your tank as it grows and changes.

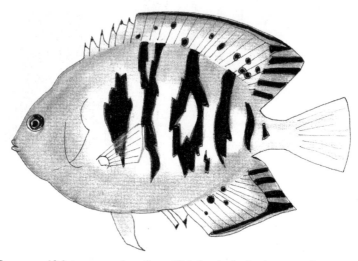

The flame angelfish is a great dwarf angelfish for the beginning aquarist.

(Courtesy Karen Talbot.)

The Least You Need to Know

♦ Don't rush a livestock purchase, even if it is a replacement animal.

♦ Adding animals beyond your initial stocking list is okay, but do so with caution after carefully researching each proposed addition.

♦ Wait at least a year before starting a second tank.

♦ When replacing an individual, be particularly careful if there are other fish of the same species already in the tank.

♦ Special attention should be paid to mated pairs and fishes that form harems.

♦ While you may need to add new invertebrates as part of your clean-up crew, do be careful when adding some invertebrates that are either territorial or incompatible with other invertebrates.

Glossary

alkalinity It is the measure of water's resistance to changes in pH. Alkalinity is synonymous with buffering capacity and is sometimes referred to as carbonate hardness.

ammonia A chemical produced in the aquarium by decaying organic matter and the natural biological processes of marine organisms. It is highly toxic even in fairly low levels.

amyloodiniosis A disease that affects fishes and is caused by a dinoflagellate called amyloodinium ocellatum. Its common names are marine velvet and coral fish disease.

aragonite Coral reef sand is aragonite because it contains calcium carbonate produced by corals.

Berlin method A method of aquarium filtration involving the use of live rock and a sump is often called the Berlin method (and the sump is frequently called a Berlin sump).

bioload A measure of waste-producing organisms in the aquarium. An aquarium with a high bioload refers to one that contains a large number of organisms. The consequence of a high bioload is a larger amount of waste per unit volume. Too high a bioload can cause a system to crash.

biological filter   A filter apparatus designed to promote biological filtration is called a biological filter. Examples include fluidized bed filters, live rock, wet-dry trickle filters, deep sand beds, etc.

black-band disease   So-called black-band disease attacks stony corals infected by cyanobacteria. It presents as a black band of dead tissue that will ultimately kill the coral.

black-spot disease   A disease caused by worm parasites that appear as black dots on fishes, black spot disease is also called black ich.

brooklynellosis   Sometimes called clownfish disease, brooklynella can affect all fish. It is caused by a parasitic protozoan called *Brooklynella hostilis*.

brown-jelly infection   While not fully understood, brown-jelly infection is thought to be the result of protozoan infection that causes tissue breakdown in corals. A brown, jellylike substance is apparent where the tissue damage occurs.

buffer   A buffer helps maintain pH stability. *See also* alkalinity.

calcareous algae   *See* coralline algae.

calcium carbonate   A crystalline substance precipitated by coral polyps and used to build coral skeletons and marine invertebrate shells, calcium carbonate ($CaCO_3$) contributes to alkalinity or water hardness in marine aquaria.

calcium reactor   A calcium reactor is a substrate reactor that dissolves subbase calcium and carbonate with the use of CO_2 in order to maintain appropriate levels of calcium and alkalinity in the aquarium.

carbonate hardness   *See* alkalinity.

clean-up crew (CUC)   The clean-up crew is the group of organisms added to the aquarium to perform basic maintenance functions.

closed-loop system (CLS)   A closed-loop system is a circulation system where water is pumped from the aquarium through a pump and wavemaking device, and then directly back to the aquarium. The system is closed because there is no way in or out of the system except for the aquarium.

clownfish disease   *See* Brooklynellosis.

coralline algae   All red algae with calcium carbonate is called coralline algae, and it is a highly desirable algae that many marine aquarists attempt to cultivate in their tanks. Coralline algae is also referred to as calcareous algae.

cryptocaryonosis   A relatively common disease that affects marine fishes and is caused by the parasite *Cryptocaryon irritans*. Although it is often referred to as marine or saltwater ich, that is a misnomer as it is not caused by the parasite *Ichthyophthirius multifilis* that affects freshwater fishes, nor is it caused by the fungus *Ichthyyophonus hoferi* (which causes reeling disease in marine fishes). Its common name is more accurately white-spot disease, or simply "crypto."

curing   Curing is the process of preparing live rock, whereby decaying and dead organisms provide food for bacterial populations essential to a stable system.

cyanobacteria   Sometimes called blue-green algae or blue-green bacteria, cyanobacteria are a type of bacteria that play a role in the nitrogen cycle.

deep sand bed (DSB)   An aquarium with a sand bed of at least 10 centimeters (4 inches) is said to have a deep sand bed, as it is deep enough to contain anaerobic areas.

denitrification   The process of converting nitrate into nitrogen-containing compounds, denitrification is a critical component of the nitrogen cycle.

detritus   Waste materials (animal waste, dead algae, and so on) bound with bacteria that provides a food source for many corals and other organisms.

dissolved oxygen   The measure of oxygen dissolved in your aquarium water.

filter   A filter is a device or mechanism that removes waste products, toxins, and potential toxins from the water column. Three types of filtration are generally employed in the marine aquarium: mechanical, biological, and chemical.

fin rot   Caused by bacterial infection, fin rot is the decomposition of fin tissue. Fin rot is usually secondary to improper handling.

flashing   When a fish repeatedly rubs against live rock or other objects in the tank; the behavior may indicate the presence of parasites on the fish's skin.

fluidized bed filter   A type of biological filter that provides good habitat (wet and oxygenated) for nitrifying bacteria in a substrate reactor.

foam fractitioner   *See* protein skimmer.

hardness   *See* alkalinity.

head and lateral line erosion   A condition resulting in erosion caused by ulcerations along the lateral line of a fish and on the fish's head. It can lead to death.

hexacoral   Hexacoral polyps have six (or multiples of six) tentacles. All stony corals (scleractinians) are hexacorals.

hole-in-the-head disease   Common name for Hexamitosis (caused by the *heximata* parasite) or Spironucleosis (caused by the *spironucleus* parasite); presents with pitting of the flesh on a fish's head.

hydrometer   An instrument used to indirectly measure salinity (specific gravity).

hyposaline   Water with a specific gravity less than natural seawater is said to be hyposaline.

invertebrate tank   A tank containing only invertebrates (coral and other invertebrates) and no fishes.

Jaubert method   A method of aquarium keeping that does not use protein skimming but instead uses a deep sand bed over a plenum.

Kalkwasser   A solution of calcium hydroxide or calcium oxide in water. Also known as "lime water," it is used to increase calcium concentration and temporarily increase the water's buffering capacity.

lateral line   A line evident along the side of a fish that serves as a sensory canal.

live rock   Rock that has been colonized by marine flora and fauna and is then used in the marine aquarium as a biological filter.

live sand   Sand that contains living flora and fauna.

LPS A hobbyist's term for "large polyp stony" corals. LPS corals are said to be easier to keep than "small polyp stony" (SPS) corals, but these generalizations are increasingly flawed and may lead to errors by beginning aquarists.

marine ich *See* cryptocaryonosis.

marine velvet *See* amyloodiniosis.

mechanical filtration Mechanical filtration is one of the three primary filtration methods employed in the marine aquarium. Mechanical filtration refers to filtration devices that mechanically remove impurities from the water (e.g., filter sponge, filter sock, protein skimmer, and so on.).

motile A motile organism is one that can move about the aquarium. It is the opposite of sessile.

new-tank syndrome The break-in period of a new tank where toxic ammonia and nitrite levels are too high to support most marine aquarium fishes and invertebrates.

nitrate The end product of nitrification is nitrate (NO_3). It is far less toxic than ammonia and nitrite.

nitrite The intermediate product of nitrification is nitrite (NO_2). In high concentrations, it is toxic to many marine organisms.

nitrogen cycle The cycle whereby toxic ammonia is converted to less toxic nitrite and finally to relatively harmless nitrate.

octocoral Polyps with eight tentacles.

open system A system using a sump (sometimes called a Berlin sump), whereby water is drained from the aquarium into an open chamber or sump where filtration occurs before being pumped back to the aquarium.

osmotic shock When an organism is placed in a fluid that has a much different solute concentration than the fluid to which that organism is acclimated, the animal may go into osmotic shock. This either presents as the animal pumping too much water into its body resulting in hemorrhaging and death, or the animal pumping too much water out of its body resulting in dehydration and death.

ozone   Ozone, tri-atomic oxygen (0_3), when used properly in the sub-base aquarium, can both reduce disease-causing organisms and improve water clarity.

pH   A measurement of how acidic or basic a solution is based on a measurement of the concentration of hydrogen ions.

phosphate   A trace nutrient found in natural seawater and a waste product that, in higher concentrations, is dangerous to marine organisms.

plankton   Microscopic or very small organisms that drift in the water, including both zooplankton and phytoplankton, which are important food sources for many marine animals.

plenum   A water-filled space beneath a deep sand bed but still within the aquarium.

polyp   The smallest whole living unit of a polypoid cnidarian.

powerhead   A submersible pump often placed directly in the tank to produce flow.

protein skimmer   A mechanical filter that uses foam fractitionating to remove organic waste from the water.

quarantine   The procedure of isolating a new animal before introducing it to the display tank.

reef tank   A tank including corals, other invertebrates, and fishes in the same aquarium.

refractometer   *See* hydrometer.

refugium   A tank separate from, but connected to, the main display tank where certain species of plants and beneficial invertebrates can live.

salinity   The degree of saltiness (dissolved salt or sodium chloride) of a solution.

salt creep   Accumulated deposits of salt on and around the aquarium.

saltwater ich   *See* cryptocaryonosis.

sessile   An animal that, for most of its life cycle, does not move beyond a single biotope. Most corals are sessile animals.

shallow sand bed (SSB)   A sand bed that is shallower than 10 centimeters (4 inches).

soft coral   Corals that do not build a calcium skeleton. Most soft corals are part of the subclass Octocorallia, order Alcyonacea.

specific gravity   A measurement of density relative to pure water. It is used as an indirect way to measure salinity.

SPS   A hobbyist term for "small polyp stony" corals. SPS corals are said to be harder to keep than "large polyp stony" (LPS) corals, but these generalizations are increasingly flawed and may lead to errors by beginning aquarists.

substrate   The material placed on the bottom of the tank if the aquarium is not a bare-bottom tank. Sometimes substrate is also the term used for the live rock, to which various organisms (e.g., corals) may be attached by the aquarist.

sweeper tentacles   Some corals have long, stinging sweeper tentacles that can be used to defend space on a reef from other corals. Particularly aggressive corals use their sweeper tentacles to go on the offensive against adjacent corals.

trace elements   Elements in natural seawater that are found in small concentrations but which may be essential for certain animals to thrive.

wet-dry or trickle filters   A type of biological filter that provides good habitat (wet and oxygenated) for nitrifying bacteria.

whirling disease   Common name for myxosporidia, a disease that causes fish to swim in circles.

white-band disease   Often called white plague or white death, this disease affects coral tissue, causing tissue recession resulting from unknown causes.

white-spot disease   *See* cryptocaryonosis.

zooplankton   Plankton without chlorophyll; an important food source for many marine organisms.

zooxanthellae   Algae that lives within the cells of other organisms (e.g., corals) in a symbiotic relationship. Organisms that contain zooxanthellae generally require high lighting intensity.

Appendix B

Reading List and Online Resources

Calfo, Anthony, and Robert Fenner. *Reef Invertebrates: An Essential Guide to Selection, Care and Compatibility*. Reading Trees, 2003.

Delbeek, J. Charles, and Julian Sprung. *The Reef Aquarium, Vols. 1-3*. Ricordea Publishing, 1994-2003.

Fenner, Robert M. *The Conscientious Marine Aquarist*. Microcosm Ltd., 1998/2008.

Goemans, Bob, and Lance Ichinotsubo. *The Marine Fish Health & Feeding Handbook: The Essential Guide to Keeping Saltwater Species Alive and Thriving*. New Jersey: TFH Publications, 2008.

Kuiter, Rudie H., and Helmut Debelius. *World Atlas of Marine Fishes*. IKAN-Unterwasserarchiv, 2006.

Michael, Scott W. *Reef Fishes Volume 1-4*. TFH Publications, 2001-2008.

———. *A PocketExpert Guide to Marine Fishes: 500+ Essential-to-Know Aquarium Species*. TFH Publications, 1999.

Paletta, Michael S. *The New Marine Aquarium: Step-by-Step Setup & Stocking Guide.* TFH Publications, 1999.

Sprung, Julian. *Corals: A Quick Reference Guide.* Ricordea Publishing, 1999.

Tullock, John H. *Natural Reef Aquariums: Simplified Approaches to Creating Living Saltwater Microcosms.* TFH Publications, 1997.

Wittenrich, Matthew L. *The Complete Illustrated Breeder's Guide to Marine Aquarium Fishes.* TFH Publications, 2007.

Web Resources

Wet Web Media at www.WetWebMedia.com

Microcosm Aquarium Explorer at en.microcosmaquariumexplorer.com

Reef Central at www.ReefCentral.com

The Reef Tank at www.TheReefTank.com

Reefs.org at www.Reefs.org

Fishbase at www.FishBase.org

Index

What's on the CD

The CD opens in your computer's Internet browser. Packed with more than 900 pictures, it is loaded with information and is very easy to use and navigate. Choose any of the fish species and you'll find its reef compatibility, care level, disposition, minimum tank size, mature size, diet, and more. Additionally, if you want to find other fish with the same type of requirements, you can also find them with just one click.